BE ONE
OF GOD'S
UNLIKELY
LEADERS

REX M. ROGERS

BE ONE OF GOD'S UNLIKELY LEADERS

LIVE WITH FOCUS, GET THINGS DONE

Also by Rex M. Rogers

Seducing America: Is Gambling a Good Bet?

Christian Liberty: Living for God in a Changing Culture

Gambling: Don't Bet on It
revision and update of *Seducing America*

Today, You Do Greatness: A Parable on Success and Significance
ebook coauthored with Dr. Rick Amidon

Living for God in Changing Times
ebook revision of *Christian Liberty*

Be One of God's Unlikely Leaders
Copyright © 2025 by Rex M. Rogers
All rights reserved.

Published in the United States of America by Credo House Publishers, a division of Credo Communications, LLC, Grand Rapids, Michigan
credohousepublishers.com

Unless otherwise indicated, Scripture quotations are from the ESV® Bible (The Holy Bible, English Standard Version®), copyright © 2001 by Crossway Bibles, a publishing ministry of Good News Publishers. Used by permission. All rights reserved.

ISBN: 978-1-62586-338-6

Cover and interior design by Frank Gutbrod
Editing by Elizabeth Banks

Printed in the United States of America
First edition

To the late C. John Miller,
stalwart friend, listener, adviser, mentor,
faithful spiritual example, beloved family man,
successful businessman, prototype board member,
truly remarkable leader.

Aside from my father and grandfathers, no man
made a greater positive impact upon my life.

Rex M. Rogers

CONTENTS

Foreword 01

Prologue: Leaders in My Life 05
Leadership Lessons 14

1 Choices: Why You *Can* and *Should* Become a Leader
Anyone, Anytime, Anywhere 16
Somebody Must Lead 17
Wanted: Corporate Leaders—Others Need Not Apply 19
Leaderless Academies 21
Where Have the Political Leaders Gone? 22
Ministry Leaders—Missing in Action 25
You Can Learn to Be a Leader 26
God's Unlikely Leaders 28
Leadership Lessons 30

2 Credibility: What a Leader *Is*
Jesus 31
Got Leadership? 32
Defining Leadership 33
Christian Perspectives on Leadership 36
Leadership Myths 39
The Spiritual Gift of Leadership 42
Leadership As Calling 43
Women in Leadership 47
Leadership "Demons" 49
Servant Leadership 50
Leadership Lessons 54

3 Confusion: What a Leader *Could Be*

Judas 55
May Another Take His Place of Leadership 56
Little "L" Leaders 56
Unlikely Leaders Who Led 57
The Unlikely Leaders' Leaders 64
God's Unlikely Leaders' Essential Characteristics 66
God's Unlikely Leadership Principles 67
Leadership Lessons 71

4 Character: Who a Leader *Is*

Joseph 73
Character 75
A Low Bar in a High Office 77
Where Do You Draw the Line? 78
No Perfect People 80
Evil Leaders 80
Bad Leaders 81
Conscience 82
Arrogance 84
Confidence 86
Courage 88
Leadership Lessons 91

5 Cause: What a Leader Is *About*

Moses 93
Purpose/Mission and Vision 95
The Vision Thing 97
The Power of Vision 100
Excellence 101
Leading Change 104
Change Without the Organization 106
Change Within the Organization 108

Change Within the Leader 111
Proactive Stewardship 112
Optimistic Realism 113
Leaders Are Never Lucky 114
Leadership Lessons 117

6 Communication: What a Leader *Says*
Joshua 119
Not Power, Not Position, But Passion 120
Inspiring Others to Aspire 123
Stories and Symbolism 126
4 Cs 130
Nuts and Bolts 131
Say It Like a Leader 136
Leadership Lessons 138

7 Commitment: What a Leader *Does*
Daniel 139
Don't Just Stand There; Do Something 140
Creativity 142
Competence 144
Energy and Work Ethic 145
Styles of Leadership 147
Transactional and Transformational Leaders 149
Making Decisions 151
The Ironies of Leadership 154
Leadership Lessons 158

8 Community: *Who* Follows a Leader
David 159
Unlikely Leaders Need Help 161
The "Right" People 166
Making the Hard Decision 168

Relationships 172
Developing More Unlikely Leaders 173
Creating a Leadership Culture 176
Giving Credit Where Credit Is Due 181
Leadership Lessons 182

9 Crises: When a Leader Is *Challenged*

Nehemiah 183
Welcome to Leadership 184
Receiving and Interpreting Criticism 185
Responding to Criticism 188
Criticism That Hurts 193
Giving Criticism 195
Hard Times 198
Keep the Faith 203
Leadership Lessons 206

10 Conduct Unbecoming: When a Leader *Fails* or *Falls*

Samson 207
When Leaders Fail or Fall 208
When Leaders Fail 211
When Leaders Fall 218
Burned Out, Bummed Out, Bounced Out 227
"The Modesto Manifesto" 231
Leadership Lessons 234

11 Continuity: What a Leader *Leaves Behind*

Gideon 235
Leaders Always Leave 236
Leaders Leave Legacies 237
Sacred Cows 241
Closeted Skeletons 244
Historic Preservation—Structure 247

Lame Ducks 249
Leadership Succession 251
Leadership Lessons 259

12 Conclusion: Why Becoming a Leader Is Not *Option* but *Opportunity*

Queen Esther 261
Leadership Maxims 262
Leaders Don't Wait, They Lead 267
What Will Your Epitaph Be? 268
Great Gifts, Great Needs, Great Opportunities 271
Leadership Lessons 277

Leadership Lessons 279
Acknowledgments 287
Selected Bibliography 289
Endnotes 301

FOREWORD

Leadership is a subject addressed frequently in Scripture. As a result, many Christian books on leadership have been written. From A. W. Tozer's *Lead Like Christ* to John Maxwell's *Leadership 101*, you will find a variety of volumes detailing the principles, secrets, laws, lessons, ways, and behaviors of Christian leadership. In fact, several years ago my friend Saji Lukos convinced me to coauthor a leadership book based on Nehemiah, *Leadership Under Fire*.

But when Dr. Rex Rogers told me about his approach to leadership, I was intrigued. *Be One of God's Unlikely Leaders—Live with Focus, Get Things Done* describes a different approach than that taken by many books. Others challenge those who have God-given, recognized leadership qualities to cultivate and develop those traits in order to become a more outstanding and effective leader. And that's a valid approach to the subject.

Instead, Rex takes the approach that, if you are a living human being, you have the capacity to influence others. Since leadership in its simplest form is influence, God wants you to become one of those "unlikely leaders." Rex uses the words "anyone, anytime, anywhere" to underscore the message of his book. Quoting President Dwight Eisenhower, he points out that all people have untapped leadership potential and thus by choice can develop their God-given abilities.

Some authors write books out of their theoretical understanding of the subject. Others primarily write from practical experience. For Dr. Rex Rogers, the correct selection is option C, all the above.

Rex introduces his subject by labeling himself as one of God's unlikely leaders. He describes how his family as well as his wife's demonstrated leadership in ways that mentored him on the subject.

Using those experiences, Rex tells how he quickly became a leader during his student days at Cedarville University. He then honed his craft as president of Cornerstone University and SAT-7 USA, a strategic ministry reaching into the Middle East and North Africa using satellite and Internet technology. Through those assignments, Rex has experienced literally every category of opportunity and challenge any leader is likely to face.

This book points to a dearth of leadership in many strategic areas in our world today, business and industry, education, politics, and especially ministry. But Rex is not simply looking to motivate those who have gifts and skills in leadership. As he puts it, "This book was written for those who think they aren't leaders, who think they can't be leaders, and even don't want to be leaders, but actually can and should be leaders."

One important point established in the book: one can exercise leadership and still be a follower. In fact, those two roles are certainly not mutually exclusive.

Be One of God's Unlikely Leaders—Live with Focus, Get Things Done approaches the subject with a thorough and biblical perspective. Each chapter begins with a scriptural example. Some, like Jesus himself, as well as Moses and David, present positive leadership traits. Others, like Samson and Judas Iscariot, present the negative side—what leadership should not be.

To me, the most important point Dr. Rex Rogers makes in this book is the premise that every one of us will exercise leadership from time to time, whether in a corporate C-suite carrying out strategic planning or in a family discussion to choose which restaurant to visit for dinner.

Having found myself placed in a number of leadership roles, including the unlikely appointment as president of my alma mater, I am a person who seeks to "live with greater focus and to get things done." That's one reason *Be One of God's Unlikely Leaders* proved an intriguing book from my perspective.

Whether you consider yourself to be a leader or not, the collection of adjectives Rex uses to describe different kinds of leaders will help you understand what's involved in leadership—and hopefully motivate you to embrace your God-given role as one of his unlikely leaders.

Don Hawkins, DMin
President/CEO, Encouragement Communications
Former President, Southeastern Bible College
Author or coauthor of over twenty-five books, including *Leadership Under Fire* and *Master Discipleship*

PROLOGUE

LEADERS IN MY LIFE

Leadership is a learned behavior. I say this because I believe leaders are more often "made" than "born." Of course, all people are born, but leadership is developed. So, what I've learned about leadership is a gift from other people.

Leaders are more often made than born.

My youth was influenced by a father and two nearby grandfathers, all of whom were leaders in different ways. They each left an indelible mark upon my life.

My father, Ernest, was both a factory worker and the proprietor of Rogers Barber Shop. One thing he liked about the factory is that you could punch out at 3:00 p.m., be home in ten minutes, and have the rest of the day to do other things. That's when he cut hair, fished, got involved with the family, or worked at the church. Later in life he served as a village councilman and a township trustee.

But if you really want to understand Dad's life you must know that he was a deacon in our local church for fifty years, much of it as chairman of the board. Dad came to Christ as a child, grew up in the Methodist church, and responded to God's call to live a spiritually productive life. If there was anything happening at the church—the Baptist church a couple of small-town blocks from our home—Dad was there, leading by serving. He led the church board, participated in workdays, helped organize church picnics and countless other events, fixed whatever was broken, and taught Sunday School. He did all this with an unassuming, humble, easygoing spirit. As a leader he never dominated nor demanded recognition. His legacy is faithfulness, tireless effort, a willing heart. He continued to build that legacy in his retirement until in his late 80s he went to sleep in his own bedroom and awakened in heaven. Dad was a *quiet leader.*

Dad's father was a farmer and a carpenter, the son of a long line of farmers and tradesmen back to the 1680s when four Rogers brothers arrived in Maryland from England. Grandpa Rogers, as I called him, Thomas to Grandma, and Tom to everyone else was a man short in stature but huge in personality. If Tom Rogers was around people knew it, as much because of the vigor of his work ethic as the strength of his persona.

Good leaders leave a legacy of faithfulness.

Grandpa Rogers's father, Lilburn, died in middle age on Christmas Eve 1915. In the habit of the times, my grandpa dropped out of school in the eighth grade to run the family farm. He grew up fast as he drove a coal wagon, farmed, became a carpenter, and provided for the family. Eventually he bought his two brothers' shares in the farm, married at age 31, and worked the land for the rest of his life.

Grandpa Rogers was not a quiet leader. He was energetic and noisy in a Teddy Roosevelt kind of way. His prodigious productivity became legendary in surrounding counties in Southeastern Ohio. The work was often hard, but he was undaunted. Grandpa led by full-speed-ahead example. He did this on the farm, on the job, at his Methodist church, as a voting precinct committee member, and in the family. He did the right thing as he saw it and expected everyone else to do the same. If they didn't (including me), they heard from him. He wasn't mean or autocratic, just bigger than life. He was a Christian who took no prisoners. Grandpa Rogers was a *gung-ho leader.*

My mother's father, Lewis Davis (or "Bones" as everyone called him), was the son of Welsh immigrants. As a young man he joined his relatives mining underground, but he didn't like it—"Too dark, too dank, and too deep," he said. So, he labored in a glass factory and a state hospital for the remainder of his career.

For thirty-eight consecutive years, and for different nonsequential years prior to this, he served as deacon in the same Baptist church as my father. In fact, Grandpa Davis and my grandmother, along with four other families, founded the church, which decades later became my home church. They took this action when the other Baptist church they attended turned from biblical teaching. In this, Grandpa Davis stepped up to the spiritual challenge of his day. He became a risk-taker and leader, a member of the "Joshua generation" who conquered a new land, a man who formed a new congregation and built a new church and remained faithful to the truth.

Bones Davis possessed only an eighth-grade education, but he could read. He read his Bible eagerly and regularly, and he read organic gardening magazines. He absorbed both sources of knowledge so well no one could determine which flourished more, his faith or his garden, but both grew and nourished others.

Effective leaders rise to the spiritual challenge of their day.

Bones' reputation for wisdom and a tremendous sense of humor was born not of formal training but of the school of hard knocks lived faithfully before the Lord. Had you said to him, "You're a leader," he would have cracked a joke and gently set that thought aside. But for many years, people traveled to his home to sit with him on his oversize back porch swing, admire his garden, and talk (ask questions) about life. I did too. Those people still remember him and some, like me, are still influenced by him. He was our family's spiritual patriarch. He was a *charismatic leader*.

I should mention my mother, Yvonne. I can still hear her saying, "Readers make leaders." I don't know where she found that phrase, but it reinforced my love of reading and foretold my interest in leadership. Mom also frequently quoted, "This is the day that the LORD has made; let us rejoice and be glad in it" (Ps. 118:24). I've never forgotten that one either. This verse comes to mind each time circumstances seem overwhelming. Mom is an encourager, a *cheerleader*.

Readers make leaders.

In high school I was a good student and a not-so-good varsity wrestler. My entry-level leadership experiences took place a little in the classroom and a lot in the church. One blessing of a small church experience in the 1960s was no one waited for you to say, "Here I am! Send me" (Isa. 6:8). Somebody usually sent you whether you wanted to go or not. So, I learned a few leadership lessons in our youth group. One of those lessons was how to pray in public. It doesn't sound like much, but proper public prayer is an act of leadership in America's pluralistic culture. I've heard too many sermons, jeremiads, or political statements masquerading as public prayer. Praying combatively may be worse than not praying at all. On the other hand, I've met too many adult Christians who will not pray in public. I learned the courage and the content of public prayer in those youth groups long ago.

University is where I really cut my leadership teeth. I attended Cedarville University (OH), where, as an undergraduate, I was elected vice president then president of a men's service club called Alpha Chi (AX). The adviser, Dr. Murray Murdoch, taught me how to lead collegially. My presidency came early, a kind of battlefield promotion when during my junior year the club president departed campus for several weeks on a mission trip in the Republic of the Philippines. As the sitting AX vice president, I was sworn in as president and the earth began turning faster.

> **Proper public prayer is an act of leadership in a pluralistic culture.**

From "day one" as a newly minted president I had to assume responsibility for the school's big spring event called "Cedar Day." Believe me, for a kid in college in that era this was a happening akin to the Olympics—or at least I thought so. The men of AX were the event sponsors/workers, and I was right in the middle of it. I had to learn fast.

I learned that some people say yes but never do what they agreed to do.

I learned some people must be begged, cajoled, pushed, babied, or maybe even shamed before they do much of anything.

I learned that some individuals would take on more than they can handle.

I learned that "more than they can handle" may refer to a person's lack of ability but much more often refers to an underdeveloped work ethic or lack of commitment.

I discovered many people must be shepherded continuously to assure their assigned task is completed well and on time.

These formative leadership lessons also taught me that some people—actually, very, very few—will say, "Yes, I'll do it," and then will complete the task and complete it well. In these instances, the one in charge never has to think about that task again. To state the obvious, these "I'll do it" people are "Doers." They get things done. They're reliable. For them, commitment + ability + hard work = accomplishment. Reliable Doers are rare. As I grow older it sometimes seems to me that reliable Doers may be an endangered species nearing extinction.

I've never forgotten one of those Doers, Kevin Sims, who now holds a doctorate and is a professor of history and political science at our *alma mater*. If Kevin said he'd do it, he did. No questions or quibbling. He did it, and he did it very well. He was reliable. His word was his bond, and his work was his blessing. I say, "God give us more Kevins."

In the years since those days in the early 1970s I've discovered that "the leadership experience" is pretty much the same at all levels and in all kinds of organizations. I now know that those early lessons were invaluable.

Other lessons came later from a few key leaders like former president Dr. Paul Dixon and former academic vice president Dr. Clifford Johnson of Cedarville University. During later years when I returned to my school as a professor, I was able to watch these accomplished leaders in action. Paul's example was one of vision, self-discipline, and profound spiritual commitment. He appointed a young professor in political science—me—first as director of academic computer resources and later as director of planning.

> **The leadership experience is similar in all kinds of organizations.**

The job description for both roles required me to work with all departments and offices, everyone on the campus, and therefore quickly afforded me an education in the need and value of communication, coordination, consensus building, and more. Paul gave me opportunity, access, and reinforcement. For this I will be forever grateful. He was a *spiritual leader*.

"Doc" Johnson's impact was more direct. "Rex," he said, "college life is a free enterprise system. People can accomplish pretty much anything if they want to. The key is whether they *want* to." And another time he shared this leadership gem with me: "Nothing happens on a college campus unless it has a champion. On this deal, you're it." Whoa. He was the Do-*er* and I was the Do-*ee* who learned to be a Doer. Doc Johnson's school of leadership imparted practical, potent advice, which I've since paid forward to others.

I don't remember Doc Johnson ever seeking credit for the good things that happened in the academic enterprise. And frankly, faculty members didn't always give him credit when and where he deserved it. I believe this happened for two reasons: one, Doc Johnson's leadership style was akin to President Dwight D. Eisenhower's, publicly laid back but privately active, and two, the spiritual maturity Doc evidenced before the faculty and staff. Doc Johnson was a *facilitative leader*.

Dr. Friedhelm Radandt, former president of The King's College in New York, gave me a chance to prove my mettle in upper-level leadership. Dr. Radandt appointed me as a 34-year-old academic vice president and overnight became an important tutor in my life. I'll always remember his genteel example. He is living proof that it's possible to combine vigorous professional tenacity with a gracious spirit. Elegance is the word that always comes to mind when I think of Friedhelm, as he liked to be called.

> **Leaders can be both professionally tenacious and gracious.**

When I was a new academic dean, Friedhelm said, "Rex, if you and I are threatened by the brilliance of our faculty, we'll never build a strong faculty." I learned my task in leadership was to recruit and develop the best people I could, then let them work while giving them the credit they deserved. Friedhelm taught me that my satisfactions as a leader should come in knowing that I helped attract talented people to our campus and that I helped build an organization in which they could work and in which they wanted to remain. Friedhelm was a *selfless leader*.

During more than sixteen years in the presidency at Cornerstone University I worked with six chairmen of the board. Each man brought to his service a different personality, leadership style, and spiritual insight. Learning to work as productive partners at the top of an organization is itself an important leadership lesson.

Leaders learn to work in productive partnerships.

My first board chairman, C. John Miller, is the gentleman to whom this book is dedicated. John was a singular individual. He was one of the best leaders I know, and it's not his success in the oil and gas industry that formed my opinion. While John's professional accomplishments cared well for his family and earned him the respect of his industry peers nationally, he was far more widely recognized and appreciated for his wonderful spirit. John's love for the Lord and his example of the Christian walk at times convicted but never failed to encourage me. He simply lived the love of Christ in a manner quickly apparent to anyone he met.

At the beginning of my leadership experience at Cornerstone University John said to me, "I want to be your partner in this." Years later I can say that he never wavered in that commitment. He repeatedly said, in good times and tense times, "I prayed for you today. I pray for you every day."

One moment stands supreme—the call John made to me during one of my most stressful times in leadership. He said, "I'm walking right beside you in this." No one could have said anything that meant more. Everyone who knew John Miller knows he was a class act. He was a *model leader*.

Another man who served as a trustee and as chairman of the university foundation became a mentor in my life. Richard Antonini is a former corporate chairman and CEO who loves his family, loves the Lord, and thoroughly enjoys life, especially hockey, ice-skating, and other winter sports. He combines a strong personality with a gift for numbers and major league leadership talent. Somewhere along the way I became a direct beneficiary of his teaching skills. We'd periodically schedule what often became two-hour breakfasts, or we'd take off on the bicycle path. I learned more about leadership in those sessions than I did from virtually any other source.

Dick is a storyteller and one of his classic stories is the one about the office visit from an employee with "a monkey on his back." Of course, the "monkey" is the employee's problem-of-the-day. So, Dick would say, "We'll put the monkey on my desk. We'll look at it. We'll talk about it. We'll discuss how we can make it grow or make it go away. But when you leave, you don't leave that monkey on my desk. You take him with you. He's your monkey." The moral of the story is: Don't let employees or colleagues leave problems or challenges in your hands that they should handle themselves. Great lesson. I wish everyone had a mentor like Dick. He is a *dynamic leader*.

Leaders need mentors too.

All these leaders helped shape my clay. God used them and others to mold the talents and interests he created in me. While my choices affect the image, God is still forming my sculpture.

I certainly don't claim to be special. Far from it. I'm a kid from a small-town, working-class upbringing. But I was blessed with a loving Christian family, support, opportunity, and models and mentors. I'm still learning as I lead. I'm one of God's unlikely leaders.

I want to continue to lead, to accomplish things for the Lord in whatever challenge and opportunity he gives me. I want to finish well.

Leaders should strive to finish well.

And I want you to become one of God's unlikely leaders who live with focus and get things done.

LEADERSHIP LESSONS

1. Leaders are more often made than born.
2. Good leaders leave a legacy of faithfulness.
3. Effective leaders rise to the spiritual challenge of their day.
4. Readers make leaders.
5. Proper public prayer is an act of leadership in a pluralistic culture.
6. The leadership experience is similar in all kinds of organizations.
7. Leaders can be both professionally tenacious and gracious.
8. Leaders learn to work in productive partnerships.
9. Leaders need mentors too.
10. Leaders should strive to finish well.

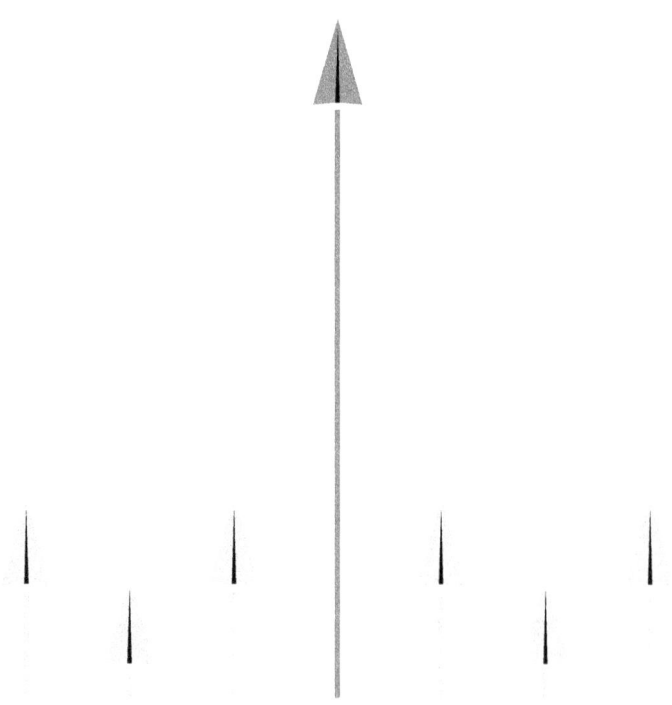

CHAPTER 1

CHOICES

Why You *Can* and *Should* Become A Leader

Two people lost in the wilderness come to a fork in the path. Which way should they go? They consider their options and eventually one says, "Let's go this way." That's leadership.

A family is traveling, and Dad says, "Where do you want to eat?" Mom and the kids debate hamburgers, submarine sandwiches, Chinese. Finally, Dad says, "Let's go to the next place we see." They all agree to this culinary adventure. He exercised leadership.

A newly appointed CEO walks into a struggling corporation with turnaround on her mind. After systematic meetings with her employees, conversations with former customers, and evaluations of marketplace trends, she launches a plan. The plan includes casting a vision, dismissing two vice presidents, reassigning some managers, and encouraging employees by implementing some of their suggestions. A new wind is blowing at company headquarters. In the next six months the CEO shows the local business community how effective leadership really works.

Five people are trapped by fallen debris in a cave. One panics. One prays. Two stand motionless and wide-eyed. One person says, "I feel a breeze. If we crawl this way, I think we can get out." The one, a child, guides four adults to safety by demonstrating heroic leadership under pressure.

A child isn't usually our idea of a leader. We think of George Washington or those other guys on our money. We think maybe of Mother Teresa, the Pope, John Wayne, Elon Musk, the President of the United States, or last year's star quarterback. We think of corporate tycoons or the latest notable red state or blue state politician.

Sometimes the leader is the one you'd pick out of a crowd. But just as often the leader is the person you'd least expect. It's these unlikely leaders who surprise us. They rise up in our midst, demonstrating once again that anyone anytime anywhere can be a leader.

Anyone, Anytime, Anywhere

Being a leader is not the exclusive domain of the rich and powerful, the famous, or the beautiful people. Being a leader isn't reserved for the super talented or the VIPs. It's not just for men, adults, a given nationality, race, or ethnic group.

Contrary to popular opinion, leadership is not a mysterious talent only some people are "lucky" enough to acquire. Quite simply yet quite remarkably, leadership is a gift of God to all of us.

Leadership is a gift of God.

This book is written for everyone who's ever thought, "How am I going to do this? I'm no leader."

That's a lot of people. Maybe it's you. You want to accomplish something, but your perception of leadership—or of yourself—makes you think you're not cut out to be a leader. You think you *can't* be a leader. This book is for you.

Then there are other people I meet who don't want to be leaders. Or at least they *say* they don't want to be a leader.

They lack confidence in themselves or their abilities. They're not sure they have "the right stuff." They fear the hassle or the pressure or the accountability or the potential embarrassment if they don't do well. But even these folks *can become* leaders, and some of them, deep down, really want to.

Maybe that's you. You'd like to lead, but you're not sure how. Remember what we said: Anyone anytime anywhere can be a leader. That includes you.

You're still breathing, so it's safe to say God's blessed you with time and talent. *So, no matter how unlikely it may seem, you can learn to lead.*

Somebody Must Lead

Let's start with the fact that "leaderlessness" does not exist.[1] Somebody always leads. If you don't lead somebody else will. So why not you?

Organizations without good leadership go nowhere. Organizations consist of people, and they need leadership to survive and effective leadership to thrive. Leaders pull people together around common goals (which is what an organization is all about), and they point the way. In fact, "the more we lack leadership, the more we hunger for it."[2] And no organization, no institution, be it religious, commercial, educational, political, or military, can be great without a great leader at the top.[3]

> **If you don't lead somebody else will.**

This doesn't mean "non-leaders" don't matter. It simply means leadership always matters.

Valley Forge was a turning point in the American Revolution because of a man named George Washington. Wendy's is a successful hamburger chain because of the entrepreneurial vision and the work ethic of a man named Dave Thomas. During the Cuban Missile Crisis of 1962, the Soviet Union backed down because of the strength of a president called JFK. The San Francisco 49ers football team dominated the 1980s because of the innovative leadership of Coach Bill Walsh and a quarterback named Joe Montana.

Look at any outstanding organization of any kind. Look at any significant political event or development and the answer is always the same. It could not have been done without strong, effective leadership.[4]

The Marines say, "Wherever there are two Marines one of them is going to be a leader." I love this quote. I wish we could paraphrase it for Christians: "Wherever you find two followers of Christ both of them are going to be leaders" (and that's a spiritual irony we'll talk about later—"followers" will be "leaders.")

Sure, the Marines have a lot of moxie, but you don't have to be a Marine to know this maxim could apply to any group of two or more human beings. Whether or not you train for it, whether you're conscious of it, leadership *is*. It may not be good leadership. It may not be leadership in the right direction. It may not be consistent leadership. But leadership is.

Leadership is.

Leadership exists because God wants it to exist. It exists because we need it to exist. "If leaders were not necessary," social researcher George Barna says, "(God) would not have included leadership among the spiritual gifts; the Bible would not provide so many incredible principles of leadership; and the Holy Spirit would not have inspired the authors of the Bible to incorporate so many examples of strong leadership."[5]

Leadership exists because God wants it to exist.

The importance of leadership cannot be overstated. Whether an art or a science, leadership is key to change, accomplishment, and success. Leadership motivates others to get things done.

The Panama Canal was successfully completed because of the vision and resolve of a man with a toothy grin named Teddy Roosevelt. Americans were the first to land on the moon because of a man named John F. Kennedy, even though he didn't live to see it. Leaders set the stage and create targets for the rest of us.

"Ask not what your country can do for you. Ask what you can do for your country."

"I have a dream . . ."

"Mr. Gorbachev, tear down this wall!"

It's not disrespectful to non-leaders, people called followers, to say, "Things rise and fall on leadership." Yes, we know leaders can't accomplish a task alone. If they do, they're not really leaders but loners. So, others are always involved. But leaders *must* be involved.

Why do we need leaders? Because . . .

1. we lack leaders.
2. the future is important, and leaders take us there.
3. we don't get along with everyone, (i.e. war).
4. organizational structures are flattening, and change is increasing rapidly.
5. management is not working well anymore.
6. technology now makes it possible to get into trouble faster than ever.
7. leaders drive agendas.
8. we're being asked to do more with less.[6]

The often-traumatic development of the world's economy recalls the old expression, "We're up to our knees in alligators." Now it's much higher—up to our necks in problems and challenges. "If you're not confused these days, you don't know what's going on." [7]

Leaders don't have all the answers. But leaders help organizations identify and make sense of the answers. We need leaders every day in every way. We need leaders in corporations, the academy, politics, ministry, and more.

Wanted: Corporate Leaders—Others Need Not Apply

When corporate scandal hit Tyco, Sotheby's Global Crossing, Qwest, Worldcom, Xerox, Arthur Andersen, and Enron it drove public regard for business and business leaders to new lows. Americans learned they couldn't trust high profile business leaders because so many of them proved untrustworthy.

A crisis in integrity morphed into a crisis in leadership. It affected and it's still affecting our economy and well-being. It threatens our children's future.

Leaders don't have all the answers.

Given that "the world is flat," the need for moral, effective leaders in the twenty-first-century global marketplace is greater than ever. "We must have working-class leaders with unyielding integrity who will transform their organizations and develop a new generation of leaders. Without such leadership, our free-enterprise society is undermined."[8] We need leaders in corporations who model the best of what American freedom of opportunity is all about.

Commercial enterprises are constantly on the lookout for effective leaders because "the scarcest resource in the world today is leadership talent capable of continuously transforming organizations to win in tomorrow's world."[9]

When Louis Gerstner showed up for work on his first day as the new chairman and CEO at IBM, April 1, 1993, more than one person thought he was an April fool. IBM suffered from an image of starchy formality, counted unhappy and angry people among its customers, and was experiencing an almost decade long precipitous decline.

Gerstner's first order of business? "I had an enormous team of executives. I would need to develop a cadre of leaders."[10] Leadership positions weren't scarce at IBM. Leaders were.

Gerstner knew that holding a leadership position isn't the same as leading. So, he banished the famed management committee, a group of vice presidents that had become a classic example of centralized control with diffused responsibility, where nothing happened and no one took the blame. Eliminating this bureaucracy helped break the rigor mortis Gerstner believed had set in at IBM.[11]

Holding a leadership position isn't the same as leading.

Gerstner created positive change because he did what *Fast Company's* John Ellis said leaders must do: Show people that "many things matter, and here's what matters most."[12]

Leaderless Academies

Twenty-first-century colleges and universities are just as hungry for quality leaders as corporations. Most educational institutions are more often administered than led. "The system"—academic bureaucracy that can "aca-demolish" any idea suggesting change—discourages leadership.

According to the Association of Governing Boards, "University presidents operate from one of the most anemic power bases in any of the major institutions of American society. Academic presidents are like other chief executives in their responsibilities. But they are unlike other chief executives in the source and reach of their authority. Academic presidents are held accountable by many powerful constituencies. . . . As a result, presidents run the continual risk of being whipsawed by an ever-expanding list of concerns and interests. Instead of a leader, the president has gradually become the 'juggler-in-chief.'"[13]

In academia, leadership is one of the few terms still considered a dirty word. "If 'leadership' means significant and lasting influence over the ideas and decisions of others, the term does not describe the work of most college presidents" because most, higher educational institutions represent "organized anarchies."[14] Consequently, "only in higher education can you be considered a successful leader simply by maintaining the status quo."[15]

Many college and university presidents have learned to be "educrats," academic professionals buried in the minutia of "administrivia" with little experience, inclination, or encouragement to lead. The result is that "passive presidents litter the landscape, and their pallid institutions reflect their listless leadership."[16] Yet we need leaders who stand for something.

> **We need leaders who stand for something.**

Community college and public university observers talk about a "crisis" of leadership, and private college and university authorities discuss an existing "challenge." They're not referring exclusively to the issues that leaders face; they're referring to a dearth of leadership talent. Not enough proven leaders are willing to assume handcuffed positions in academia and not enough new leaders are being developed within academic ranks.

Leadership is always a high-wire act without a net, perhaps nowhere more so than the academy. Colleges and universities facing a highly volatile competitive environment need academic daredevil "Flying Wallendas" who are willing to risk a fall in order to accomplish amazing feats to get where they need to go.

Where Have the Political Leaders Gone?

Each election cycle produces a new wave of presidential and other public office wannabes who claim to be tanned, rested, and ready to lead. Whether Republican or Democrat, candidates say they're neither tainted by the politics of Washington nor beholding to special interests. They point to their résumés and tout experience or values they say make them the ideal next "Decider."

FDR and his reluctant successor Harry Truman hailed from incredibly different backgrounds, yet both are rightly remembered for the leadership prowess each demonstrated via significantly different personal styles during a succession of national crises—the Great Depression, World War II, and the Korean War.

Dwight D. Eisenhower is remembered for his victories as Supreme Allied Commander and for navigating safely the beginnings of the Cold War abroad while enjoying relative economic well-being at home.

Pundits didn't think he did much besides play golf. But historians are giving him credit for being an active leader behind the scenes.

Ronald Reagan was optimistic about the country's future, "a shining city on a hill." He was kind to his staff, and he was comfortable delegating responsibility. He was a remarkable visionary even when he sometimes seemed lost in a few details. With the fall of the Berlin Wall and the USSR, and the ending of the Cold War, he engineered a transformational impact upon the global village. He ultimately left the Oval Office respected by his supporters and liked by those who disagreed with his politics.[17]

Leadership is a high-wire act without a net.

Each man's personality, preparation, and political philosophy differed. But they led with vision and vigor. Today, Democrats yearn for another FDR or Truman, Republicans for another Eisenhower or Reagan. Both parties wonder where all the leaders have gone.

American politicians have always disagreed on policy perspectives. Yet historically, politicians have generally acknowledged an underlying consensus of basic values about what's good for America's future and its children. In our sound bite culture today, however, contemporary politicians can't seem to agree on *how* to tell right from wrong, let alone *what is* right or wrong. And to make matters worse, many of them seem to loathe one another. They attack not just the merits of another politician's argument but the integrity of the speaker.

To get reelected, politicians become risk-averse, flip-flop on issues with the prevailing political winds, and fail to cast a compelling larger vision for the good of society. They become brokers, not leaders, apologists for special interests or ideological viewpoints rather than statesmen or stateswomen speaking for the greater good.

A Chinese proverb says, "May you live in interesting times." We do. The threat of terrorism from without and ideological civil war from within ratchets to a new level America's need for inspirational, principled political leaders.

Upon his election as prime minister in May 1940, Winston Churchill told the British House of Commons:

> "I have nothing to offer but blood, toil, tears and sweat. We have before us an ordeal of the most grievous kind. We have before us many, many long months of struggle and of suffering. You ask, what is our policy? I can say: It is to wage war, by sea, land, and air, with all our might and with all the strength that God can give us; to wage war against a monstrous tyranny, never surpassed in the dark, lamentable catalog of human crime. That is our policy. You ask, what is our aim? I can answer in one word: It is victory, victory at all costs, victory in spite of all terror, victory, however long and hard the road may be; for without victory, there is no survival . . . But I take up my task with buoyancy and hope. I feel sure that our cause will not be suffered to fail among men. At this time, I feel entitled to claim the aid of all, and I say, "Come then, let us go forward together with our united strength."[18]

A year and a half later, FDR told a shocked and angry American people, "The only thing we have to fear is fear itself."

Both men gave their countries hope even as they called them to dreadful action. Our presidents and other public officials will not always be, God willing, forced to ask the American people to sacrifice. But our political leaders will always be required to lead, and the question remains, will they be ready?

Ministry Leaders—Missing in Action

Warren Wiersbe said, "Everything rises or falls with leadership, and this includes what we call 'the work of the Lord.'"[19] Churches, mission agencies, rescue missions, and church or youth camps need effective leadership too. So do other nonprofit organizations like zoos, museums, hospitals, and foundations.

Yet for some reason many religious organizations in general and Christian agencies in particular suffer for lack of leaders.

Christian researcher George Barna pulls no punches. "The American church is dying due to a lack of strong leadership. In this time of unprecedented opportunity and plentiful resources, the church is actually losing influence. The primary reason is the lack of leadership. Nothing is more important than leadership."

> **America needs principled leaders who use power wisely.**

Barna also observes, "The Church in America is in a crisis time. Most of all, we have a crisis of Christian leadership. I contend that all these other crises would not be crises but simply opportunities for radical transformation—if we had true leaders leading the Church. . . . The Church would infiltrate American society to its very core if we had leaders in charge, people who experiment, take risks and create new possibilities through casting God's vision. Leaders are the missing link to the health of the Church."[20]

These men aren't blowing smoke. They are themselves leaders looking in their rearview mirrors and they aren't seeing many new leaders coming along behind them. Insufficient leaders in the church will result in both a negative social and spiritual impact.

Echoing Barna's lament, a concerned religion editor said this: "If churches were to pool their efforts to pitch one message on billboards across the continent, that message might be 'Send us young people who can lead.'"[21]

Christian educator Kenneth O. Gangel describes the problem from a different angle: "Churches, mission boards, colleges and seminaries, parachurch organizations and scores of other Christian organizations suffer in these crisis times because of mis-leadership. Not because of bad people. . . . They suffer because of ineffective leadership."[22]

The church is not consistently developing leaders.

In a time when people are looking for leaders they can trust, too many Christian leaders have failed them—or simply been missing in action. And the church is not consistently developing leaders. Yet the church is God's organization for the care and feeding of Christian people, who in turn God commissions as "salt" and "light," his influencers of culture. Who will feed and care for the sheep if there are no shepherds?

Charles Haddon Spurgeon said, "Let this be the burning passion of your souls, to be leaders and champions."[23] God wants us—you and me—to lead those around us toward him and the blessed life he promises.

Yet the church, who knows the source of faith, hope, and love and who should be developing leaders for the front lines, is too often missing in action.

You Can Learn to Be a Leader

In a letter to his son at West Point, General Dwight D. Eisenhower said, "The one quality that can be developed by studious reflection and practice is the leadership of men"—and women.[24] The leader of D-Day should know. What he was saying is that all people have untapped leadership potential[25] and all people can by choice develop their God-given abilities.

But, you say, "I don't have anywhere near the leadership talent of my friend."

Maybe. But remember, "Although it's true that some people are born with greater natural gifts than others, the ability to lead is a collection of skills, nearly all of which can be learned and improved."[26]

It doesn't matter whether your friend possesses more perceived natural leadership abilities than you. What matters is whether you want to develop your own ability to lead. What matters is your own will, your choice.

Coauthor of *The Leadership Challenge* Barry Posner said, you can learn to lead the same way you learn to throw a ball:

1. If you are willing.
2. If you practice.
3. If you get good coaching.[27]

All people have untapped leadership potential.

You can learn to lead by making a choice to do so, by experience, and by learning from others. Posner explains that because leadership is *observable*, it is *learnable*. He said leadership development isn't so much about raising the bar as lowering the bar, getting down where people live and discovering what they really want to do.[28] In other words, learning to lead is not as difficult or as scary as it may appear.

James Maxwell built his leadership writing and teaching reputation on the idea that while "not everyone will become a great leader . . . everyone can become a better leader."[29] If you're a "4" in leadership ability, Maxwell repeatedly says, you can become a "5" or maybe a "7." If you're a "7" you can become an "8." For that matter, if you're a "1" you can become a "2."

If you're a living human being, you influence others. And if you influence others, you are or can be a leader—or you can become a better leader. If you're a Christian, you can become one of God's unlikely leaders.

God's Unlikely Leaders

The Bible is filled with stories of everyday people who learned to lead for the Lord. I call them "God's unlikely leaders." They were people just like you and me. Really. We say that, but it's genuinely true. Moses and Peter were flesh and blood men, talented, temperamental, tough, scared—all rolled into leaders who accomplished great things for God despite their weaknesses.

Biblical leaders aren't typically people we would've chosen. They're not always the ones their contemporaries chose or wanted to choose. They weren't always the best and the brightest.

God's leaders are a strange list of characters from all walks of life. The only trait God's leaders hold in common is the fact that it's unlikely they would ever be chosen to lead.

We think biblical leaders are an "unlikely" bunch because we look for people we think *are* leaders while God looks for people who *will be* leaders. God doesn't think like we think. God looks for obedient people he can form into leaders.[30]

> **God looks for people who *will be* leaders.**

In the story of Saul, the first king of Israel, and his successor, David, we discover the fundamental key to God's definition of an unlikely leader.

If we'd chosen the king, we would've picked the tall, good-looking Saul.

He was a hunk, a Tom Selleck or Russell Crowe or Matt Damon in Old Testament times. He looked like a leader right out of central casting. He seemed to be everything Israel needed in a leader. He was the people's choice.

God knew better, but he let his people learn a hard lesson.

King Saul proved to be insecure, threatened, beset with a poor self-image, lacking in integrity, and of greatest concern, spiritually weak. He was a poor person. He became a poor leader.

When at least some of the people began to understand this, including the great prophet Samuel, God reminded them that his standards for leadership selection are different from ours.

"Man looks on the outward appearance," God said to Samuel, "but the Lord looks on the heart" (1 Sam. 16:7).

Through Samuel God anointed the minstrel David as the next king of Israel. A mere youth, David hadn't led anything other than sheep. His leadership credentials included killing a lion and a bear. That was good, yet that seemed to be the extent of his leadership résumé.

The Lord looks at the heart.

But wait. David possessed one more attribute that even Samuel missed. God said, "I have found in David the son of Jesse a man after my heart, who will do all my will" (Acts 13:22).

The people looked at Saul's physique and persona and failed to see who he was. God looked at David's heart and saw who he was and who he would become.

We get sidetracked with skin-deep characteristics. We respond too easily to the latest celebrity *du jour*. Or we look at accomplishments when we should be looking more at attitudes and values.

We're tribal. We often clannishly opt for people like us, missing potential leaders unlike ourselves. And we're self-righteous. Sometimes we forget about redemption and consign people who've made poor choices to a lifetime ban on leadership.

God didn't do any of this in biblical times. He doesn't work like this today. He uses unlikely leaders to achieve his purposes—which means you and I can be one of God's unlikely leaders.

LEADERSHIP LESSONS
1. Leadership is a gift of God.
2. If you don't lead someone else will.
3. Leadership is.
4. Leaders don't have all the answers.
5. Holding a leadership position isn't the same as leading.
6. Leadership is a high-wire act without a net.
7. The Church is neither leading nor developing leaders.
8. All people possess untapped leadership potential.
9. God looks for people who *will be* leaders.
10. You can be one of God's unlikely leaders.

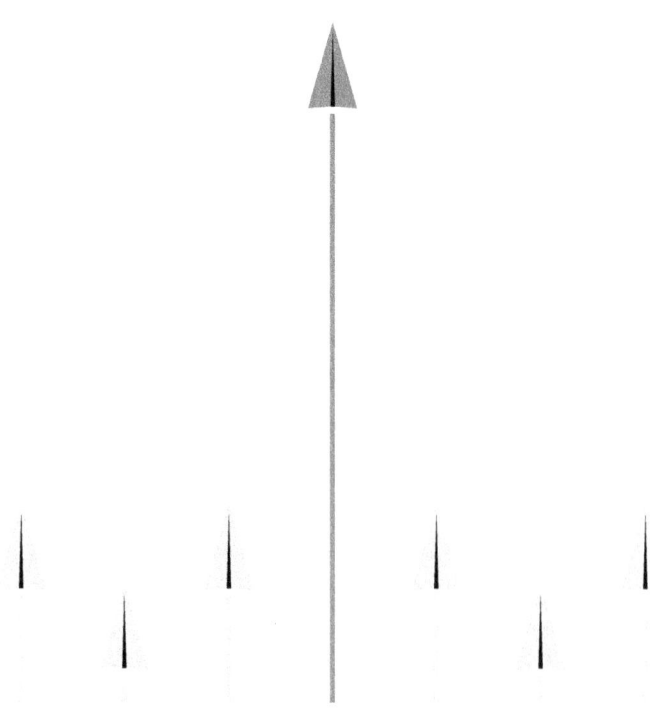

CHAPTER 2

CREDIBILITY

What A Leader *Is*

JESUS

Jesus is the greatest leader who ever lived. He's the greatest example of what a leader is and what leadership should be.

Although he never led an organization, Jesus launched a movement that spans eternity. His leadership focused upon principled moral statements rooted in the character, will, and word of God.[31] Jesus provided hope like no other leader before had ever done and no leader since will ever be able to do.

Humanly speaking, Jesus was an unlikely leader. Though he is the Son of God, Jesus was born in a cave and placed in a manger by a poor Jewish mother named Mary. She was espoused to a poor carpenter named Joseph, but they were not yet married. Since no man played a role in the conception and therefore Joseph was not Jesus's father, Jesus was born under a cloud of suspicion and ridicule.

Jesus's future hometown, Nazareth, wasn't considered the best neighborhood. Except for a temple incident at age twelve, until his thirtieth year Jesus labored in obscurity before becoming the rabbi of twelve men of dubious character. He certainly did not fit the dominant religious expectations of his day, and he did not emerge as a leader of the religious establishment.

But Jesus was and is the Good Shepherd (Ps. 22), the Great Shepherd (Ps. 23), and the Chief Shepherd (Ps. 24). He is the way, the truth, and the life (John 14:6), and he is the light of the world (John 8:12). His example as well as his instruction formed the core of his leadership.

Jesus demonstrated that one may love and lead. That loving and leading are not contradictory. That one may evidence compassion while establishing standards of excellence and expectation. That transformational change is best promoted based upon enduring values. That being and doing are both important to God and that what one does is rooted in who one is. Jesus demonstrated that sacred and secular are inseparable.

> **Jesus demonstrated that one may love and lead.**

Jesus was an unlikely leader who taught his followers to be leaders, unlikely choices though they were. He invested first in the Twelve and then through them countless others including you and me. Jesus led by example. He never condemned good leadership. He modeled it.

Got Leadership?

"Got milk?"—the old advertisement asked. Maybe.

Got leadership? Definitely. The capacity to lead resides within all of us. Jesus as Creator God placed it there.

Leadership sometimes shows up, so to speak, unexpectedly. And it's possible to seek leadership or be sought by it—or to simply find yourself leading. It's also possible to lead at one time in your life and not another.

Maybe you haven't led recently. Maybe you've never led, or at least not perceived yourself as leading. But your time to lead will come. Sooner or later, everyone is presented with an opportunity to lead. Many people shrink from the opportunity, but leaders respond. They answer the call.

It's also possible to lead in one part of your life while not leading in others. A father, for example, may lead his family but choose not to lead in his local church. A woman who leads in the workplace may choose other group involvements outside of work where she's not a leader. On given occasions, a person may lead temporarily but not permanently.

> **Sooner or later, everyone is presented with an opportunity to lead.**

There's nothing wrong with this. It's okay to be a periodic leader. You don't always have to lead. Followers are part of God's plan too. Still, the need for leaders is never ending, and demand exceeds supply. Both social problems and good causes want for leaders. This is an opportunity. If you want to lead you can find your niche in which to do so.

Defining Leadership

Before we go further, to make sure we're talking the same language we need to take time to define this thing called leadership. It's not rocket science so identifying a workable definition should be easy. Then again it can be complex because leadership is something everyone understands but seemingly no two people define the same. Put the classic twenty people in a room and you'll get twenty-five definitions of leadership. And to make it more problematic, many of those definitions will come with a suspicious or negative tone.

Perhaps this happens because there's something about human nature that makes us long for strong leaders even as we rebel against anyone who dares to tell us what to do.[32] It happens in politics where politicians rise to positions of leadership on waves of substantial support only to see their approval ratings plummet as soon as they begin making decisions. It happens in higher education where it's sometimes said, "Faculty want leadership until they get it." Same can be said for the Old Testament Israelites.

When it comes to leadership, "We're all Israelites." We all sometimes resist leadership. We all sometimes dream up boogeymen when we think of leadership, which is why God reminded us he ordained authorities for our own good (Rom. 13:1–5). But it's human nature to defy what's good for us, leadership included, so leadership is the focus of a lot of illogical and strange ideas.

The need for leaders is never ending, and demand exceeds supply.

Later in this chapter, we'll take time to examine some of these strange ideas about leadership, what I call leadership myths and "demons." For now, though, let's consider some definitions of "leader" and "leadership."

The word "leader" comes to us from the Old English word *lithan,* meaning "to travel," "to go before," "to cause to go with one," or "to show the way or guide." Leaders point the way from one place to another. "Perhaps the image that best captures the meaning is of the pioneer who blazes a trail for others. Vivid illustrations of this sense of leadership populate US history."[33] In a classically American image, a leader is a trailblazer, a pathfinder.[34]

If a leader is a trailblazer, what's "leadership"?

—Leadership is a set of attitudes and skills, not one thing. Leadership is about liberating skills and attitudes within people that are already there. Leadership is not so much a set of traits as a mentality, a way of thinking.[35]

—Leadership is more than tools and methodologies—it's thinking, judging, acting, motivating. "Leadership reflects a person's mindset and his or her approach to the world."[36]

—"The very essence of leadership, going out ahead to show the way . . ."[37]

—"Leadership is the capacity to get things done through others by changing people's mindsets and energizing them to action."[38]

—Leadership is influence, the ability to get followers.[39]

Leaders point the way from one place to another.

—Dwight D. Eisenhower said that leadership is "the art of getting *someone else* to do something that *you* want done because *he* wants to do it."[40] He put it slightly differently another time, saying, "The art of leadership is making the right decisions, then getting men to want to carry them out."[41]

—Leadership sets a direction, aligns people, and requires motivating and inspiring.[42]

—Leadership is the development of vision and strategies, the alignment of relevant people behind those strategies, and the empowerment of individuals to make the vision happen, despite obstacles. Management involves keeping the current system operating through planning, budgeting, organizing, staffing, controlling, and problem solving.[43]

—"There are more than 200 definitions of leadership in the literature. Eventually, leadership is about character—value-based, with no single definition of leadership or a single delivery system."[44]

These definitions look at leadership from different angles. Some definitions involve the *characteristics of leadership*, including skills, actions, influence, vision, long-term thinking, discomfort with the status quo, creativity, work ethic, calling, etc. Some definitions focus upon the *character of the leader*, like values and attitudes. Both ways of looking at leaders or leadership are helpful. Neither is complete.

Leadership is at once simple and complex. It's natural giftedness and it's learned experience. It is art and science. Leadership is the act of inspiring others toward a goal. Leadership involves characteristics anyone can display and which can be taught. Good leadership is an act of inspiring others toward a goal for good reasons. Good leadership requires character only some people display, which must be caught from our understanding of who God is and who we are in relationship to him. Indeed, "it is impossible to assess whether a leader is good without recourse to moral values."[45]

> **Leadership is the act of inspiring others toward a goal.**

Political scientist James MacGregor Burns insists, "There is nothing neutral about leadership; it is valued as a moral necessity."[46] In Burns' view, leadership is both essential and worthy. Leadership—good leadership—is a good thing. Burns, however, cites only self-interest and a pursuit of happiness as the reasons why people want and benefit from leadership. Consequently, though he was right about the moral necessity of leadership he missed its moral character rooted in God's eternal values.[47] God's moral teachings help us determine what "good" leadership is.

Christian Perspectives on Leadership

From a Christian point of view, I believe "the call to leadership from God's Word is embodied in both the fulfillment of the creation mandate and the fulfillment of the Great Commission."[48] In the creation or "Cultural Mandate," God charged Adam and Eve—and through them the human race—with the responsibility to develop human and earthly resources for his glory and our good (Gen. 1:28). He followed up this Old Testament command, which remains in place today, with the New Testament's "Great Commission" in which God said to go into all the world and teach others to be followers of Christ (Matt. 28:19–20).

These two far-reaching commands require God's followers to "do good" in what God intended to be a good world. But as we all know evil exists. In the garden of Eden, Satan's treachery and Adam's fall from grace introduced sin into the world (Genesis 3). Since the fall each human being has been born into sin and lives in a world fully influenced by sin.

The presence of sin in the world inevitably means evil will collide with good. It means not everyone behaves with his or her own best interest and certainly not the best interest of others at heart. It means we experience pain and suffering, afflictions and disease, wars and rumors of wars, and death.

God's plan for victory over sin is described in the Bible's redemptive story. This narrative is God's way of restoration provided through the virgin birth, sinless life, sacrificial death, burial, and resurrection of God's Son, Jesus Christ (John 3:16; 1 Cor. 15:3–5).

> **God wants Christians to care for the world by carrying his message.**

When a person who is "dead in sin" accepts Christ as Savior and Lord, he or she becomes God's "ambassador of reconciliation." This "born again" man or woman, now a Christian or "Christ follower," becomes one of God's change agents (2 Cor. 5:14–21). God wants those of us who are Christians to care for the world by carrying his message of reconciliation. He commissions us to help change the world. We do this by sharing God's message of forgiveness with other sinners and by communicating his message of hope for a troubled world.

When we become God's ambassadors we *stand out* (Eph. 5:8). And when we become God's ambassadors, we must make the most of every opportunity, which is to say we should *step up* (Gal. 6:10; Eph. 5:16; Col. 4:5).

God is always concerned about our *being*—our attitudes, values, and philosophy of life that cause us to *stand out*. But he also wants us to be *doing*—our actions that speak louder than words when we *step up*. This is how God accomplishes his purposes, how we reflect his image, and how our lives are blessed with meaning.

> **If we become God's ambassadors, we'll *stand out* and *step up*.**

Maybe Aristotle was speaking metaphorically when he said, "Man is a political animal." But if he wasn't, he got it wrong. We may be political, but human beings are not animals. We possess what is called a "God-consciousness." That's our realization that there's more to us than us. It's an acknowledgment of what Francis A. Schaeffer called "the God Who is there." Deep in our hearts we know God exists, the Sovereign Creator who gave human beings moral understanding and eternal significance, neither of which he bestowed upon animals.

So, our lives matter. What we do matters. How we live our worldview in our culture (way of life) matters. And not only does what we do matter, it should aid others and bring us fulfillment.

God entrusts us with the time, talent, opportunity, and responsibility to reflect his creativity, to contribute. And as clichéd as it may sound, God commands us to "make a difference."

Consequently, "to aspire to leadership is laudable (1 Tim. 3:1). . . . Christian leadership is undertaken for the sake of other people, as a conscious act of stewardship. . . . No blueprint for Christian leadership exists; a variety of styles and flavors and approaches are satisfactory. Yet, all must emerge from intentional reflection on biblical principles."[49]

Godly ambition is possible, a "noble and worthy" ambition as opposed to the "selfish ambition" referenced in Scripture (2 Cor. 5:9; Gal. 5:20; Phil. 2:3; 1 Tim. 3:1). J. Oswald Chambers noted, "A desire to be great is not necessarily in itself sinful. It is the motivation that determines its character. Our Lord did not discount or disparage aspirations to greatness, but he did pointedly expose and stigmatize unworthy motivation."[50] So a desire to lead based upon spiritually sound aspirations is a worthy ambition. And if we don't lead, we may deny ourselves a level of fulfillment that may come to us in no other way.[51]

> **A desire to lead based upon spiritual aspirations is a worthy ambition.**

I could not disagree more strongly with those who suggest leadership is not a Christian concept or that Christians should never want to be a leader. Leadership is an essential ingredient in God's plan, a divine expectation. Leadership allows us to influence for good a world gripped by evil. Leadership is one way to *step up*. It's how we change the world.

Leadership Myths

As I mentioned earlier, let's look at leadership myths. For all our presumed understanding of what a leader or leadership is we seem to work with a lot of leadership mythology—curious ideas developed over time like urban legends.

Leadership myths are pervasive and persistent. What makes them troubling is that people who believe them usually fail to reach their leadership potential—and they sometimes hold others back as well. The myths get in the way like barriers on an obstacle course.

Let's clear away some barriers by reviewing a few leadership myths:

- Leaders are born.
- Leaders are men.

- Leaders are wealthy.
- Leaders are especially charismatic.
- Leaders are White.
- Leaders are superb communicators.
- Leaders are just managers who have more power.
- Leadership is authority.
- Leadership is hierarchical or positional.
- Leadership is a spiritual gift only a few possess.
- Leadership is a special call from God.
- Leadership is not open to Christian women who must be in "submission."
- Leadership can't be taught.

You may be able to cite single examples for all these statements, but one example does not make a law. On the other hand, one example to the contrary will invalidate what someone thinks is a law, and we can point to plenty of exceptions. None of these statements may be generalized to all leadership in all times and cultures.

> **Believe leadership myths; fail to reach leadership potential.**

For example, I've never met a leader who hadn't been born; so proclaiming "leaders are born" like it's a breakthrough discovery is silly. But many people still believe leadership attributes and skills are instilled at birth and that's it. If you didn't get the leadership gene from the stork, so the argument goes, you're never going to be a leader.

This is a devastating concept.[52] It's reminiscent of the feudal perspectives of the Middle Ages all the way back to the divine right of kings. But claiming leaders are born and never "made" doesn't stand the test of experience.

Leaders are men, and wealthy men at that. Oh really? Joan of Arc was neither a man nor wealthy. Same can be said for Harriet

Tubman and Mother Teresa. Have a disproportionate number of leaders been men and have many leaders been wealthy? Sure. But this historical fact says more about lack of access for women in certain times and cultures, including our own, than it does about innate ability. And more than one wife has led from behind the scenes when her husband, the elected or expected leader, wouldn't or couldn't lead. Ask Mrs. Woodrow Wilson.

Leaders aren't leaders unless they exude charisma. Wrong again. President Calvin Coolidge was a smart man, but charisma certainly isn't a word associated with his memory. Interestingly, though, "charisma isn't an essential leadership quality. Many leaders, despite a lack of charisma, still manage to inspire trust and loyalty in others, and in that way get things done."[53] That's what "Silent Cal" did.

Leaders are as different in personality and gifts as the leaves in a forest of trees. Gifted Native American speakers Tecumseh and later Chief Joseph were leaders in a lost cause, and they weren't White. Neither was Martin Luther King Jr., an orator of the first rank and the most important leader of the American Civil Rights Movement. The biblical Moses, arguably one of the greatest leaders who ever lived, at least initially struggled with poor communication skills.

> **Leaders are as different in personality and gifts as leaves in a forest of trees.**

Leaders are just hyped-up managers. No, leaders may be good managers, and some managers may possess leadership skills. But leaders are more than just managers with more clout. Warren Bennis famously said, "Leaders are people who do the right things. Managers are people who do things right."[54] Leaders lead, and managers, well, they manage. We need them both.

Leadership isn't just for those who possess formal authority, have amassed power, or hold a position. Talent and tenacity trump titles any day. That's one lesson from the American Revolutionary War.

Ragtag colonists took nearly eight years to do it, but they succeeded in chasing the Redcoats and chastening the king. Women without power or position—yet leaders—from Elizabeth Cady Stanton to Susan B. Anthony, worked throughout the nineteenth century to secure American women's right to vote, finally granted in 1920 in the Nineteenth Amendment of the United States Constitution. Even "title-less" leaders get things done.

The Spiritual Gift of Leadership

Another leadership myth is that a spiritual gift of leadership is only given to some people, so only they are equipped to lead. This is a delicate one, because we don't want to do damage to the Scripture. Interpreting the Bible correctly should always be paramount in our decision-making. But Christian people regularly trip over this myth. You'll hear it everywhere you go and it's hurting the church.

According to the Scripture some individuals in the community of Christian faith are given a spiritual gift of leadership or administration. God said, "Having gifts that differ according to the grace given to us, let us use them: . . . the one who leads, with zeal" (Rom. 12:6, 8).

Unfortunately, some Christians misapply this scriptural teaching. Since the spiritual gift of leadership is given to certain individuals, they reason, it must be an *exclusive* or *unique* gift, not given to others, including maybe not to them. They adopt a kind of zero-sum interpretation of spiritual gifts. If you get the gift, I don't.

This point of view doesn't do justice to God's teachings about spiritual gifts in Romans 12:6–8; 1 Corinthians 12:1–13:13; and Ephesians 4:7–16. If we believed God gave us a complete list of spiritual gifts in these passages of Scripture, we'd be forced to conclude that these gifts are the only ones God has with which to work. But the Sovereign God is not limited. God gave to us an *illustrative* list of spiritual gifts, not an *exhaustive* one. God bestows far more gifts upon the church than the examples he cited in his Word.

> **The Bible gives us an *illustrative* list of spiritual gifts, not an *exhaustive* one.**

The Bible says that every follower of Christ is given at least one spiritual gift (1 Peter 4:10). The Scripture never says Christians are restricted to one gift each. Nor does the Scripture state that once a spiritual gift like leadership is given to one person in a community of faith it won't be given to another. If this were true, then a gift of teaching given to a friend means I cannot and may not ever exercise that gift. By this interpretation, if the gift of mercy is given to you, then I'm free never to be merciful, because "I don't have the gift." If you possess the gift of giving or generosity, I don't have to give? No way.

> **Every follower of Christ is given at least one spiritual gift.**

In these biblical passages God said he wants Christian people to act in unity of heart and belief even though the church is incredibly diverse, including every nation, tongue, race, and personality. God informs us that each member of the church is differently gifted (Rom. 12:6; 1 Cor. 12:11, 18). Then he admonishes us to exercise these spiritual gifts in love for the glory of God (1 Cor. 13).

So, if you've been blessed with the spiritual gift of leadership, you'd better exercise it diligently, that is, with zeal. God has given you something more, and "Everyone to whom much was given, of him much will be required, and from him to whom they entrusted much, they will demand the more" (Luke 12:48). If you haven't been blessed with the spiritual gift of leadership, then you've been blessed with other gifts, and you'd better exercise them. Plus, you're still free in Christ to develop your capacity to lead for his kingdom.

Leadership As Calling

Christians often speak of one's life purpose as a "calling" and over the years the idea that God conveys a "special call" has affirmed some people while confusing a lot more. Some individuals have bought into the myth that only "called leaders" lead. These individuals are, therefore, reluctant to lead or to even consider leading because they believe to lead one must have received a special call from God to become a leader. "How can I lead if I don't have the call?" or, "How can I be sure I'm called to lead?" they ask. It's too bad, because their confusion is rooted in a hurtful misunderstanding or misinterpretation of Scripture.

The idea that a person must receive a special calling from God to pursue a given profession or vocation, or the idea that only those called of God to lead may lead, is not biblically supportable. It's true, a few Old Testament leaders like Abraham, Moses, and Jeremiah were specially called by God. It's also true that the idea of a "special call" is used once in the New Testament, depending upon how one interprets the use of the word "call" (1 Cor. 7:17–24).

> **The idea only called leaders may lead is not biblically supportable.**

The Old Testament giants of the faith lived in a time when God spoke directly, sometimes visually or aurally, to his chosen leaders. In the New Testament, the 1 Corinthians passage speaks more about salvation and one's spiritual walk than it does one's employment or professional position. Nowhere in Scripture does God use the word "call" or "calling" to describe a specific vocational assignment, career choice, or leadership for you or me today.[55]

But as I said, this idea is firmly planted in the evangelical Christian landscape and won't go away soon. It's an idea promoted by a long list of Christian notables, including social researcher George Barna: "A Christian leader is called by God. . . . The vast majority of God's human creation are followers."[56]

Here's Barna again: "If you have not been chosen by Him to lead His people, it does not matter how wonderful your character or how well skilled you are for the task, you will never become a great Christian leader. You may lead, of course—our political system, educational institutions and corporations are packed with people who are leading despite not being called by God to be spiritual leaders. The difference is that we are not talking about leading God's people to higher profitability, or to greater efficiency, but to superior godliness and to spiritual truth. Further, we are not talking about meddling in human affairs to make incremental gains for worldly purposes, but about investing in people such that they recognize and maximize the ways God has called, gifted and seeks to refine them."[57]

> **Nowhere in Scripture does God "call" us to a vocational assignment or career choice.**

Now to be clear, George Barna is talking about people called of God to lead the Christian church, what he calls "spiritual leadership," as opposed to other kinds of leaders. But even with this distinction noted, his treatise on leadership is still confusing. Barna's demotion of other forms of leadership to second-class status is biblically unjustifiable and another in a long line of erroneous teachings separating "worldly" or "secular" pursuits from the ostensibly "godlier" ones in "Christian service." Barna presents the old "sacred/secular dichotomy."

Martin Luther first battled this false dichotomy at the inception of the Protestant Reformation, because he recognized that a truly biblical idea of calling has nothing to do with career choice or position, clergy versus laity, and certainly not leadership. Luther wrote that contrary to the prevailing viewpoint of his era, all Christians are members of the "spiritual estate," and all are part of "the priesthood of all believers," not just the ruling, contemplative, priestly, special upper class. Luther made no spiritual or any other evaluative distinctions between farmer and priest, homemaker and businessperson, or a host of other moral pursuits.[58] So "one does not disobey God by choosing any one worthwhile secular occupation over another, or by retiring at 60 rather than at 65."[59]

In fact, the Scripture says, "What does the LORD require of you but to do justice, and to love kindness, and to walk humbly with your God?" (Micah 6:8). God's expectations are surely a high and holy standard, but they're stated in terms of what we are "to be" and "to become," not what we are "to do."

> **What does the Lord require of you? To act justly, to love mercy, and to walk humbly.**

Students of the Bible have sometimes referred to this divine command to be/to become as our "primary call." In other words, our primary call—our life's purpose or mission—is to be/become God's obedient and devoted followers. In Os Guinness's classic book on the subject, *The Call: Finding and Fulfilling the Central Purpose of Your Life*, Guinness reminds us that our primary calling is to *someone* (God) not *something* or *somewhere*.[60]

Guinness further notes that students of the Bible also talk about a "secondary call." In Guinness's words, "Our secondary calling, considering who God is as sovereign, is that everyone, everywhere, and in everything should think, speak, live, act entirely for him."[61] Our secondary call—whatever we choose in Christian liberty to do in and with our life—is to serve God with our talents in the time and place and opportunity he sets before us.

Consequently, neither my "primary call" nor my "secondary call" is really a "special call" that is exclusively for me but not you, or for you but not the next person. And disappointing as it may be to some, the truth is, you and I won't generally identify our secondary calling through some miraculous occurrence like Moses's burning bush, or God's writing on the wall at King Belshazzar's feast, or the light shone upon Saul-who-became-Paul on the Damascus Road. We may experience a humble personal epiphany as something dawns upon us someday, but that's what it is, our developed thinking, not typically a "special call" of God.

> **We won't generally identify our secondary calling through some miraculous occurrence.**

More likely we'll identify our secondary calling and perhaps our life's work by applying our understanding of the Word of God to the God-given talents, interests, and opportunities of our lives; or, by asking questions of those older and wiser, by walking the walk with our eyes open, one step of faith, one sound moral judgment, at a time.

It pleases God when we make good choices about how to use our gifts to fulfill our purpose, including as unlikely leaders. He gives us the liberty and responsibility to do so. You can choose to make leadership your secondary calling.

Women in Leadership

Some Christians have also misinterpreted God's teachings about the spiritual gift of leadership in another way, this one involving women. Simply put, they believe women should never—anywhere, ever—assume authority over men. The rest of the argument goes something like this: God commanded women to be demure examples of Christian womanhood. Since leadership generally involves authority over men—and apparently attitudes and behaviors considered inconsistent with Christian femininity—Christian women cannot and may not lead.

This is a spurious scriptural interpretation. Frankly, it is an absurd chauvinism, one that has harmed not only many women but also societies that missed the benefits talented women could have demonstrated if they had not been denied access to leadership.

Nowhere does the Bible suggest that a woman's enterprise, even leadership, will somehow detract from her femininity. In fact, in Proverbs 31 the Bible suggests the opposite.

Nowhere does God say Christian womanhood and leadership are mutually exclusive concepts.

Nowhere does the Bible say women are the property of the men of her family or that she must always take second or lower place in the presence of men.

Nowhere does the Bible say women cannot own property, vote, participate in civic or organizational decision-making, or "speak up" when men are present.

Nowhere does the Bible state that women should be second-class citizens or anything less than men.

Nowhere in the Bible does God say women should not or cannot lead.

> **Nowhere in the Bible does God say women should not or cannot lead.**

The Bible does reference relationships within the family and within the local church, encouraging both men and women to submit voluntarily to one another, to "bear one another's burdens" (Gal. 6:2) and to live in mutually supportive community (1 Cor. 11:3–16; Eph. 5:22–24; Col. 3:18–19; 1 Tim. 2:9–15; 1 Peter 3:1–7). These passages address specific and limited circumstances in worship and in husband-and-wife relationships, not relationships in society and culture.

Whatever you believe the Bible teaches about "submission" between a husband and a wife, you must agree the Scripture does not say a woman must be subject to every man she meets. By the same token, the Bible most emphatically does not give a man carte blanche authority over every woman he meets.

There is no doctrine called "Keep a woman in her place." That attitude is a form of chauvinism that is not biblically justifiable, nor is it socially justifiable.[62]

There were godly women leaders in biblical times—Abigail, Anna, Lydia—and there've been godly women leaders in every age since.

Many were not high profile. Even more were never given the credit they deserved. That's the case with many female missionaries today. If women pulled out of missions, international Christian outreach would collapse. Not just because the nurses and teachers went home but because women perform leadership roles all over the world.

Simply put, it is not unbiblical for women to lead. Positively put, women should be encouraged to lead and developed as leaders. Another way of looking at it is to recognize that roughly 50 percent of the unlikely leaders out there are women. Women *should* lead. We *need* women leaders.

Leadership "Demons"

Aside from myths, leaders and leadership are often "demonized," either blamed for evil in the world or looked upon with suspicion. Here are a few such demons:

- Leaders are robber barons.
- Leaders are anti-democratic.
- Leadership is Machiavellian, (i.e., manipulative).
- Leadership is tyrannical.
- Leadership is intimidation or coercion.
- Leadership is controlling, dictating.
- Leadership contradicts service or "servanthood."

For some reason, our ideas about leadership get twisted up with our image of "bad guys" and their desire to conquer the world. Lex Luthor in the Superman comic books and movies. Adolph Hitler in real history. Some people can't seem to think about leaders without wincing. In this view, leaders are self-promoters, "politicians" who can't be trusted. Only "the people" will ultimately be in the right.

Some of this attitude toward leadership is fostered by American democratic culture. We haven't fully trusted a leader since we threw off England's King George and our George left the first presidency.

> **Our ideas about leadership get twisted up with
> our image of "bad guys."**

Some of this suspicious attitude is justifiable. A few leaders haven't deserved the allegiance and power they commanded or usurped, and some leaders have left lasting bitterness in their wake. Richard Nixon may be America's highest profile if not worst-case example. And historically, the world has certainly endured evil leaders—from the Old Testament King Jehoram, about whom it was said, "He departed with no one's regret" (2 Chron. 21:20), to Genghis Khan to Nero to Pol Pot to Saddam Hussein to Kim Jong-Il. Sadly, the rogue's gallery has many members.

Dishonest, anti-democratic, manipulative, tyrannical, coercive, and dictatorial demagogues are the bad people who don't fit James MacGregor Burns's prescriptive definition of leadership. Yet their record shows us morally questionable *individuals* holding leadership positions, not a record of something intrinsically irredeemable about leadership in general.

Leadership is a tool. As free moral agents, human beings can use leadership for good or for evil. Leadership always gets back to character.

Servant Leadership

Another perspective on leadership that's gained prominence in recent years is called "servant leadership." The idea of servant leadership is taken from Scripture and was popularized as a leadership model beginning in 1970 by Robert K. Greenleaf.[63] In the time since, servant leadership has become its own cottage industry with companies like Starbucks Coffee, Herman Miller, 7-Eleven, ServiceMaster, and others implementing service leadership models in their approach to decision-making and personnel development.

In Scripture, the story begins when the mother of two disciples, James and John, approached Jesus, requesting he place her sons in positions of honor and authority in relationship to him (Matt. 20:25–28; Mark 10:35–44). Later, during the Last Supper, a similar discussion arose among the disciples as to who would be greatest (Luke 22:24–30).

Leadership always gets back to character.

On both occasions, Jesus responded, "But whoever would be great among you must be your servant, and whoever would be first among you must be slave of all. For even the Son of Man came not to be served but to serve" (Mark 10:43–45). Then he provided a timeless picture of a servant's heart by washing his disciples' feet (John 13:1–17).

With this statement Jesus made it clear that leaders are not better than their followers. That leadership is not about the leader but about others. That leadership is a form of stewardship, not a means of lording over others but a means of enabling them.[64] That leadership is about humility as well as hierarchy. That biblically informed leadership may involve ambition but never selfish ambition (Phil. 2:3–4).

Some writers, even people who do not embrace Christianity, now contend servant leadership is *the* model of leadership. To hear them talk you'd think no other model will suffice. However, nowhere in his earthly ministry did Christ ever use the term "servant leadership," nor did he offer it as a full-fledged model exclusive to all others. This point is not meant to disparage servant leadership as a model for leading. It's just a reminder that there's much we can learn from other models of leadership, if we remember Christ's injunction about our motives.

Leadership is a form of stewardship.

Meanwhile others, especially some Christians, misapply the servant leadership model by suggesting it requires leaders be subservient or submissive. Their approach yields a weak leader Jesus wouldn't recognize, for not only did he act decisively when required, he never equated being a servant with being servile. Jesus said, "Blessed are the meek, for they shall inherit the earth" (Matt. 5:5), but he didn't commend weakness to his followers. Meekness and weakness are not synonymous. And one can demonstrate the Christian virtues of humility and selflessness without neutering his or her ability to lead.

Still others argue that to implement a servant leadership model in an organization you must decentralize authority and power. Proponents of this view prefer a consultative, relational, or shared-power approach to community decision-making. This view is more prominent in the academy than the corporation where academic tradition suggests faculty and possibly staff members should be the ones running the university, not administrators. But if this approach is skewed it can strip leaders of their ability to lead.

"Servant leadership flipped the paradigm upside down from the followers serving the leader to the leader serving the followers. A leader's purpose morphed into becoming an emotional healer and facilitator of social acceptance."[65]

While a servant leadership approach surely does not preclude a relational, shared-power method of decision-making, neither does it necessarily require it. Jesus never condemned authority, the use of power, or the idea of leadership. Indeed, he ordained their use for our good (Rom. 13:1–5).

Jesus never condemned authority or the use of power.

What Jesus did was demonstrate that leadership and service are not contradictory, and he approached all that he did, especially leadership, with an ethic of love. For Jesus, "the style changed but the purpose did not, because his leadership had only one goal, to do the Father's will by bringing in the kingdom of God."[66] In this he set a standard for all of us, for "servant leadership is more about character than style."[67]

We lead best when we become shepherds who serve the Good Shepherd by serving others.[68] For God's unlikely leaders Jesus is our prototype.

LEADERSHIP LESSONS
1. Sooner or later, everyone is presented with the "need to lead."
2. Leadership is the act of inspiring others toward a goal.
3. Leadership is one way to *stand out* and *step up* as God's ambassadors.
4. Believe leadership myths; fail to reach leadership potential.
5. Leaders are as different in personality and gifts as leaves in a forest of trees.
6. Every follower of Christ is given at least one spiritual gift.
7. Nowhere in the Bible does God say women should not or cannot lead.
8. Human beings are free moral agents who can use leadership for good or for evil.
9. Leadership always gets back to character.
10. Jesus never condemned authority or use of power but led with love.

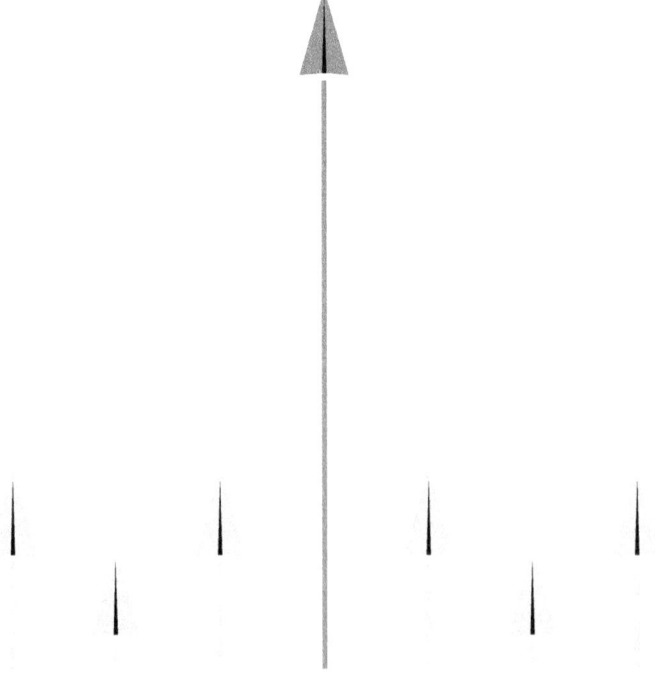

CHAPTER 3

CONFUSION

What A Leader *Could Be*

JUDAS

Judas Iscariot was the bad disciple. He's the poster boy for disloyalty. He was one of the Twelve, but his name lives in infamy as the man who betrayed Jesus Christ for thirty pieces of silver.

One of the things we learn from Judas is that "leadership has less to do with position than it does disposition."[69] Judas enjoyed the same leadership position and prospects, training and opportunity, as the other disciples. Like them, he sat under Christ's teaching, but he didn't give the Lord his heart. Like them, he was a flawed character. Unlike them, Judas was a spiritual fake who remained unredeemed, religious but lost. He never embraced values different from those in the world around him (Luke 6:16; 22:2–6, 47–48).

Judas was apparently good with money, or at least was interested in it, for he kept the disciples' moneybags and acted as treasurer for the group. To have maintained his credibility with the disciples for so long Judas must have performed some of the acts of ministry they performed. Even so, he didn't become the example of spiritual transformation his colleagues became. He squandered his leadership opportunity.

After Judas betrayed Jesus, the Savior still greeted him as "friend" (Matt. 26:50). To the very end, Jesus kept the door open for Judas to repent. But evil had so darkened his soul that Judas responded with remorse rather than repentance and took his own life (Matt. 27:3–5; Acts 1:15–20). Ultimately, in a chilling summation, the Scripture says Judas "turned aside to go to his own place" (Acts 1:25).

May Another Take His Place of Leadership

In Acts 1:20, Judas Iscariot's passing is observed with the heartrending but amazing statement, "Let another take his office" or "place of leadership."[70] The sadness of this verse points to potential unfulfilled, to blessings unbestowed.

Yet incredibly Judas's position as a disciple is still described as a "place of leadership." In God's providence even this bad apple was permitted for a season to hold a position of leadership. In God's grace the disciples were given an opportunity to choose a new leader.

Leadership matters to God.

Judas's story is an indictment of the leader, not a condemnation of leadership. Otherwise, God would have eliminated Judas's position. Judas failed to become the leader he could have been. Why the Sovereign God chose Judas may not make sense to us, but the lesson remains: leadership matters to God.

Little "L" Leaders

Leadership isn't capitalized in the Bible, most notably in the Acts 1 passage referencing Judas and his successor. Except for a few godly kings of Israel, throughout biblical history God used "little l" leaders to accomplish his purposes. We're told, for example, that Matthias takes Judas's place as one of the twelve apostles. This is a momentous transition at a turning point in the development of Christianity and the inception of the early church. Yet nothing is known or said about Matthias before or after his appointment. The only thing we may infer from Scripture is that Matthias was a man with a right heart because the disciples prayed, "You, Lord, who know the hearts of all, show which one of these two you have chosen" (Acts 1:23–26). Matthias was an unlikely "little l" leader who stepped up and served without accolade when opportunity called.

Leadership isn't capitalized in the Bible.

The Bible's leaders were almost all "regular people" like you and me. Not just superstars, spiritual giants, or brainiacs. Sure, God makes well-known people into well-known leaders. But he blesses leaders among the "little people" too.

The Bible is a record of ordinary people accomplishing extraordinary things for God. He pointed them toward the task. If they hesitated, like Jacob, Jonah, or Jeremiah, he reminded them of their God-given talent, encouraged them, said he would be with them, and held them accountable. Then he placed them in leadership—as unlikely as it may seem.

Unlikely Leaders Who Led

The typical biblical leader was an unlikely leader. Even some of the greatest started rather low on the social ladder.

Rahab was a harlot living in Jericho, one of the more wicked and powerful cities of the day. Rahab's rendezvous with history began when the Israelites approached the city and Joshua sent spies to reconnoiter. When two spies were threatened with discovery Rahab courageously intervened, hiding them and making possible the future conquest of the city. At this strategic juncture of her life, she saw the big picture and willingly embraced an enormous personal risk. She was not a traitor. She took sides in her culture's battle of good versus evil and is commended in Scripture for her faith. Rahab is one of the most unlikely leaders in the Bible but was honored later in her life with a maternal place in the lineage of Christ.

> **In the Bible, ordinary people accomplished extraordinary things for God.**

Caleb was a man with a possibly questionable pedigree, a Kenizzite, a descendant of Esau rather than Jacob. We learn, though, that his courage and character were far more important than his ancestry. Early in the Israelites' exodus Moses sent twelve men to spy upon the promised land. In their report, only two spies, Caleb and Joshua, had the faith and courage to recommend proceeding into the land despite the giants they had seen. God was displeased and he judged the people for their lack of faith by sending them wandering (and at times "wondering") in the wilderness for forty years. All that generation eventually died short of their goal, except for Caleb and Joshua.

Years later under Joshua's leadership the Israelites took the promised land, and the now eighty-five-year-old Caleb reminded Joshua, "Give me this hill country of which the Lord spoke on that day, for you heard on that day how the Anakim were there, with great fortified cities. It may be that the Lord will be with me, and I shall drive them out just as the Lord said" (Josh. 14:12).

Undoubtedly to Joshua's great satisfaction his friend Caleb defeated the very people who'd decades earlier terrified their peers. Caleb, the Bible says, was a man who "wholly followed the Lord, the God of Israel" (Josh. 14:14). Caleb measured his giants by faith in God not by fear of failure, and his leadership didn't waffle in the face of majority opinion. He cared more about where he was going than where he was from, and so did God.

Deborah the judge and prophetess was a woman in what then was a "man's world." She was a wife, homemaker, and counselor who rose to denounce the lack of leadership among the men of her era. In response to her people's oppression by a foreign enemy she summoned the military commander, Barak, and commissioned him to amass an army of ten thousand men. In one of the more amusing male/female anecdotes of Scripture the great general Barak said he'd go to battle only if she went with him. She did and thus inspired one of the earliest known martial anthems on record (Judges 5). Deborah is the only woman in the Bible placed in power by the people. She led with wisdom in peacetime, courage in war, and always with faith in the Lord. Her leadership is witness to the fact that biological sex is morally and spiritually irrelevant.

Jephthah was the son of a prostitute who was rejected by his half brothers but emerged as a mighty warrior in God's service. It's not *who we were*. It's with God's help *who we become*.

Ruth was a humble yet decisive widow who evidenced profound faith in God, loyalty, an admirable work ethic, and a concern for justice. That she did all this as a Gentile woman in a Jewish patriarchal society makes her achievements even more remarkable. Ruth eventually became a great-grandmother of King David and therefore a member of the lineage of Jesus. She never led a nation or an organization, but leading a family is still leadership.

> **Courage and character are far more important than ancestry.**

Surely these unlikely leaders don't seem very impressive. Yet they did great things for God. And interestingly, maybe even ironically, in our eyes the accomplishments of "less impressive" leaders is an impressive thing. The unexpected catches our attention. We notice when the tortoise defeats the hare, and God properly receives even more glory.

Josiah was only a boy when he began to serve God and lead his people, beginning his reign as king of Judah at eight years of age.

As a teenager he embarked upon his spiritual odyssey and "he did what was right in the eyes of the LORD and walked in all the way of David his father, and he did not turn aside to the right or to the left" (2 Kings 22:2). At age twenty he purged Jerusalem and Judah of idols and false priests. Then at age twenty-six he repaired the temple of God, rediscovered the Law of Moses, and renewed the people's covenant with God. He died from a battle wound at thirty-nine years of age and the Scripture says, "Before him there was no king like him, who turned to the LORD with all his heart and with all his soul and with all his might, according to all the Law of Moses, nor did any like him arise after him" (2 Kings 23:25). His leadership is testimony to the fact that age is morally and spiritually irrelevant.

Elijah is an example of a great leader who called an entire nation to account. He's an incredible example of what one life sold-out to God can accomplish. A bit odd, sometimes fearless sometimes fearful, he was always a high-impact miracle-worker. For much of his prophetic career he was the daring spiritual nemesis of King Ahab and Queen Jezebel, probably the wickedest royal tandem in ancient Israel. There was nothing low profile about Elijah. When his time came God took Elijah to heaven on a whirlwind in a chariot of fire.

Leading a family is still leadership.

Elijah's protégé, *Elisha*, was by comparison an unknown and rather reserved farm boy. But Elisha watched and learned, and his later exploits rivaled his mentor's remarkable service for God. Neither man cared for silver or gold. Both men were agents of righteousness. Both men were the most powerful voices of their generation.

Throughout Scripture God taps one odd character after another, compelling and enabling them to lead. To say the least, Jonah was an unenthusiastic leader. His life is a case study of a woebegone underachiever who God still used in unique historic ways. *Hosea* was another strange choice and his circumstances were stranger. Hosea's marriage to Gomer was marred by her unfaithfulness, but when Hosea and Gomer reconciled, God used the marriage as a living illustration of his love for his people. Awkward as these men may have been, they "were made strong out of weakness" as God used their unlikely preparation and personalities to fulfill his purposes (Heb. 11:34).

God taps one odd character after another, compelling and enabling them to lead.

Jeremiah was a reluctant servant. First, he echoed Moses by protesting he didn't know how to speak, then he argued he was too young to lead. But God had other plans. For more than forty years God enabled Jeremiah to proclaim his law in the face of consistent opposition, beatings, and imprisonment.

Jeremiah must have been one tough fellow. Think again. Jeremiah never evidenced the strength of personality of a Joshua. He showed no iron will or strong ambition. He was lonely and melancholy, he shed tears freely—he's been called "the weeping prophet," and he didn't see much in the way of results. One might say he was "unsuccessful," except for one principal thing. Through it all Jeremiah set his eyes upon the Lord: "'The LORD is my portion,' says my soul, 'therefore I will hope in him.' The LORD is good to those who wait for him, to the soul who seeks him" (Lam. 3:24–25).

Jeremiah led with his speech, by walking around with an ox yoke on his shoulders—what today we'd call a prop—and through his own prayerful introspection. Jeremiah was frequently frustrated but always faithful. His life demonstrates one can lead without fitting the modern conception of leader-as-alpha-male.

In the New Testament church era—still a "man's world"— *Priscilla* becomes known throughout Christendom as one of the most influential women of her era. She taught the teacher Apollos, the early church assembled in her home, and she became a scholar of the Word. She became a friend and confidant of the apostle Paul. Priscilla led by doing, both as a tentmaker with her husband Aquila and in their evangelism.

> **One can lead without fitting the modern conception of leader-as-alpha-male.**

The New Testament *disciples*, Jesus's handpicked followers, were a motley crew comprised of rough fishermen, a wealthy and probably dishonest tax collector, and several local laborers. None of us would have selected any of them, especially not as close associates. This so-called letter to Jesus from a fictional Jordan consulting agency humorously illustrates the point:

To: Jesus, Son of Joseph
Woodcrafter's Carpenter Shop
Nazareth 25922

From: Jordan Management Consultants

Dear Sir:
Thank you for submitting the résumés of the twelve men you have picked for managerial positions in your new organization. All of them have now taken our battery of tests; and we have not only run the results through our computer but also arranged personal interviews for each of them with our psychologist and vocational aptitude consultant.

The profiles of all tests are included, and you will want to study each of them carefully.

It is the staff opinion that most of your nominees are lacking in background, education, and vocational aptitude for the type of enterprise you are undertaking. They do not have the team concept. We would recommend that you continue your search for persons of experience in managerial ability and proven capability.

Simon Peter is emotionally unstable and given to fits of temper. Andrew has absolutely no qualities of leadership. The two brothers, James and John, the sons of Zebedee, place personal interest above company loyalty. Thomas demonstrates a questioning attitude that would tend to undermine morale. We feel that it is our duty to tell you that Matthew had been blacklisted by the Greater Jerusalem Better Business Bureau; James, the son of Alphaeus, and Thaddaeus definitely have radical leanings, and they both registered a high score on the manic-depressive scale.

One of the candidates, however, shows great potential. He is a man of ability and resourcefulness, meets people well, has a keen business mind, and has contacts in high places. He is highly motivated, ambitious, and responsible. We recommend Judas Iscariot as your controller and right-hand man. All of the other profiles are self-explanatory.

We wish you every success in your new venture.

Sincerely, Jordan Management Consultants[71]

The Twelve, including the future betrayer Judas, followed Jesus willingly if often fearfully. They weren't spiritual storm troopers. In their early years they consistently demonstrated both an individual and a collective lack of faith. They offered mundane advice when spiritual insight was required, they grumbled, and they squabbled over who would be the "greatest." They doubted, slept when they should have watched, and eventually ran in fear from those who arrested Jesus. Nevertheless, Jesus persevered. He loved them. He chose them. He taught them. He led them.

Jesus loved them, chose them, taught them, led them.

Jesus looks for *could be* and *would be* leaders. He saw what the disciples could be and would be in him. In time via the grace of God, they said, "We believe." Then in Jesus's name the disciples performed miracles, launched "the Way," and, ultimately, suffered martyrdom for their faith (John 6:69–71; Acts 9:2; 24:14).

Long before the disciples met their end, one of the first to be martyred for his Christian faith was a man named *Stephen*. He was a man "full of grace and power" (Acts 6:8) and a deacon who performed miracles, preached in Jerusalem, and defended himself against false accusations. For all this Stephen was finally stoned to death while a young man named Saul, the man God would later commission as the apostle Paul, looked on with approval. Stephen's leadership was an example of faith, service, courage, and saintliness.

Jesus looks for *could be* and *would be* leaders.

The apostle Paul's spiritual apprentice, *Timothy*, was a youth, probably in his late teen years, when he assumed responsibility for his first church. Paul told him, "Let no one despise you for your youth, but set the believers an example in speech, in conduct, in love, in faith, in purity" (1 Tim. 4:12).

The Unlikely Leaders' Leaders

Shortly after Christ's ascent into heaven and Matthias's election replacing Judas, disciples *Peter* and *John* emerged as leaders among the Twelve in the birth of the early church. The church was founded on the day of Pentecost in response to Peter's impassioned preaching. Peter and John worked together in the healing of the lame man at the temple, sharing the gospel of Jesus's resurrection, and experiencing the first recorded arrests and persecution of believers.

In an act of civil disobedience Peter and John respond courageously—"Whether it is right in the sight of God to listen to you rather than to God, you must judge, for we cannot but speak of what we have seen and heard" (Acts 4:19–20). Local religious leaders were astonished, primarily because they accurately if arrogantly considered Peter and John "uneducated, common men" (Acts 4:13).

This is Peter, the rough, uncouth, impetuous fisherman. This is John the mere youth, "the disciple whom Jesus loved" (John 21:20). This is the same Peter who in fear denied Jesus three times, the same John who ran away with the rest of the Twelve during the events preceding the crucifixion. These men were truly unschooled and ordinary. But lack of education and common roots doesn't disqualify people from leadership.

> **Uneducated and common doesn't disqualify people from leadership.**

Peter became a dynamic presence in the life of the early church and was directed by the Holy Spirit to write two books of the New Testament. John survived all his apostolic contemporaries to live a long life and write as many as six books of the New Testament including the book of Revelation.

Peter summarized his energetic leadership philosophy in 1 Peter 4:10–11: "As each has received a gift, use it to serve one another, as good stewards of God's varied grace: whoever speaks, as one who speaks oracles of God; whoever serves, as one who serves by the strength that God supplies—in order that in everything God may be glorified through Jesus Christ."

Peter and John used the talents God gave them. They fed and they led Jesus's sheep, demonstrating once again that God's unlikely leaders often come from unexpected, unimpressive backgrounds.

God's Unlikely Leaders' Essential Characteristics

God's unlikely leaders shared at least two essential characteristics:

- Faith—While they did not always understand, they trusted God.
- Willing heart—They obeyed God.

The people listed in the faith "hall of fame" of Hebrews 11 from Abel to Samuel and the prophets were all unlikely leaders in one way or another. Through faith they "conquered kingdoms, enforced justice, obtained promises, stopped the mouths of lions" (Heb. 11:33). All of them responded to God's call. Many of them went about "in skins of sheep and goats, destitute, afflicted, mistreated," to the point Scripture said of them "the world was not worthy" (Heb. 11:37–38).

Like Isaiah who said, "Here I am! Send me," God wants our willing submission (Isa. 6:8). He wants us to choose to serve him. He provides all the rest an unlikely leader needs, even in the face of severe trials.

Lead with the strength God provides.

God's unlikely leaders were all beginners at some point. They all started somewhere. They all learned "on the job" in a process of time. Their leadership experiences were not always glamorous or noble. They took risks and made mistakes—sometimes big ones. They were sinners in need of God's grace, just like the rest of us. They led in different ways. They didn't sit around waiting to "have it all together" before they lead. They did meditate and pray. They did get away from their followers occasionally.

God's unlikely leaders took risks and made mistakes.

God's unlikely leaders led by being, telling, and doing. They learned to deal with negativity, pessimism, and various versions of "You can't do that" or "We've never done it that way before." They expressed virtually every human emotion. They weren't always courteous, cheerful, brave, clean or otherwise able to affirm much less embody the twelve points of the Boy Scout Law. They used mind and muscle. Some led patiently, some like their hair was on fire. They "raised the bar," "went to the next level," "painted a new picture," and lived their vision "24/7."

God's Unlikely Leadership Principles

God's unlikely leaders did all those things but not all at once and not all by one leader. Along with recognizing the foundational importance of faith and a willing heart we can learn a few more things from studying God's unlikely leaders. I call them "God's Unlikely Leadership Principles." Here are a few:

1. *Men and women of God must be godly men and women.* A person may be an unlikely leader, but he or she won't be one of God's unlikely leaders without godliness. Like Jeremiah, God uses people with broken and contrite hearts (Ps. 51:17). The quality of our leadership will be directly related to the quality of our fellowship with God. "We lead best when God is leading us."[72]

2. *Character and competence count more than countenance or connections.* In the oldest biblical text on record, Job is remembered as a man of integrity, not just as a man of riches, achievements, notable friends, or success (Job 1:1, 21–22). While countenance and connections are blessings, gifts from God to use in his service, they become hollow

without a clear conscience. God's unlikely leaders recognize their character, confidence, and competence "is from God" (2 Cor. 3:4–5).

3. *Don't get hung up on a presumed lack of talent but vigorously use the talents God provides.* God's unlikely leaders knew there is no "leadership gene." They worked with what God gave them. Like the poor widow who gave God all she had to live on, "two small copper coins," God's unlikely leaders invest whatever moral and intellectual capital they have in his service (Luke 21:1–4).

4. *Access the power of prayer.* Unlikely leaders in the Bible recognized their limitations and sought God's help daily, like Daniel, or before a significant action, like Esther. The Bible says, "The prayer of a righteous person has great power as it is working. Elijah was a man with a nature like ours, and he prayed fervently" (James 5:16–18). When Elijah prayed, God answered, Elijah was emboldened, and his leadership was empowered.

5. *Stand for something.* What God's unlikely leaders stood for matched God's expectations. They knew that "where there is no prophetic vision the people cast off restraint" (Prov. 29:18). So, they aligned their leadership with the people's need to refocus upon God's wisdom and will. This is something Abraham's nephew Lot never did. He wasted his leadership opportunity in Sodom primarily because he stood for nothing. Lot never measured up. He absorbed the values of the culture in which he lived, and he lost his family, his fortune, and his honor (Genesis 19).

6. *Lead when others are not yet following.* Risk and ridicule were part of the experience of God's unlikely leaders, but so was reward. Jesus said, "A prophet is not without honor except in his hometown and in his own household" (Matt.

13:57–58). Of course, leaders must take care not to get so far out in front of their troops they're mistaken for the enemy and "shot in the back."
7. *Believe that leadership works.* God's unlikely leaders recognized that leadership could accomplish objectives, is practical and functional, and gets things done. They also recognized that *the* leadership, meaning the leader, must demonstrate a work ethic, put in time, exercise a labor of love, be an example. They lived what James observed: "So also faith by itself, if it does not have works, is dead" (James 2:17).
8. *Understand the central issues and needs of the day.* Moses became a liberator. Joshua conquered a land. Elijah led in opposition. Leaders change things. They make things happen. God's unlikely leaders were present throughout history. Joseph led during the ancient Egyptian sojourn. Deborah led during the period of the judges. Josiah led during the time of the kings. The twelve disciples launched a movement in the time of the Roman Empire.
9. *Change things.* God's unlikely leaders lived a Christian worldview that centuries later became known as the "Serenity Prayer": *O God and Heavenly Father, Grant to us the serenity of mind to accept that which cannot be changed; the courage to change that which can be changed, and the wisdom to know the one from the other, through Jesus Christ our Lord, Amen.*

A humble priest named Martin Luther had no idea he was launching the Reformation when he tacked the Ninety-Five Theses on the door of Castle Church in Wittenberg. He only knew he believed the Bible taught "justification by faith," not justification by works or indulgences as taught by the dominant church culture. So, he acted. He spoke for others who could not speak. God multiplied this unlikely leader's courageous investment of talent, expanding one man's convictions into a movement that yet influences the entire world.

You and I probably won't alter the course of Western civilization by becoming an unlikely leader for God like Martin Luther. But you never know. If God knows the number of hairs on our head, it's not much of a stretch to think he cares about every step we take.

Remember, unlikely leaders have faith and a willing heart. A "willing heart" is more than "Lord, I'll do this if you want, but do you really want me to step up?" Turn the idea of a willing heart on its axis. It's not passive. It's active. It's David's statement to King Saul in the face of the Philistine giant, "Let no man's heart fail because of him. Your servant will go and fight with this Philistine." And it is David's challenge to Goliath, "I come to you in the name of the Lord of hosts" (1 Sam. 17:32, 45). Life doesn't just happen *to* you. God's unlikely leaders become unlikely leaders because they make a choice.

The great English pastor Charles Hadden Spurgeon said, "We accomplish little because we have no idea of doing much. I would to God we had more pluck."[73] He was talking about what unlikely leaders *could be*.

LEADERSHIP LESSONS
1. Leadership isn't capitalized in the Bible.
2. Leading a family is still leadership.
3. Uneducated and common doesn't disqualify people from leadership.
4. God's unlikely leaders took risks and made mistakes.
5. Men and women of God must be godly men and women.
6. Character and competence count more than countenance or connections.
7. Don't get hung up on a presumed lack of talent but vigorously use the talents God provides.
8. Access the power of prayer.
9. Stand for something.
10. Lead when others are not yet following.

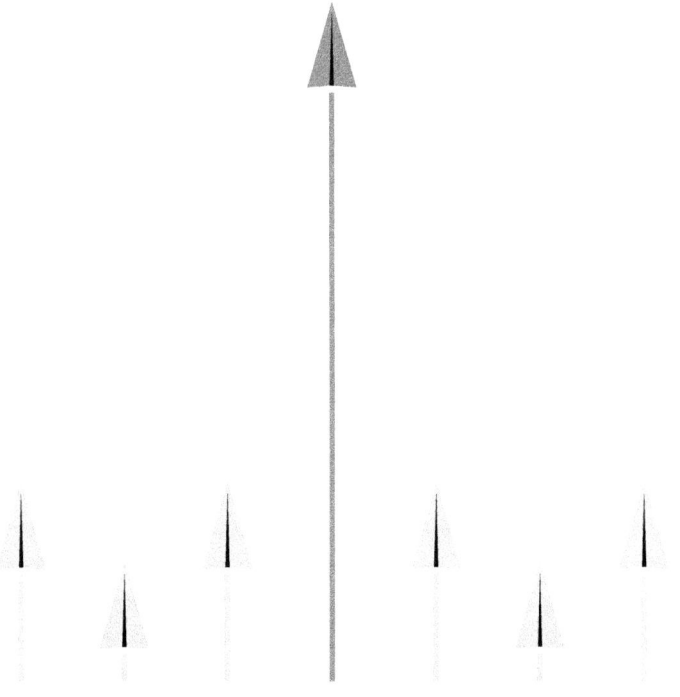

CHAPTER 4

CHARACTER

Who A Leader *Is*

JOSEPH

Joseph is one of the most beloved characters in the Bible. He begins life as a shepherd, then follows a providential path from shepherd to slave to convict to master of Pharaoh's Egypt.

Long before he understood his destiny Joseph was a man of principled faith and impeccable character. He trusted God despite the unpleasant circumstances in which he often found himself. As a direct result of this spiritual commitment, throughout all his considerable trials and temptations Joseph "kept his record clean." And "when the days of honor followed days of humiliation, he did not yield to pride."[74]

Joseph demonstrated unswerving faith in God.

Joseph's early life was a series of unwarranted troubles. His ten older brothers despised his grandiose dreams suggesting they might someday bow down to him and they envied their father's love for Joseph. To remedy their problem, they tossed Joseph into a pit and sold him to passing slave traders. The traders took Joseph to Egypt and sold him to a master who soon learned to trust him and promoted him accordingly. But trouble came to Joseph again when his master's wife attempted to seduce him and then lied about him after he refused her. Feeling betrayed and angry, Joseph's master committed him to prison.

The warden quickly recognized Joseph's leadership qualities and entrusted him with privileged authority. But Joseph remained in prison until the Egyptian ruler's advisers called upon him to interpret Pharaoh's disturbing dreams.

God revealed to Joseph the meaning of the dreams as well as the wisdom to know how to prepare for the years of plenty and famine the dreams predicted. Recognizing talent when he saw it, Pharaoh immediately appointed Joseph second in command in Egypt, chief administrator of the empire's stores of food.

During thirteen years of slavery and imprisonment the Bible says God "was with him and that the LORD caused all that he did to succeed in his hands" (Gen. 39:3; see also vv. 2, 21–23). Joseph remained faithful in the face of unfair treatment without knowing whether his life would ever change for the better. In fact, Joseph's character was so well formed by godliness that he never evidenced bitterness toward his brothers' treachery. Through all those years of servitude he never burned with a desire for revenge. He didn't live for the day he could kill his brothers. He lived for God.

> **Joseph's character was formed by godliness.**

Despite the erratic trajectory of his life, Joseph one day—incredibly—found himself in a position of near absolute authority, looking down from a throne upon a band of supremely distraught brothers fearing for their lives. Here at last was Joseph's chance for justice, yet he chose mercy. He spoke gently with love, spiritual wisdom, and compassion, saying, "As for you, you meant evil against me, but God meant it for good, to bring it about that many people should be kept alive, as they are today" (Gen. 50:20).

You meant it for evil, Joseph said. God meant it for good. You meant it to hurt me. God meant it to help you. Clearly Joseph understood the sovereignty of God.

Aside from Jesus, Joseph is the only major figure in the Bible about whom no sinful attitudes or behavior are recorded. Joseph teaches us "that what life does to us depends on what life finds in us."[75] Though he achieved the pinnacle of political eminence in the ancient world Joseph is remembered more for his character than for his statecraft.

Character

Joseph was given leadership opportunities because of his character, and he performed his leadership tasks with character. He was a living testimony that "life-ship"—meaning how leaders live, their character, and their reputation—is central to leadership. How leaders live their lives is key to what they do and who they become.

Leading shows what a leader is made of. In fact, "the higher you go the more visible your integrity, or lack of it, becomes."[76] People see leaders before they see where leaders want to lead, so "credibility is the foundation of leadership. If people don't believe in the messenger, they won't believe the message."[77]

Consequently, a leader's earned trust, and therefore potential effectiveness, is directly rooted in his or her character. "The real leader increases trust and action among followers. His (or her) leadership is character in motion with trust as its fuel."[78] Trust doesn't come from one's job or authority anymore; it must be earned.[79] Thus, guarding your own character as a leader is job one.[80]

> "Life-ship" is central to leadership.

People aren't going to wonder for very long what a leader is really like. They're going to know. Ralph Waldo Emerson once said, "What you are speaks so loudly I cannot hear what you say."[81]

Irish evangelist Gypsy Smith said, "There are five Gospels, Matthew, Mark, Luke, John, and the Christian, and some people will never read the first four."[82] Making a similar point for a different reason, Saint Francis of Assisi famously observed, "Preach the Gospel at all times, when necessary, use words."

Unfortunately, American culture is becoming a wasteland littered by public figures, leaders of varying types, politicians, celebrities, illicit priests or other religious figures, athletes, and these do not scratch the surface of the host of lesser known state and local leaders mired in mud of their own making—who lied, engaged in wanton sexual immorality, stole money, cheated with performance enhancing drugs, or otherwise evidenced a lack of character. It's a sad state of affairs, no pun intended.

What leaders do on the outside tells people what's on the inside. And we're all human, so succumbing to hurtful behaviors is easy to do. Some of the perils to leadership include pride, egotism, jealousy, popularity, infallibility, indispensability, elation, and depression.[83] Selfishness, lack of humility, lying, greed, dishonesty, stealing, sexual immorality, bitterness, malice, delusions of grandeur, complacency, vengefulness, insecurity; the list is as long as the creativity of the sinful human heart.

Who a leader *is* matters. A leader with a faulty moral compass will invariably lead his or her people in wrong (unethical, illegal, immoral) directions.

And leaders with poor character are a danger to themselves. They shipwreck their own reputations and careers on the shoals of shallow integrity.

The list of political leaders who squandered their influence and reputations for short-term adulterous sexual adventures is so long it has its own Wikipedia page.[84] Some, like Arnold Schwarzenegger, John Edwards, or Al Franken paid a price for their misbehavior in their political careers. Others like President John F. Kennedy didn't live to see his extramarital White House affairs exposed to the public, but his legacy suffers for it today.

And all these occurred before the impact of the #MeToo movement that resulted in more men bounced from political and professional leadership because of the way they mistreated women.[85]

Who a leader *is* matters.

Not all leaders lose their jobs or damage their reputations because of sex scandals. Some go down because of conspiracy to commit bribery, mail fraud, tax evasion, wire fraud, racist comments, perjury, influence peddling. The list is endless, which is one reason Americans are often cynical about politicians, corporate tycoons, and every other kind of leader. Money, sex, and power, a leader's temptations, have been around since Adam and Eve walked out of the garden. The truth eventually emerges, and guilty leaders become victims of their own devices.

A Low Bar in a High Office

When it comes to questionable character in a leader President Bill Clinton is exhibit A. During his second term, he endured a presidential impeachment trial, racked up millions in legal fees, and was disbarred because he lied under oath—which all started in the scandal of his "inappropriate relationship" with a White House intern.

Despite considerable political skills and much political success during his presidency, President Clinton is most remembered for his hubris in conducting an affair in or near the Oval Office, ambiguous definitions of words like "sexual relations" and "is," glib lies to the American people, and squandered political leadership opportunities.

The sex scandal reintroduced an important question. Does a leader's private choices inevitably affect his or her public actions? Politicians, pundits, and professors debated whether it's possible for a leader to act with such mind-bogglingly questionable judgment privately while acting with astute judgment publicly.

Money, sex, and power—a leader's temptations.

In the United States historically, private character and public action were considered inextricably linked. Yet at the time of President Clinton's impeachment, some 70 percent of the American people did not want Congress to pursue the matter.[86] So the Senate's vote during the trial fell short of conviction and President Clinton was spared the ignominy of being bounced from office. Whatever your thoughts on the outcome of this trial, we can say that the American people's inclination to separate private from public character is a choice with consequences not yet fully understood.

The lasting ripple effects of the Clinton affair only history will tell. But it's neither a partisan comment nor a cheap shot to say that the impact of one leader's poor character choices can greatly and negatively affect a nation—or an organization. For example, how this history influenced voters' attitudes toward serious sexual allegations (regarding incidents before they took office) made toward President Donald Trump, then later against President Joe Biden is anyone's guess. But clearly, it's increasingly difficult to find front-runners from either political party whose character is without question.

Where Do You Draw the Line?

What kind of poor character choices should cause us to disqualify a person from leadership? Where do you draw the line? According to the present American mindset private sexual immorality is apparently okay. But what private character choices are not okay for a leader or potential leader, particularly in public office?

President Clinton, for example, was not a traitorous man. He was not an autocrat or a murderer. He did good things in office, even as a sexually immoral man. He is charismatic and many people like him. Some people seem to like him *because* he's a rogue. So, his "not-so-bad-just-like-the-rest-of-us" immorality tends to be written off with softer descriptors like antics or peccadilloes.

But still, the problem remains. Which character fault lines in a leader's heart should give us pause? What about a candidate for office who's known or shown to be a congenital liar? (This is now routinely alleged about candidates if not incumbents in both political parties.) What about a candidate who evidences some of those other character perils we listed above?

Which character fault lines in a leader's heart should give us pause?

What about a nominee for leadership who admits to illegal behavior but explains it away as one of his or her "youthful indiscretions"? Allow me to say it again, where do you draw the line? Should private behavior be ignored? How does a political leader (or you or me) separate his or her moral being into private and public personas?

From a Christian perspective, the short answer is "You can't." Yet that's what our culture now seems to believe.

Should private behavior be ignored?

"Americans too often fall for the phony distinction that so long as they do not influence public acts, flaws in candidates' character should be disregarded. . . . Human beings do not consist of two spheres, a public and a private one. Poor judgment, hypocrisy, deceit, arrogance, and corrupt tendencies displayed in one's personal life inevitably manifest themselves in public life. . . . 'No man can climb out beyond the limitations of his own character,' Viscount John Morley wrote."[87]

Albert Einstein agreed, saying "Whoever is careless with the truth in small matters cannot be trusted with the important matters."[88] He was right, but based on that credo Einstein couldn't have supported any number of American leaders.

No Perfect People

You see, it's tough. We're all sinners. Any of us who are leaders or leader-aspirants have already established a record of wrong choices in our lives. We're human. We were born in sin, and we've committed varying levels of wrongdoing ever since.

We know it's impossible to select perfect leaders because there are no perfect people, so we work with a sliding scale. We place character choices (often subconsciously) on a continuum running from acceptable to unacceptable. Where a character choice sits on that continuum varies based upon our cultural values at a given point in time. Before President Ronald Reagan, for example, candidates for the highest office in the land were not taken seriously if they'd ever been divorced. Now it doesn't seem to matter.

> **It's impossible to select perfect leaders because there are no perfect people.**

We know that good and bad behavior exists and, consequently, we know that good and bad leaders exist. But as a culture we sometimes struggle with where one fades into the other.

Evil Leaders

In the extreme it's easy to recognize. Adolph Hitler was an effective leader in a terrible sort of way. He grossly misused his God-given leadership abilities for evil purposes. He was most emphatically not a good leader. He was worse than bad. He was wickedly, criminally evil.

God says that "like a roaring lion or a charging bear is a wicked ruler over a poor people. A ruler who lacks understanding is a cruel oppressor" (Prov. 28:15–16). Evil leadership is a tragedy. It debilitates, devastates, and destroys.

Evil leaders like Genghis Khan, Joseph Stalin, Mussolini, Mao Tse-tung, and Idi Amin populate history and some, like Osama bin Laden or Ayatollah Ali Hosseini Khamenei, periodically walk the earth today until their time comes. They demonstrate that evil character results in evil leadership. We must contend with them.

Bad Leaders

But most of us, praise God, will not live under regimes led by evil leaders. More often we'll struggle with bad leaders. Or we'll face the question of our own character and therefore what kind of leader we want to be.

Bad leaders are those who may not accurately be categorized as evil (actually, not even remotely close to being evil on the level of the worst-in-history gallery we just mentioned). But bad leaders still evidence a pattern of poor moral choices in their lives and leadership.

> **Bad leaders evidence a pattern of poor moral choices.**

How do you recognize bad leaders? They lack integrity. They allow fundamental flaws to fester in their character. These flaws are not the vague "He's struggling with his demons" you read about in media, as if something or someone else is responsible. No, these flaws are sinful attitudes and behaviors sprung from the leader's own heart.

There's generally a pattern of wrong moral choices in a bad leader's character. Bad leaders don't tell the truth, the whole truth, and nothing but the truth. Bad leaders live for their own self-aggrandizement. They *take from* rather than *grow with* the people.

Bad leaders' lives and leadership are a running story of ethical lapses and duplicity.

Bad leaders always exact a price from their nation or their organization. They can destroy in a matter of months what took years to build.

In the Old Testament book of Proverbs, God reminds us that, "When the righteous increase, the people rejoice, but when the wicked rule, the people groan" (29:2). Good leaders and good leadership are a blessing. Bad leaders and bad leadership are a curse.

> **Good leaders and good leadership are a blessing.**

Long after President Gerald R. Ford's administration, former Senator Alan Simpson summarized well the importance of a leader's character when he introduced Mr. Ford at Harvard University. Simpson said, "If you have integrity, nothing else matters. If you don't have integrity, nothing else matters."[89]

Conscience

The continuum of acceptable to unacceptable character choices we tolerate in our leaders is a picture of how Americans think about values, character, and leadership. It's not a trustworthy guide for how God thinks about these matters. Nor should it be our standard. In Christian terms, good enough is not good enough.

God's moral standard for leadership is high. He said, "Everyone to whom much was given, of him much will be required, and from him to whom they entrusted much, they will demand the more" (Luke 12:48). His standards are high, but he didn't leave us without help.

> **Good enough is not good enough.**

God enables us to learn right from wrong in several ways: our conscience, reasoned observation of creation, and hearing God speak directly from his Word, the Bible.

Our conscience is one way we differ from animals. It's that part of us that compares our actions and behaviors with standards of morality we've either innately recognized, or we've learned. Our conscience is a God-given asset, but since Adam's fall from grace our conscience has been affected by the sin of the human race (Genesis 3). So, our conscience is helpful but not always trustworthy.

Similarly, our reasoning capacity is also affected by sin, so our understanding of nature's laws may not always be accurate. Reason is an incredibly powerful tool, but reason alone cannot give us trustworthy moral direction. For that we need divine revelation (Jer. 17:9; Rom. 2:14–15; 1 Peter 1:2).

In God's special revelation, the Bible, the Sovereign Creator speaks through time and space to answer the great questions of life and to tell us the truth. He plainly communicates foundational principles upon which he commands us to build our lives. In the Bible we learn who made us, why we're here, what we're like, what we can become, and where we're going. We learn about good and evil, and we learn how to discern truth from error in the real world.

To help us understand, the Scripture writers used both the word "conscience" and the word "heart," to describe our moral consciousness. For example, the Scripture says that "the aim of our charge is love that issues from a pure heart and a good conscience and a sincere faith" (1 Tim. 1:5). The Scripture also says, "Keep your heart with all vigilance, for from it flow the springs of life" (Prov. 4:23–27).

Again, the Scripture speaks: "For no good tree bears bad fruit, nor again does a bad tree bear good fruit. . . . The good person out of the good treasure of his heart produces good, and the evil person out of his evil treasure produces evil, for out of the abundance of the heart his mouth speaks" (Luke 6:43, 45).

Our conscience informs our character which informs our leadership. A conscience and character enslaved by sin produces one kind of leader, while a conscience and character liberated by biblical moral values yields another.

It's simple, really. What's in the well comes up in the bucket. Who a leader *is* affects everything that he or she does. That fact of life, for good or for ill, includes biblical personalities, former President George W. Bush, business leaders like Martha Stewart or Elon Musk, athletes Patrick Mahomes or Riley Gaines, former Secretary of State Condoleezza Rice, Presidents Donald Trump or Joe Biden, you and me, and every other leader.

> **Our conscience informs our character which informs our leadership.**

God gave us the capacity to choose. We get to decide whether our character will be recognized as good or bad and, therefore, what kind of leaders we can be. If we want to lead well, we won't base our choices on the common denominator of whatever culture happens to find "acceptable." We'll be guided by a conscience instructed by God's standard of holiness (1 Peter 1:13–16).

Arrogance

One of the great temptations of leadership is arrogance. It appeals to our basic human nature, what the Scripture calls the "pride of life" (1 John 2:16). Arrogance is the beginning of many a leader's downfall.

President Lyndon B. Johnson believed the country needed a larger-than-life leader and acted accordingly. He often sought to humiliate people through such means as interviewing staff members while he used the toilet. He made ridiculous demands, raged over not enough Root Beer on Air Force One, threw his drink on the carpet if it wasn't mixed properly, changed his clothes to the point of nakedness in front of his male and female aides, regularly lost his temper with the plane's crew if his meal wasn't cooked to his liking, involved himself in immoral liaisons, had a chair built especially for his use that would raise or lower so he could dominate his guests, and more. Former Air Force One steward John Haigh said, "President Johnson's attitude was, 'I'm from Texas and I'm the bull of the pasture.'"[90]

Arrogance is the beginning of many leaders' downfall.

The book wasn't written then, but President Johnson would have benefited from reading Rick Warren's *Purpose Driven Life.*[91] The best thing about that book is its first sentence, "It's not about you." President Johnson never learned that basic lesson. His administration's leadership would have been far more effective, and he would be more fondly remembered if he'd recognized that "the office of leadership is bigger than the person who holds it."[92]

President Gerald R. Ford took a different approach than Johnson's because Ford was a humble man. At his confirmation hearings to become vice president he humorously observed that he was "a Ford, not a Lincoln." Mr. Ford understood that the point is to "take your job seriously but not yourself."[93]

Johnson's eccentric behavior may be rare but unfortunately his attitude is not. Arrogant leaders are more common than perhaps we imagine.

Bill Pollard, the longtime chairman of ServiceMaster, talked about one example of leadership arrogance, what he called "the arrogance of ignorance," the feeling that one does not have to learn.[94] Arrogance is a self-imposed blindness (like Hans Christian Andersen's Emperor who had no clothes), stemming from a lack of humility.

Successful leaders face another temptation to arrogance. They all too frequently begin to believe the praise heaped upon them by a grateful public. They begin to think more highly of themselves than they ought to think (Rom. 12:3). They've never learned that those who toot their own horn don't have much to toot about (Prov. 25:27).

There are many practical ways to avoid arrogance:

- Give credit to others where credit is due.
- Thank others publicly.
- Accept praise graciously while recognizing it as a blessing of God, not a right.
- Don't talk about yourself and your accomplishments any more than is necessary.

> **Those who toot their own horn don't have much to toot about.**

Arrogance isn't pretty. Humility is more becoming than arrogance, especially in a leader. Chuck Swindoll makes this point describing the life of Elijah. "The most vulnerable moment is right after a great victory. Humility does not follow readily on the heels of awards and achievement. Yet Elijah, who had just come through the greatest and certainly the most public victory of his life, was not arrogant. He went right back to Mt. Carmel—back to the very site of that triumph—and humbled himself before God."[95]

Confidence

Arrogance is a deadly threat to effective leadership, but it shouldn't be confused with confidence. A leader must avoid the first while developing the second. Arrogance is ugly. Confidence is attractive.

For a leader, confidence is an enabler. No leader ever accomplished much if he or she didn't have the confidence to point the way.

Historian Stephen Ambrose recounted General Dwight David Eisenhower's experience with the burden of leadership. Eisenhower "wrote that it was at his first command post, in Gibraltar in early November 1942, 'that I first realized how inexorably and inescapably strain and tension wear away at a leader's endurance, his judgment, and his confidence.' No matter how bad things got, no matter how anxious the staff became, the commander had to 'preserve optimism in himself and in his command. Without confidence, enthusiasm, and optimism in the command, victory is scarcely obtainable.'"

"Eisenhower realized that 'optimism and pessimism are infectious, and they spread more rapidly from the head downward than in any other direction.' He learned that a commander's optimism 'has a most extraordinary effect upon all with whom he comes in contact. With this clear realization, I firmly determined that my mannerisms and speech in public would always reflect the cheerful certainty of victory—that any pessimism and discouragement I might ever feel would be reserved for my pillow.'"[96]

Confidence is often one of the missing ingredients in people's initial perceptions of their leadership potential. They don't have the confidence to lead. In their minds they're not an unlikely leader, they're an inconceivable leader.

But confidence is born of experience with one's God-given abilities. Confidence can grow as experience grows. Confidence can be developed, and it's a good thing.

> **Confidence is born of experience with one's God-given abilities.**

Confidence is neither crippled by humility nor strengthened by arrogance. Joseph and Elijah knew this. Abraham Lincoln knew this. Some corporate leaders apparently do not.

Leadership books ghost written for celebrity business tycoons like the late and dynamic Lee Iaccoca of Chrysler fame, Starbucks's Howard Schultz, or *Shark Tank*'s Mark Cuban are frequently devoid of any idea of humility. Leadership is cast as "Lead, follow, or get out of the way." But leadership is not machoism.

A few celebrity leaders' comments are worth hearing. Take, for example, retired Indianapolis Colts Coach Tony Dungy. His book,

Quiet Strength, shares a philosophy of life and leadership based upon Coach Dungy's faith in the Lord.[97] The title alone distinguishes confidence from arrogance, the former so constructive the latter so destructive.

Leadership is not machoism.

Confidence is an outgrowth of humility rooted in the spiritual understanding that "every good gift and every perfect gift is from above" (James 1:17). This theological truth protects a leader from arrogance even as it liberates a leader to confidence. Our strengths, our opportunities, are of and for the Lord.

Courage

Who a leader *is* may be measured by character, confidence, and courage. Leaders with character accomplish things for God. Leaders with character and confidence accomplish more for God. Leaders with character, confidence, and courage accomplish most for God.

On 9/11, when Todd Beamer said to his fellow passengers resisting terrorists on United Airlines Flight 93, "Are you guys ready? Let's roll," he demonstrated courageous leadership and became an American hero.

When Jimmy Stewart left Hollywood to enlist, he became one of the first major motion picture stars in uniform during WWII. As the leader of his squadron, he eventually flew more than twenty missions deep into Nazi territory. His courage earned him the Distinguished Service Medal, Croix de Guerre with Palm, Distinguished Flying Cross, and several other medals. For decades thereafter his men consistently described him as he appeared on screen, humble, self-effacing, morally upright, and a leader they'd follow anywhere.[98]

Leaders with character, confidence, and courage accomplish most for God.

John C. Maxwell once said, "It's not the size of the project that determines its acceptance, support, and success. It's the size of the leader."[99] Beamer and Stewart proved the point in very different ways and so have others.

Former president of Poland, Lech Walesa was asked what makes a good leader. Without hesitation he replied, "Courage." In 1974, within thirty days of taking office President Gerald R. Ford announced his decision to pardon the Watergate-disgraced Richard M. Nixon. Many political leaders and columnists, and many within the public, strongly criticized him. But in 2001, Mr. Ford received the John F. Kennedy Foundation's Profiles in Courage award for making a decision now considered one of the nation's gold standards for political courage.[100]

Even JFK's brother, Sen. Teddy Kennedy, said of Mr. Ford at the presentation, "I was one of those who spoke out against his action then. But time has a way of clarifying past events, and now we see that President Ford was right. His courage and dedication to our country made it possible for us to begin the process of healing and put the tragedy of Watergate behind us. He eminently deserves this award, and we are proud of his achievement."[101]

People want leaders with courage. Country or corporation, it doesn't matter, people hunger for leaders with courage born of conviction.

It's not that leaders are not ever afraid or even should not ever be afraid. The apostle Paul openly evidenced both courage and fear (1 Cor. 2:3; 2 Cor. 7:5). Leaders sometimes suffer from cold feet and self-doubt, weariness of the flesh and the spirit, anxiety, and stress.

The best leaders develop not only the courage to change their circumstances but also at times to change themselves.[102] The book of Psalms is a record of how the psalmist David linked his fears to his faith and, consequently, to God's empowerment.

Great challenges are great opportunities wearing a mask. At least that's what the youthful shepherd David thought.

> **Great challenges are great opportunities wearing a mask.**

"The only backdrop against which Saul viewed Goliath was the landscape of the present. But David looked back into his own past and into his people's history, and he saw something beyond the giant Goliath. He saw a vision of what Israel was all about, a vision that beckoned him forward, that turned the valor of yesterday into tomorrow's possibility. He saw God in his life and in the life of his people, and he saw the capacity for change and new vitality. Therefore, he saw Goliath not as a menace or a deadly threat but as a mandate for the expression of faith."[103]

Courageous leaders with depth of character—Martin Luther, William Wilberforce, Clara Barton, Theodore Roosevelt, George Washington Carver, Martin Luther King Jr.—have changed history, organizations, and families. Character defines leaders; courage distinguishes them.

LEADERSHIP LESSONS

1. "Life-ship" is central to leadership.
2. A leader's private choices inevitably affect his or her public actions.
3. Leaders cannot rise above the level of their own character.
4. Be guided by a conscience instructed by God's standard of holiness.
5. Confidence is born of experience with one's God-given abilities.
6. Those who toot their own horns don't have much to toot about.
7. Leadership is not machoism.
8. Leaders with character, confidence, and courage accomplish most for God.
9. Great challenges are great opportunities wearing a mask.
10. Character defines leadership; courage distinguishes it.

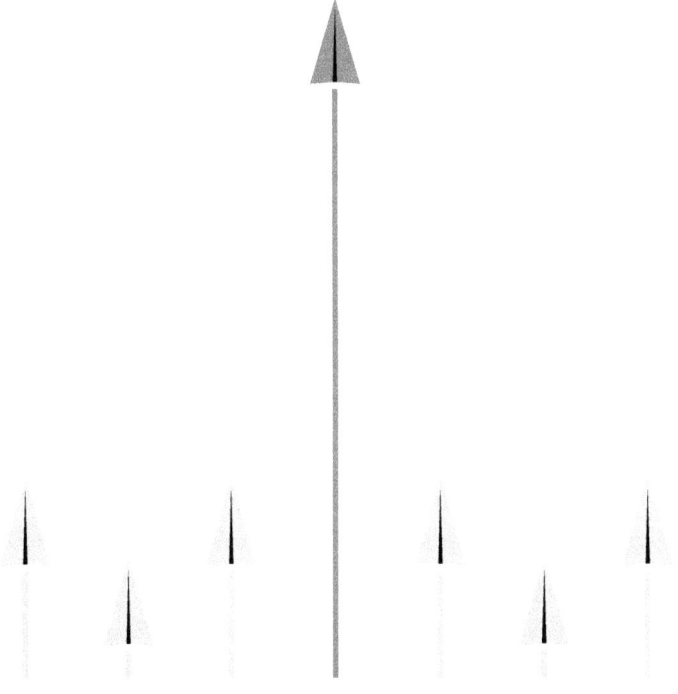

CHAPTER 5

CAUSE

What A Leader Is *About*

MOSES

Moses led two to three million Israelite people in the ancient Exodus, arguably the greatest leadership challenge in history. He wrote the *Torah*, the first five books of the Old Testament. He received from God the Ten Commandments, then delivered the law to his people. He established and codified their customs, directed construction of the tabernacle, organized the twelve tribes, and by the power of God worked spectacular miracles protecting, feeding, and healing his people.

For his achievements as lawgiver Moses's image became the subject of countless iconic statuary and paintings throughout history. For decades his visage has graced the chamber wall in the United States House of Representatives.

But for all this, Moses began life floating in a basket on the Nile River, his sex and his ethnicity making his very existence illegal. His name means "drawn up from the water," signifying the most celebrated adoption ever recorded when baby Moses was taken from his floating basket and placed in Pharaoh's daughter's arms (Ex. 2:5–6, 10).

After a young lifetime in the presence of royalty, at forty years of age Moses's life took a sudden turn. Walking among the Israelite slaves one day, Moses lost his temper, took the life of an Egyptian guard he'd seen beating a slave, and then fled to live as a fugitive in the wilderness. With four decades behind him of outstanding palace preparation for regal leadership, Moses spent his next forty years in wilderness graduate school, learning the ways of the desert and learning to be a shepherd leader.

At eighty years of age, Moses experienced the defining moment of his life. While caring for his sheep he saw an inflamed-but-not-consumed burning bush on Mt. Sinai. More amazingly, God spoke from the bush, commissioning Moses to lead the Israelites away from what had become 430 years of oppression in a foreign land. Poor communicator, fearful fugitive, sheep herder, Moses hardly evidenced typical leadership traits. So, he logically said, "Oh, my Lord, please send someone else" (Ex. 4:13). But God fortified him with the necessary strength, words, and direction.

Returning to the palaces of his youth, Moses demanded Pharaoh let God's people go. While it took ten horrible plagues to convince the Pharaoh, in the end he relented, and Moses found himself in charge of the liberated, fledgling nation of Israel.

Moses's stature may cause us to overlook the fact that under the pressure of responsibility he became first a controlling, then an overwhelmed leader. Observing this, Moses's father-in-law said, "What you are doing is not good" (Ex. 18:17–27). To his credit, Moses took Jethro's advice and appointed assistants, truly becoming a leader when he learned not only to cast vision but to delegate.

> **Moses truly became a leader when he learned to delegate.**

Moses was called a "friend of God" and is listed among the heroes of the faith in Hebrews 11. The last verses of the *Torah* records Moses' unique epitaph: "And there has not arisen a prophet since in Israel like Moses, whom the Lord knew face to face, none like him for all the signs and the wonders that the LORD sent him to do . . . for all the mighty power and all the great deeds of terror that Moses did in the sight of all Israel" (Deut. 34:10–12).

Purpose/Mission and Vision

Though Moses never made it into the promised land he led with the vision of bringing his people to a better life in the promised land. Moses applied God's message to create a hope, a destination, and a future for his people. A worthy purpose and a stirring vision remain the most enduring traits of leadership.

Former longtime vice president of the Billy Graham Evangelistic Association, Leighton Ford, said, "Centered in any great leader's soul is a sense of transcendent purpose."[104] That's pretty lofty, but then again, "without a transcendent purpose, understood and enunciated from on high, the company's direction is at the mercy of the winds of corporate fads and fancy."[105] For company, organization, or nation-state, purpose and vision are essential.[106]

> **Purpose and vision remain enduring traits of leadership.**

You should know that "purpose" and "vision" are often used interchangeably, which is admittedly confusing. Both words suggest a desirable future—what the leader or the organization is trying to accomplish—which is the source of the easy substitution of one word for the other in daily conversation. But purpose and vision may also be distinguished.

Purpose speaks to activities:
- what business you're in,
- what an organization does, or
- why an organization exists.

Purpose implies *mission*.

Vision speaks to direction:
- where the organization is headed,
- what the organization's idealized tomorrow looks like, or
- what is the organization's destiny.

Vision implies *movement.*

Visions envision. "Foresight," Robert K. Greenleaf said, "is the 'lead' that the leader has."[107] Leaders think about the future, and their ideas about the future translate to vision.

The great British statesman and political theorist Edmund Burke considered leadership and vision two sides of a coin. "The great difference between the real leader and the pretender," he said, "is that the one sees the future, while the other regards only the present; the one lives by the day and acts upon expediency; the other acts on enduring principles and for the immortality."[108]

Purpose implies *mission*; vision implies *movement*.

In these simple definitional distinctions, purpose or mission (also interchangeably used words) becomes the core of an organization's existence, something that typically doesn't change much or often. Vision becomes a picture of an organization's possibilities, something that may change often, especially under the stewardship of different leaders.[109]

Purpose is about perspiration—doing the job today. Vision is about inspiration—conceiving the job tomorrow.

Think of it this way. Beginning in 1966, every *Star Trek* science fiction television episode, including its later television spin-offs and films, began or ended with one of several versions of this stirring narration:

"Space... the Final Frontier. These are the voyages of the starship *Enterprise*. Her ongoing mission: to explore strange new worlds, to seek out new life and new civilizations, to boldly go where no one has gone before."

Is this a statement of purpose/mission, vision, or both? Probably both, but does it really matter? William Shatner's (and later others like Patrick Stewart) voice and passion transformed mere words into a compelling and enduring vision that's captured the public's imagination for more than fifty years.

Purpose is about today; vision is about tomorrow.

The lesson: don't get lost in definitional minutia. Your task is to lead, perhaps to boldly go where no one has gone before.

The Vision Thing

In 1992, President George H. W. Bush was a respected incumbent running for reelection. He served because it's what his Greatest Generation believed was and what his patrician upbringing taught him was the right thing to do. But until it was too late, he failed to understand that serving for serving's sake wasn't enough. Voters wanted to know not so much what he *had done* in an accomplished political life—including helping win the Gulf War—as much as what he was *going to do* in the next four years. They wanted to know more about what he struggled to articulate, what he called "the vision thing." There were other factors in President Bush's loss, to be sure, but the absence of a stated vision was a key ingredient in the untimely end of the first Bush Administration. President Bush was a leader, but he couldn't sustain his leadership in part for lack of a compelling vision.

In the 1860s, during America's most anguished time, President Abraham Lincoln provided a different leadership example. Most citizens, even most scholars, believe Abraham Lincoln was the right man at the right time. He was a truly singular leader, though in many ways an improbable one. He wasn't particularly handsome; actually, some contemporaries called him "homely." He was a man of humble beginnings, and he carried a homespun quality with him throughout his life. He lost elections repeatedly before he finally won.

The "Vision Thing" articulates what you're going to do.

So, what made Abraham Lincoln a great leader? Well, for one, he apparently was a good judge of character. Though he later struggled to find the right general, the "team of rivals" he appointed to his cabinet proved a masterstroke of what historian Doris Kearns Goodwin called "political genius."[110] Lincoln was blessed with an uncanny memory enabling him to recall scores of stories and anecdotes at just the right time, either lightening the moment or making a potent point. His integrity was impeccable; indeed, "Honest Abe" was both a campaign slogan *and* a reality. His grasp of Scripture, the nature of good and evil, and the providence of God easily made him the greatest "civil theologian" ever to hold this nation's highest office.

But more than any other factor, the thing that made Lincoln a great leader was his vision. He knew what he wanted to accomplish, and he stuck to it resolutely.

During his presidency, in the providence of God, history handed Lincoln a supreme national crisis and in response his two-part vision quickly focused—to save the Union and to preserve a government of free peoples. For four terrible years Lincoln's vision remained strong and sustaining in the face of setbacks for the Army of the Potomac, wrenching body counts reaching tens of thousands on given days, generals who wouldn't pursue the enemy, and of course, relentless criticism. Yet Lincoln never failed to make decisions rooted in what he believed the future should be. And he shared his vision eloquently, especially in his most famous orations, the Gettysburg Address and the Second Inaugural Address.

Leadership scholar Warren Bennis said, "The single defining quality of leaders is their ability to create and realize a vision." Lincoln's leadership epitomized this point.

People don't typically become leaders "just to lead." Something else motivates them—power, fame or fortune, service, self-aggrandizement, faith, a cause. For George H. W. Bush, it was service. For Abraham Lincoln, it was the cause. Both men recognized that "leadership is not about a position or a place. It's an attitude and a sense of responsibility for making a difference."[111] Effective, and certainly outstanding, leaders lead for reasons that reach beyond technique, beyond themselves, beyond today, and beyond tomorrow.

> **Leaders reach beyond technique, themselves, today, and tomorrow.**

Leaders don't just go *anywhere*; they go *somewhere*. Leaders cast visions imbued with direction. James MacGregor Burns summarized it thus: "Leadership is morally purposeful. All leadership is goal oriented. The failure to set goals is a sign of faltering leadership. Successful leadership points in a direction; it is also the vehicle of continuing and achieving purpose."[112]

If you want to be a leader, you must point the way. You must understand, and more importantly, apply Leonard Sweet's maxim: "A leader's mission is to enlist people in a mission they care about—one that will change history, go down in history—and then get the mission going."[113] This is true in any kind of organization.

> **Leaders don't just go *anywhere*; they go *somewhere*.**

In 1959, Richard DeVos and Jay Van Andel founded the Amway (American Way) Corporation in a friend's basement. They supported their vision, "Helping People Live Better Lives," with a dynamic partnership, a direct sales and marketing plan, and a respect for people, initiative, and free enterprise. Their vision and work ethic created a unique and highly successful venture that's still attracting emerging populations of free peoples worldwide.

If you want to lead, learn the power of vision.

The Power of Vision

In *Leadership Is an Art*, Max DePree succinctly said, "Leaders have ideas."[114] Visions are nothing more than ideas, good ones to be sure, but nevertheless just ideas.

Powerful ideas powerfully communicated translate to powerful visions. People could say in a single sentence what Lincoln's, FDR's, and Reagan's presidencies were all about.[115]

In 1963 on the steps of the Lincoln Memorial, Martin Luther King Jr. boldly presented a powerful vision in his masterfully eloquent "I Have a Dream" speech. Even in print decades hence in a new century this speech remains fascinatingly irresistible. In video and audio, featuring Dr. King's charismatic presence and the unmatched timbre of his baritone, "I Have a Dream" easily ranks as one of the great American speeches—President John F. Kennedy reportedly thought so, watching via television from the White House.[116]

"I Have a Dream" didn't launch a movement. It leveraged a movement. The Civil Rights Movement owes its soul to this speech. Dr. King clearly and beautifully articulated a vision no moral or compassionate human being could ultimately deny, demonstrating the wisdom of Victor Hugo's observation that "Nothing else in the world . . . not all the armies . . . is so powerful as an idea whose time has come."[117]

Max DePree said, "Giants see opportunity where others see trouble."[118] Great leaders, giants in DePree's words, take risks and make a difference.[119] They create and cast worthy visions built upon trustworthy ideas. Leaders know that people yearn for meaning, so they craft visions that appeal to people's hearts and uplift their spirits.[120] Martin Luther King did this in a moment for a movement that yet reverberates around the world.

> **Great leaders take risks and make a difference.**

In 1979, Margaret Thatcher became the first female prime minister of the United Kingdom and served three terms until 1990, the longest continuous tenure since 1827.

She had been a member of Parliament for twenty years, so she was not an unknown. But the sweep of Thatcher's vision and the extent of the change she brought to Great Britain, and eventually to the world, were yet to unfold.

Thatcher became a catalyst for free markets and free minds, what became "Thatcherism." She believed in self-reliance, initiative, and responsibility, so she promoted individual choice, downsized government, curtailed the power of trade unions, privatized nationalized industries, and stepped into the breach against Soviet imperialism. In so doing she revived the British economy. Both British Airlines and British Steel, unprofitable and weak, once privatized, became leading companies in the world.

Thatcher became "Maggie" to most of the British people. Her leadership style included wit, perseverance, and a remarkable willpower that earned her the sobriquet "the Iron Lady."

Margaret Thatcher's leadership exemplifies the power of vision. In British historian Paul Johnson's words, Thatcher was "the daughter of a small shopkeeper, who proved that nothing is more effective than willpower allied to a few clear, simple and workable ideas."[121] People followed her because she gave them a vision worth following.

Excellence

"The quality of a person's life," Green Bay Packers Coach Vince Lombardi once said, "is in direct proportion to their commitment to excellence, regardless of their chosen field of endeavor."[122]

We can apply Lombardi's observation to leadership. If a leader's vision doesn't aim for excellence, it isn't a leader's vision. There's no place for mediocrity in leadership.

> **If a leader's vision doesn't aim for excellence,
> it isn't a leader's vision.**

Certainly, for the Christian, leadership and excellence go hand in hand.[123] "Christians were never told to be mediocre. They were told to run the race to win, with humility."[124]

Excellence is not an option. Excellence in how and to what end leaders lead is one way we tell the world who God is. God created the world and called it "very good," so he set the standard for quality. Dr. Paul Dixon, the university president under whom I cut my leadership teeth, often said, "Everything done in the name of Jesus Christ should have quality stamped all over it." He was right.

God charges his followers with continuous growth. Christians are supposed to be better today than they were yesterday. Excellence reflects the very character of God and should be the Christian way of doing things.[125]

Excellence isn't the same as expertise. Don't ever confuse expertise with excellence or ethics. A lot of people develop expertise. Fewer develop their ethics. Remember political adviser David Gergen's observation, "More than one of our presidents has been a congenital liar; Jerry Ford was a congenital truth-teller. And his staff took their cues from him."[126] Leaders set an example, one way or another. Expertise might spring from the head or the hands, but excellence can only spring from the heart.

For leaders, excellence is a perpetual goal leaders should always seek to accomplish yet a goal that always remains before them.

Walt Disney was renowned for demanding his visionary amusement park, Disneyland, be scrupulously clean—"picture perfect"—and safe for families at all times, and his customers treated as guests. During one of his frequent park visits he noticed some poor maintenance and directed a wholesale repainting be completed—by morning. After his death, Walt's philosophy of excellence was applied in all of Disney's parks and resulted in the world-class staff training program called Disney University.

Excellence is a perpetual goal.

Excellence appeals to the better angels of our nature. Followers get excited about something better, not same ol', same ol'. Which leader sparks more interest, the one offering a get by, muddling through approach, or the leader offering something new and improved—even if you must sacrifice and work for it?

Lord Chesterfield reportedly said—to be emulated later by everyone's Grandma: "Whatever is worth doing at all is worth doing well." And as they say, excellence breeds excellence. So, leaders who extol excellence really are bestowing upon their organization a wonderful legacy for the next generation.

Outstanding leadership is always about excellence. Coauthor of the bestselling *Leadership Challenge*, Barry Z. Posner, noted, "Leadership is about doing it differently and better than ever before. . . . Leaders are fundamentally restless people, never quite happy with the status quo. Xerox Corporation says it this way, 'We're in a race in which there is no finish line.'"[127]

In the academy, few better examples of excellence in leadership can be found than Reverend Theodore Hesburgh. In 1952, when Hesburgh became president of Notre Dame University at thirty-two years of age, he found a university with a reputation built more upon the record of the football team than upon the academic accomplishments of the faculty. This was painfully illustrated during his first press conference when a reporter tossed him a football and asked him to hike it for the cameras—which he refused to do.

During what was to become an internationally recognized presidency, Hesburgh modeled his own leadership statement: "The very essence of leadership is that you have to have vision. You can't blow an uncertain trumpet." From the beginning, Hesburgh cast his vision of taking Cardinal Newman's nineteenth century "idea of a university" and using it to transform Notre Dame into "America's first truly great Catholic university."

> **Followers get excited about something better, not same ol', same ol'.**

Hesburgh's thirty-five-year presidency is still a record. But it wasn't longevity that transformed Notre Dame University, it was leadership—leadership that cast a vision of excellence.

Since Adam and Eve left the garden of Eden, nothing in this world or in this life has been truly perfect. There's always room for improvement. And because God wired us in his image, a leader's vision for excellence always:

- lifts hearts,
- encourages spirits,
- rejuvenates old processes, and
- distinguishes a product or serves an organization competitively.

Excellence is a leader's friend, both a tool and a goal. It helps leaders jettison "good enough is good enough" in favor of "the best." Excellence helps raise the bar, pointing the organization toward the changes needed to go to the next level.

Leading Change

Real leaders take organizations to the next level. Going to the next level requires change. Change requires leadership. Leaders, therefore, are about change.

James MacGregor Burns said, "The ultimate test of practical leadership is the realization of intended, real change that meets people's enduring needs."[128]

> **Excellence is a leader's friend, a tool and a goal.**

On December 1, 1955, in Montgomery, Alabama, Rosa Parks quietly refused to obey her bus driver's command to give up her seat to make room for a white passenger. In this simple act of courageous civil disobedience, she helped set in motion profound social change resulting in her eventually being called the "Mother of the Modern-Day Civil Rights Movement." She didn't lead an organization, but she was a leader who stimulated change.

Leaders come in all kinds of packages. At first glance you might not choose Bono, the lead singer of U2 and an international rock star, as an example of a change-agent leader. But glance again. For several years he used his celebrity to leverage access to a long list of Western leaders, encouraging decisions aimed at assisting the poor in Africa. He is a cofounder of DATA (Debt AIDS Trade Africa) and of the ONE Campaign to fight poverty. He's been nominated for the Nobel Peace Prize three times, knighted by Queen Elizabeth II, and named Person of the Year by *Time* magazine in 2006. But it's not accolades that make Bono a change-agent leader. It's his vision and effectiveness. In his words, "The world is more malleable than we think. We can bend it into a better shape. Ask the big questions, demand the big answers."[129]

Real leaders take organizations to the next level.

Change, like leaders, also comes in different packages. In fact, it's possible to identify at least three kinds of change:

1. *Change leaders experience "without" an organization*—external change generated primarily but not entirely by the marketplace.
2. *Change leaders encourage within an organization*—internal change generated primarily but not entirely by leaders and personnel.
3. *Change leaders evidence within themselves*—change generated by leaders to enlarge their own capacity to lead.

Change Without the Organization

Leaders demand change but change also creates a demand for leaders. Contemporary culture is experiencing that kind of change right now. Increasingly rapid, global social change is a hallmark of our times.

Extensive and intensive change in the marketplace puts pressure on organizations to respond and adjust. Simply put, to compete in changing times organizations must "keep up." They must change too.

Organizations must be agile, flexible, innovative, adaptable, which is to say, be able to change quickly. Organization must be built to change, not built to last.[130]

Some wag once said, "He who marries the status quo will soon be a widower." The wag was right on. Organizations that can't or won't change will decline and won't be around long.

Ronald Reagan understood this about government and used it to his advantage, observing with typical wit, "Status quo is Latin for 'the mess we're in.'"

> **Leaders create change and change creates a demand for leaders.**

Even success can breed complacency. In his book, *Work in Progress*, Michael Eisner, longtime successful chairman and CEO of the Walt Disney Company, referenced this concern. To encourage continuing organizational viability and excellence, he worked with two motivating goals: (1) "Survive success by continuing to risk failure," and (2) "Advocate change but protect the brand."[131]

Eisner's "protect the brand" comment acknowledges that not all change should be embraced. The key is to discern between novel change and needed change.[132]

Not all the cultural changes we're witnessing have been or are particularly healthy, wealthy, or wise. But this is our new reality, so we look for a certain kind of leader. As Newt Gingrich said, "We hire leaders to change reality to fit our values, not to change our values to fit the newest failed reality."[133]

In the 1970s, fundamentalist pastor Reverend Jerry Falwell emerged as one such leader. He grew tired of how religious conservatives were being ignored in the nation's political arena and weary of how their values were being trampled in the culture wars. So, he applied his considerable vision and organizational skills to founding Liberty University, establishing national radio and television ministries, organizing the Moral Majority, and eventually becoming the principal figure in the New Christian Right of the 1980s and 1990s. Falwell's leadership awakened a sleeping religiously conservative giant eventually called "values voters" and changed the face of American religion and politics.

Leading is no cakewalk anymore. Changing times create a demand for quality leaders who're willing to tackle leadership opportunities fraught with uncertainty.

In year 2020, leaders in all walks of life were blindsided by a global coronavirus pandemic, government induced lockdowns, economic slowdowns and consequent unemployment, and considerable societal angst about safety and the future. Organizational leaders who responded to this new normal with adaptability, courage, and vision helped their organizations survive or even thrive.

Rita El-Mounayer, CEO of SAT-7 International, a media ministry broadcasting and streaming online Christian content in Arabic, Farsi, and Turkish throughout the Middle East and North Africa, used the forced downtime resulting from the 2020 pandemic travel restrictions to establish new practices, set new goals, and launch new initiatives:

A weekly prayer Zoom was created with more than one hundred international staff to promote connectivity.

- Two new professionals were recruited with expertise in video on demand and social media making new tipping point initiatives possible.
- New leadership was appointed in the organization of critical functions serving viewer responses and concerns.
- More time was spent with staff and donors using online video platforms than she'd ever been able to experience spending time in the airport and in the air.
- Other organizational leaders were empowered to set in motion upgrades of the planning and budgeting processes.

At year's end, she said, "This might have been my best year ever." Ironic perhaps in a COVID year, but leaders who see opportunity rather than obstacles in challenges make things happen. In times of uncertainty, leadership matters more than ever.

Leading is no cakewalk.

Organizations are inescapably influenced by change "without" the organization. Change without demands change within.

Change Within the Organization

Change within an organization may be the result of external cultural or economic influences, like for example, the emergence of the Internet. Or change within an organization may be the product of intentional transformational efforts by leaders and personnel attempting to position the organization for growth and competitive advantage.

Instigating or implementing any kind of intentional change, especially genuine transformational change, doesn't just happen. It requires a leader to lead it. It's hard work, in part because human beings are creatures of habit—sometimes to the point of inertia. "Powerful vested interests will resist the impending reforms. The more likely change becomes, the more fiercely and vocally these negative influencers—both internal and external—will fight to protect their positions, and their resistance can seriously damage, even derail, the reform process."[134]

> **Change "without" organizations requires change within organizations.**

To woo and win change-resisters, change-agent leaders sometimes find it's better to take incremental as opposed to revolutionary steps toward change:

1. Establish a sense of urgency.
2. Form a powerful guiding coalition.
3. Create a vision.
4. Communicate the vision.
5. Empower others to act on the vision.
6. Plan for and create short-term wins.
7. Consolidate improvements and produce still more change.
8. Institutionalize new approaches.[135]

While revolutionary steps may attract more press and in times of crises may be the preferred course of action, Jim Collins demonstrated in *Good to Great* that successful transformational change in organizations more often takes place at an evolutionary or methodical pace.[136] This approach allows time for dynamic, visionary leaders to persuade a critical mass of followers to join the parade.

When I joined Grand Rapids Baptist College and Seminary as president in the fall of 1991, its ship was listing badly to the side and taking on water fast. We needed to change and change quickly to survive, let alone thrive.

During a board of trustees meeting the following spring I remember making a presentation with what now seems like a rather pretentious title, "The Acts 1:8 Strategy." The premise of that presentation was GRBC&S must change, or it will die.

> **Successful transformational change is more often evolutionary than revolutionary.**

Via the leadership of trustees like Board Chairman C. John Miller, Charles Alber, and Randy Hekman, to name a few, the board embraced a new vision for the school's identity and marketplace niche, directing it to be repositioned:

- *from* a fundamentalist, denominational Bible/liberal arts college
- *to* an evangelical Christian university of liberal arts and professional studies.

Faculty and staff members worked diligently and professionally toward the new vision and goals and God blessed. In time, some of the key organizational changes implemented included:

- Setting a "good enough is no longer good enough" standard and changing the modus operandi from a "Mom/Pop" to a professional organization.
- Engaging with the off-campus community to get the college "up and out," dispelling the community's perspective of the college as "that little school that wanted to be left alone."
- Transitioning the school's approach to spiritual formation from a rules-oriented model to a "spiritual discernment" model.

These critical internal changes provided a backstop for the external change the public finally noticed—the name changes:

- *from* Grand Rapids Baptist College and Seminary *to* Cornerstone College and Grand Rapids Baptist Seminary (1994),

- *to* Cornerstone University and Grand Rapids Baptist Seminary (1999), and finally,
- for the seminary, *to* Grand Rapids Theological Seminary (2003).

As Desmond Tutu said, "You can't eat an elephant in one bite." To accomplish an ambitious list of essential changes takes time and is usually better tackled bit by bit, or maybe bite by bite.

Of course, the university's faculty and staff "worked smarter" over many years to position the university for growth. The university changed to attain the institutional founders' vision, a thriving school offering a quality Christian higher education.

> **An ambitious list of essential changes takes time.**

In sailing, you chart your course and set your boat's heading accordingly. All is well until the weather knocks your craft off course with buffeting wind and waves. Now what do you do? You adjust your heading. You change—not to arrive at a *new* destination, but ironically, to assure the journey ends at your *original* destination.

Leaders must look to the "weather, wind, and waves," and as needed, change the organization's heading, sometimes dramatically, to get where they want to go.

Change Within the Leader

Leaders also must continue to change and keep growing, themselves. John C. Maxwell pulled no punches on this point, saying, "If you want to keep leading, you must keep changing."[137]

But amazingly, a lot of leaders resist changing, illustrating a point I once heard Rev. Haddon Robinson make in a three-way conversation, "After a while, the chief obstacle to innovation can be the chief innovator." In other words, if leaders have been around long enough to have touched most of the organization, they sometimes become reluctant to change anything they've done. When this happens, they've put a lid on the organization's capacity for growth.[138] They may not know it, but as leaders, at least if it goes too far, they're dead men walking.

> **After a while, the chief obstacle to innovation can be the chief innovator.**

To keep growing (changing), leaders must be learners. In fact, in a "flat world" leading and learning go hand in hand as never before. In Thomas L. Friedman's bestseller, *The World Is Flat: A Brief History of the Twenty-First Century*, he cited Colin Powell as a learning leader. Then Secretary of State Powell noted how new technology had changed how he performed his tasks. He no longer needed information from his staff—he could get that himself on the Internet—he needed action from his staff. And without staff assistance he could talk to world leaders directly anytime he wished. This meant the secretary had to learn a new style of communicating. He had to adapt. So did his coworkers who the secretary now expected to provide him with even more intelligence and analysis.[139]

Leaders who do not change are not leaders. They're only administrators marking time.

Proactive Stewardship

Former New York City mayor Rudolph Giuliani said, "A leader should be anticipating all the time."[140] I like that comment because it presupposes my favorite word—"proactive."

Proactive is the opposite of *reactive*. Proactive is a form of thinking and a style of behavior emphasizing awareness, forward orientation, imagination and innovation, and, most of all, an entrepreneurial bias for action.

> **Leaders must be learners.**

A proactive leader is one who does what Giuliani recommends. He or she anticipates changes in the marketplace and acts on the change before the change acts on the organization. A proactive leader is like the men of Issachar in the Old Testament "who had understanding of the times, to know what Israel ought to do" (1 Chron. 12:32).

A proactive leader doesn't just respond or wait for something to happen; he or she leads. Proactive leaders tend to operate as if the ball's always in their court.

Since the late 1980s, I've used the term "proactive stewardship" to describe my own leadership philosophy. I base this philosophy upon God's Word found in the book of Matthew 24:42–51; 25:1–30—four parables in which God says he expects us to be *watchful, ready, wise, faithful,* and *working*.

While I consider proactive stewardship a commendable way of life for anyone, I believe it's especially potent for leaders. The degree to which leaders think and act proactively is the degree to which they're protected from falling into unexamined habits, or worse, ruts. Proactive stewardship pushes leaders to think about what's next (proactive) and what's best (stewardship).

Optimistic Realism

Proactive stewardship also involves "optimistic realism." This is the idea that Christians recognize the world is fallen, cursed by sin—that's the realism—but also appreciate the fact that we "know the end of the story," the truth that the Sovereign God is in control and has provided a means of redemption—that's the optimism (or in theological terms, the hope).

Optimism is a central ingredient of leadership. Christian leaders can truly be optimistic realists. We don't go along ignoring problems and pain in some Pollyannaish fashion. But then again, we need not succumb to pessimism either.

> **Leaders should be optimistic realists.**

Proactive stewardship encourages a healthy view of risk, recognizing that without risk change is impossible. Leaders who work with the knowledge that they're accountable stewards are more likely to seek counsel, weigh apparent opportunities or proposed actions carefully, and avoid taking foolish risks. By the same token, their ability to execute appropriate leadership initiatives will not as likely be debilitated by risk aversion rooted either in their personalities or in their organizational culture's penchant for paralysis by analysis.

Bureaucratic and political personalities are risk-averse, but leaders take risks. Winston Churchill knew that without great risks and the possibility of failure, no great achievements would be possible.[141]

Robert K. Greenleaf said, "The leader . . . ventures to say, 'I will go; come with me!' He initiates, provides the ideas and the structures, and takes the risk of failure along with the chance of success. He says, 'I will go; follow me!' when he knows that the path is uncertain, even dangerous."[142]

Leaders Are Never Lucky

Proactive stewardship leaves no room for luck. I mention this because leaders and celebrities in our morally relativistic culture continually refer to luck. From Oprah to talk show guests to cable news anchors to politicians, pundits, and the public luck seems to be the ultimate explanation offered for what went right or wrong.

> **Without risk change is impossible.**

Saying something is "lucky" or "unlucky" is a way of avoiding saying something about God or religion, or individual responsibility, or you guessed it, accountability.

If it was just bad luck when the corporate leader's greedy choices destroyed his company's pension fund, then he's not really to blame. Let him go. But the bad luck isn't evenly distributed. The company is unlucky, and the pension fund member is unlucky. But the unethical leader is laughing all the way to the bank.

If a political leader was just unlucky when he got caught with his pants down, isn't it overkill to expect him to resign his office?

If it was just good luck that accounts for a retiring academic leader's prolonged record of achievements at her university, does it really matter who the board chooses to follow in her footsteps?

If it's all about fate or luck, what good are leaders anyway? Why don't we just roll the social dice and hope we get lucky?

But we have a problem. *There's no such thing as luck.* Sure, things happen beyond our control or even understanding, but that's because we are finite creatures. We are not omniscient. But the infinite, Creator God is. Nothing happens outside his providence.

A Sovereign God and the idea of luck are mutually exclusive concepts. You cannot believe in both. Luck is fantasy.

Leaders are never victims of bad luck or beneficiaries of good luck. Quite simply, leaders are never lucky. They are individually responsible for their actions.

This fact isn't discouraging. It's empowering. It means leaders' actions can and do have real impact. If that's true, then leaders' contributions are measurable, and progress is possible. Leaders' lives and their work have meaning.

A Sovereign God and luck are mutually exclusive concepts.

Proactive stewardship gives you the sense that you are not a Lone Ranger. But you are expected to lead and to do it dynamically with as much energy, emotion, and effectiveness as you can, not as a matter of luck but as unto the Lord.

LEADERSHIP LESSONS

1. Moses truly became a leader when he learned to delegate.
2. Purpose implies *mission*; vision implies *movement*.
3. Leaders reach beyond technique, themselves, today, and tomorrow.
4. Leaders don't just go *anywhere*; they go *somewhere*.
5. There's no place for mediocrity in leadership.
6. Excellence is a perpetual goal.
7. Leading is no cakewalk.
8. After a while, the chief obstacle to innovation can be the chief innovator.
9. Leaders should be optimistic realists.
10. A Sovereign God and luck are mutually exclusive concepts.

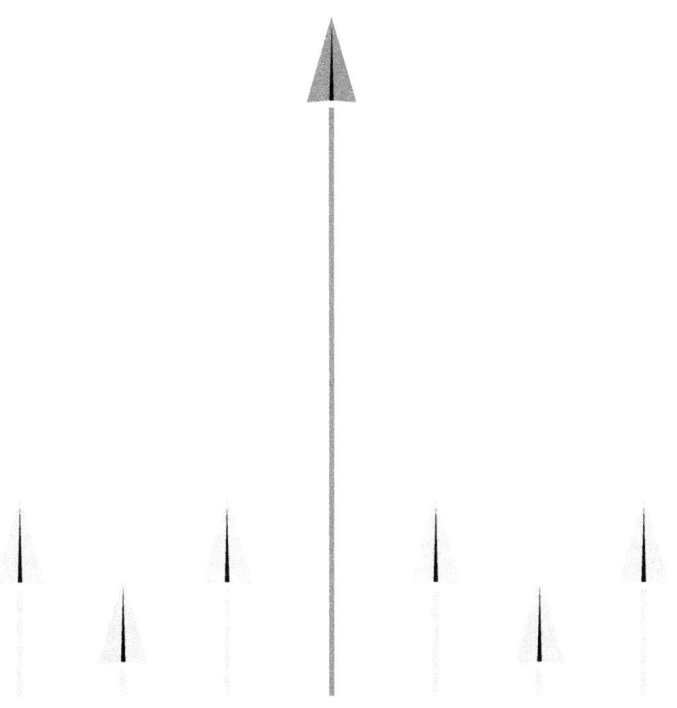

CHAPTER 6

COMMUNICATION

What A Leader *Says*

JOSHUA

Joshua was a slave, a soldier, a statesman. He entered history as one of the great military leaders of all time. He was mentored by Moses, serving as a key apprentice long before he led the nation of Israel (Ex. 24:13; 33:11). Later, God selected Joshua as Moses's successor, giving him the difficult assignment of following the greatest of all leaders. Through it all Joshua was a soldier-saint who enjoyed the presence of God, was filled with the Spirit of God, and was obedient to the will of God.[143]

As a younger man Joshua was deployed as one of the twelve spies Moses sent to reconnoiter the promised land. When the spies returned, Joshua and his friend Caleb distinguished themselves as the only spies making an encouraging "Let's roll" report. But the Israelites' fear got the best of them. They balked at following the Lord into the promised land and paid the price for their doubt by wandering for forty years in the Sinai Desert (Numbers 13–14).

God knew that "it often takes a new leader to challenge and guide a new generation." When Joshua finally came to power at the end of the forty years of life in the Sinai, God told him "Every place that the sole of your foot will tread upon I have given to you, just as I promised to Moses" (Josh. 1:3).[144] Three times, God said, "Be strong and courageous" and once he said, "Do not be frightened, and do not be dismayed, for the LORD your God is with you wherever you go" (Josh. 1:6–7, 9). Through faith Joshua believed God. He went where God told him to go and he led Israel in defeating thirty-one pagan kings.

On two occasions Joshua ran ahead of the Lord by failing to pray, wait, and walk by faith (Josh. 7–9).[145] But each time, Joshua returned to the Lord for forgiveness, wisdom, and strength, and renewed dependence upon God's promises (Josh. 7:6–9; 10:12–14).

Joshua reminded his people "to love the LORD your God, and to walk in all his ways and to keep his commandments and to cling to him and to serve him with all your heart and with all your soul" (Josh. 22:5).

Joshua was a godly leader, stating unequivocally, "But as for me and my house, we will serve the LORD" (Josh. 24:15). In large part due to Joshua's example Israel served God all the days of Joshua and "all the days of the elders who outlived Joshua" (Josh. 24:31).

While leadership is always in short supply, godly, effective leadership is in even shorter supply. Joshua answered the call.

Godly, effective leadership is in short supply.

Clearly Joshua was a strong personality. He had to be to survive for decades working with Moses and the Israelites, not to mention leading armies against armed forces in Canaan. But his effectiveness as a leader was rooted not in his persona but in his passion for the Lord's purpose for the nation of Israel— "as for me and my house, we will serve the LORD." He got *the right things* done because he led with *the right heart*.

Not Power, Not Position But Passion

Leaders who accomplish "great things" are motivated by a driving desire to fulfill a dream, a vision. Whatever the dream or vision, it's the leader's passion more than power or personality that predicts success. It's the leader's passion that determines the size of the leader.

It's the same intangible human quality you see in evenly matched sports teams during competition. Who wins often isn't determined by ability as much as who wants it most.

How many speeches, presentations, or sermons have you heard and wondered if the speaker believed what he or she said? In 1999, I attended a political event featuring Dan Quayle, former vice president, then running for the presidency. Because of what happened I've never forgotten. At that event, Mr. Quayle spoke in an unemotional monotone. Before and after the speech I shook his hand and both times he looked past me with a limp-wristed handshake. To be fair, I know that candidates must protect themselves physically by avoiding strong grips, but I also know that in those encounters and during the speech I thought, "He's not into this." Not long thereafter Mr. Quayle dropped out of the race.

> **The leader's passion determines the size of the leader.**

What leaders say matters. But how leaders say it matters too.

"Leadership is a matter of the heart. It's emotional not just rational. Leaders are in their jobs to *do something*, not in their jobs for *something to do*."[146]

So, if you wish to be a leader you need to discover—or release—your passion. You don't have to channel a Robin Williams manic personality. That's not passion. And you don't have to be somebody else. But you do need to answer the question, what is it that you most want to do? What is it you most want to accomplish?

Once answered, you tackle your vision with a passion: obvious, overt, sustained, eagerness in doing what you are trying to do. Passion keeps the work alive. Passion keeps it enjoyable. Passion is contagious.

Passion is contagious.

Louis Gerstner discovered the value of passion in his experience leading IBM: "Most of all, personal leadership is about passion.... As a student going through Harvard Business School, I would never have guessed that passion would be the single most important element of personal leadership. I don't recall the word ever being spoken during my classroom time at Harvard."[147]

Let me give you another illustration of passion. A friend of mine is a good Christian man. He cared for his family by selling cars for a living. He never stood in front of audiences. He never organized rallies, made speeches, raised funds, or spoke to the news media. He never aspired to do these things.

But then certain gambling interests decided to locate a casino in his community. Since he considered gambling a moral affront to his faith, since he didn't want a casino located minutes from his home, and since no one else stepped up—he did.

His passion made him a force for "casiNO." He became the citizen-leader of an anticasino organization in the state of Michigan. Media regularly quoted him. He spoke to supporters and debated opponents. His emerging leadership talent benefited his community.

My friend shared his passion with others, and others followed. He didn't compel anyone. His passion moved people to act.

James MacGregor Burns said, "Leadership *mobilizes*, naked power *coerces*."[148] He knew that effective leaders don't demand, they enthuse, and they do this via their own passionate commitment to ideas greater than the task at hand.

Effective leaders don't demand but enthuse.

Passion, though, can be dangerous when it's unbridled or built upon a foundation of questionable values.

In the Old Testament King Saul is a sad example of a man who presumed to lead with a warped passion. "From the start, Saul's great concern was his own prestige, his own popularity, his own grip on the reins of power. . . . It was the trappings of power and not the calling that fueled his imagination. . . . Saul did not view the state of his sheep as something significant to him. His focus, as executive, was upon himself and his perks and his problems. . . . Saul does not inspire, he demands; he does not lead; he dictates and he cajoles; he does not build for the future but reacts to the crises of the day. . . . He had authority, but little influence. *Saul was a king, but he was not a leader.*"[149]

The moral of Saul's story is that leaders who lead with passion for themselves rarely move people for the greater good. The same is true of leaders who depend upon personality or mere power. They don't motivate people; they lure or force people. Rarely do such leaders accomplish anything history considers worthy.

Saul was not God's choice for king. Now we know why.

God's unlikely leaders, though, were people of passion who changed the world. They inspired people. I want to be one of them. You want to be one of them. And you can be.

Inspiring Others to Aspire

They say, "It's lonely at the top," but leaders never work alone. Leaders who accomplish things do so by inspiring others to aspire, to move in a new direction, to change the future.

The word "inspire" means to breathe life into or to encourage. The more capable a leader becomes at inspiration the more likely followers will fulfill their aspirations. Warren Bennis said, "Leaders are sentenced by their sentences."[150] In other words, leaders must learn to communicate with urgency and emotional energy.

Leaders inspire others to aspire.

Leaders who lead well inspire a shared vision. As Noel Tichy observed, "In organizations, people don't have to work against you;

they just have to stand around. . . . (We don't say) everyone open their hymnbooks to whatever page you want. What are the chances of harmony? No, we say 'Everyone open to page 57'—all sing from the same page."[151]

Learning to communicate a vision, or simply to sell one's ideas about change, is something every leader must do to be effective. It's something with which President George W. Bush struggled throughout his public life.

President Bush held tenaciously, at times admirably, to his principles. As president he was generally decisive, but his capacity for accomplishing his goals was often undermined by his underdeveloped or quirky communication skills.

On a few occasions President Bush communicated memorably, most notably just after 9/11, standing atop the rubble of Ground Zero with a megaphone when he said, "I can hear you. The rest of the world hears you. And the people who knocked these buildings down will hear all of us soon." Days later September 21, 2001, President Bush also communicated remarkably well to a joint session of Congress in a historic address about terrorism. He was prepared, his heart was on his sleeve, and people were scared and ready to listen.

But much of the time President Bush did not communicate with verbal and emotional power. This challenge was rooted in more than his famous malapropisms like "misunderestimated" or "strategery." Some would say his limitations as a communicator stemmed from his persona, including a penchant for odd jokes at odd times, body language that conveyed an ironic discomfort with public life, and a tendency to make misstatements in public policy discourse. Whatever the source, and however decent a person President Bush likely is, his communications skills did not typically reinforce his leadership.

President Ronald Reagan was, on the other hand, renowned for his communications skills, even earning the sobriquet "The Great

Communicator." Reagan expressed his vision by focusing upon the future, instilling hope and a sense of destiny. He separated things that mattered from the peripheral and kept his eye on the big picture, not allowing himself or the American people to get buried in the details.[152] Reagan seized the "bully pulpit" and preached a message of progress through freedom and hard work. Whether or not you agreed with him you had to listen. President Reagan could move people reading a tax code.

Leaders like Reagan help followers think the impossible is possible. Leaders as change agents act "not just out of a conviction that the message is right, but that it is essential, that the very future hangs upon the thread of today's decisions."[153] Leaders clarify, communicate, persuade, enthuse, and foster conviction. They create a sense of urgency, hopefully before there is a bona fide emergency. By their verbal and body language, a vital component of effective communication according to "master teacher" Robert L. Debruyn,[154] leaders help followers "build a cathedral" not just "cut stone."[155]

Leaders help followers think the impossible is possible.

To borrow from Nike, leaders "Just Do It." Passionate leaders don't require a lot of technique. President Lincoln never took a Myers-Briggs test and Ghandi never got "360-degree feedback."[156] For effective leaders, inspiring others to aspire is an everyday occurrence.

Rudolph W. Giuliani, former New York City mayor, is rightly noted for his encouraging rhetoric and example in the tense days following 9/11. But his inspirational brand of leadership was evident before this crisis. In the early days of his first term, facing the possibility of municipal bankruptcy and the hard decisions needed to prevent that outcome, the mayor went around City Hall, talked with the media, and took his case to the people. If his plans were to have any chance at all, Mayor Giuliani knew that he had to communicate with the city's residents boldly, truthfully, directly, and often. So, he did—embarking upon a torrid pace that at times demanded multiple speeches per night.[157] He did what he had to do to get the job done, and what he had to do more than anything else was communicate hope.

IBM's Louis Gerstner did the same thing, saying later, "No institutional transformation takes place, I believe, without a multiyear commitment by the CEO to put himself or herself constantly in front of employees and speak in plain, simple, compelling language that drives conviction and action throughout the organization."[158]

It may surprise you to note that Jesus used a similar approach to lasting advantage. When the top layer of religious leaders resisted everything, Jesus taught, he went around and over and under and through them like Living Water and reached the people, everyone who had "ears to hear."[159] His three and a half years of ministry featured near nonstop teaching.

Great leaders have always understood, almost intuitively, the need to inspire by their attitudes, words, and actions. Recalling FDR, Frances Perkins, former secretary of labor said, "His capacity to inspire and encourage those who had to do tough, confused, and practically impossible jobs was beyond dispute. . . . It was not so much what he said as the spirit he conveyed."[160] During the Great Depression, he buoyed an entire nation, telling them in soaring, powerful, but personal rhetoric, "The only thing we have to fear is fear itself."[161]

Napoleon understood this. He believed that "a leader is a dealer in hope."[162] Leaders who become adept at inspiring others to aspire, who give people a sense of the possible, accomplish more.

Stories and Symbolism

Leaders inspire best when they tell stories: "Who I am" stories, "Who we are" stories, and "Where are we going" stories. These stories need to lead not just rationally but emotionally.[163]

Stories "put a human face on success," and are a critical part of a leader's journey finding his or her own "authentic voice" toward creating a powerful leadership experience.[164]

The key is to "put very profound ideas into very simple terms."[165] Aim rhetoric at the heart rather than the head. Speak of principle not policy.[166] Use symbolism more often than statistics. Create a cause célèbre, some soul, a deeper or more profound meaning for what you are doing, and people will respond with unbelievable commitment, sacrifice, and concerted endeavor.

Sometimes just give them some well-timed bravado like General Tony McAuliffe did during the Battle of the Bulge when the Germans asked him to surrender, to which he famously—and inspirationally replied—"To the German Commander, NUTS!, The American Commander."[167] But you'd better back it up like McAuliffe did.

Use symbolism more often than statistics.

JFK understood the power of symbolism. He's the one who first publicly called the presidential jet "Air Force One" and ordered "United States of America" painted in large letters on the side of the plane. Jackie Kennedy chose the plane's light blue body color that is still used to great impact today.[168]

Reagan communicated his vision in stories and pithy comments. His standard description of government: "If it moves, tax it. If it keeps moving, regulate it. And if it stops moving, subsidize it;" or, saying the scariest and most dangerous words in the English language were "Hi, I'm from the government, and I'm here to help." And then there's this one, "A recession is when a neighbor loses his job. A depression is when you lose yours. Recovery is when Jimmy Carter loses his."[169]

Reagan, perhaps more than any other recent president, worked with a well-defined political ideology. He had what Noel Tichy calls a "teachable point of view," a set of clearly developed ideas and values, which may be communicated with emotional energy as well as used to guide the tough yes/no decisions every successful leader must make. The very act of creating a teachable point of view, Tichy maintains, makes people better leaders.[170]

Leaders who teach make things happen. "This is why Roger Enrico's leadership school at Pepsico was so successful. He ran it himself, with no consultants and no professors. It was just Enrico. . . . Jack Welch's secret (at G.E.) was that he was constantly teaching."[171] Teaching is a path to inspiration, which is a path to achievement.

Leaders who teach make things happen.

General George C. Marshall, FDR's chief of staff during WWII and later a member of the Truman Cabinet, once said, "A leader in a democracy must also be an entertainer." Leadership scholar Warren Bennis seconded this notion by observing that effective leaders manage people's attention. FDR, Generals George C. Patton and Douglas MacArthur, and business giant Lee Iaccoca were all excellent entertainers. One cheeky university president said, "A leader's ability to comfortably tell jokes and humorous anecdotes is important because it makes him appear warm and accessible (even when he's not)."[172]

Leaders should add spice and emotion to their presentations. "Telling compelling stories is one of the most powerful tools there is for establishing a close bond with his followers and for inculcating his vision among them. . . . Effective leaders are able to create, manipulate, and exemplify not only stories but symbols, slogans, and mantras as well. All of these communication tricks help define in the minds of followers the essence of the leader's vision and his character. Moreover, the leader often becomes a symbol in and of himself. His actions tell followers a great deal about who he is and where he's taking the organization."[173]

Consider these academic leaders with contrasting leadership styles. The University of Chicago's Robert Maynard Hutchins acquired a degree of fame in his life for advocating the "Great Books" approach to learning and for becoming president at thirty years of age. After more than two decades in the presidency, he resigned in 1951, "more sympathized with than emulated." His was a style of high-handed, overpowering personality, brilliant, arrogant, impatient, and in the end a largely unsuccessful academic administration.

During a forty-year presidential tenure at Harvard University Charles Eliot introduced the elective course system still used today in virtually all higher education. John Hannah of Michigan State University and Clark Kerr of the University of California built large, national universities. All three men in very different eras were more successful in leadership than the renowned Hutchins. Why? They were better managers—directing the operations effectively so the institution could accomplish its purposes. But more importantly, they were better leaders—creating a story that made sense to a variety of constituents.[174] Eliot, Hannah, and Kerr all enjoyed greater academic accomplishment because they learned to tell their university's story in a compelling way.

> **The central importance of telling an organization's story cannot be overstated.**

So, the central importance of telling an organization's story in a compelling manner cannot be overstated. It is more than simply repeating the mission or the latest graphics. The best stories are informational, interesting, and inspirational. The institution's story enunciates values that will not change even as the realities of the present marketplace change continuously.

The story is not simply the leader's product. Rather it is his or her distillation of what the community has said, what it believes, and what it stands for.[175] An organization's story is its history, future, and meaning wrapped in one package.

4 Cs

When I first arrived at then Grand Rapids Baptist College and Seminary, now Cornerstone University, I found an institution unsure of its identity and uncertain of its future. After a few months of listening and learning what the school was and what I, at least, thought it ought to be, I began using what became known as the "4 Cs" speech. (This listening period is one of the most important things I did as a leader.) During my first years in the presidency, I used this speech so often many staff and faculty eventually quoted passages of it back to me in good-natured needling. Even my own children could give the speech.

> **An organization's story is its history, future, and meaning in one package.**

It was simple. It worked. It captured the essence of the institution's core commitments and vision in a few words the constituency could understand and embrace.

The "4 Cs" provided focus throughout the school's transformation from a fundamentalist liberal arts college and seminary with Bible college roots to an evangelical Christian university. Sometimes, depending upon the audience, I stopped with "3 Cs" but usually the speech included four.

I'd begin saying, "Grand Rapids Baptist College and Seminary," then later, "Cornerstone College is committed to unchanging biblical principles in a rapidly changing world. The college is a . . .

1. ***Christian College***, Capital C on both words. We are and we strive to be thoroughly Christian in all that we do, all of which is designed to help students develop their Christian

worldview. So, we care about spiritual things . . . but we care about academic things, too, because we're a college, so we're committed to academic quality . . .
2. **Conservative**, now I'm not talking about politics, I mean 'theologically conservative,' that is we believe the Bible is what it claims that it is, the Word of God, and our guide for faith and practice . . .
3. **Comprehensive**, meaning we're not a Bible college or even now simply a liberal arts college but an institution of higher learning built upon a wide array of programs including liberal arts, professional, and graduate studies."

We're Christian, a College, Conservative, and Comprehensive.

The "4 Cs" is an example of what some call an "elevator speech," what you could say about your organization's mission and vision in the time it takes to ride to the top floor. The "4 Cs" may not sound inspiring, but in the context of the times and this school's development, the "Cs" sent a simultaneous message about strengthening core values and repositioning for a brighter future.

The "4 Cs" speech had a seven-year shelf life. I retired the speech when it no longer told the university's story. In fact, eight years into my presidency when the college became a university, parts of the speech still rang true, but its poetry didn't work anymore. When at last it was time for a new speech, the old one was not a victim of age but progress. Good things are happening when leaders wear out their best speeches.

Nuts and Bolts

So, when you develop an inspirational-if-not-inspired vision for your organization, what next?

Communicate vision clearly, concisely, practically, passionately, repeatedly.

You communicate your vision clearly, concisely, practically, most definitely passionately, and repeatedly.

For years I've enjoyed listening to speakers of all types, trying to identify what makes them successful. Many preachers have developed their skills to a level of fine art, like the late Warren W. Wiersbe, Charles R. Swindoll, or Joyce Meyers or David Jeremiah. Civic and political leaders typically lag far behind religious leaders in polish and presentation, with rare exceptions like President Barack Obama. Whoever they are, leaders would do well to forever work at improving their communication skills.

Here are a few practical nuts and bolts:

1. *Speak.* The first law of communication is to communicate, so if you want people to get the message, share the message. And you must speak in a vocabulary—as simply as possible—and manner others can understand. Don't do what some professors attempt to do, impress the audience with multiple syllable words. Doesn't work. When the crowd goes home, the only thing they remember will be your hubris. Jesus said, "I am the way, and the truth, and the life. No one comes to the Father except through me" (John 14:6)—doesn't get much simpler than that.

2. *Don't apologize for speaking.* It's one thing to hear an infrequent speaker offer a nervous apology on the church platform. It's quite another to hear this from a leader. If speaking makes you nervous get over it or get another job. Your apologies for being ill at ease makes everyone else ill at ease. The more comfortable you are "in your own skin" the more comfortable your audience will be with your presentation.

3. *Convey confidence.* Take charge of the speaking opportunity and treat listeners with respect. Say "thanks," but don't gush. Do whatever it takes to develop your confidence: prepare properly, practice, use notes, etc. Stand physically relaxed and avoid signaling nerves by odd gestures or extraneous movement.
4. *Connect with the audience.* Smile. Look directly at people individually and collectively. Scan the entire audience in a natural and measured way so everyone feels you are speaking to them. On the way or at the event, be alert for a development unique to the occasion, then mention it at the beginning of your talk. Former presidential candidate Gary Bauer is a master at this. Every time, dingy old high school auditorium or the Waldorf Astoria, he finds something to say that's distinctive and complimentary to his listeners and their venue. I heard him do this on our campus. Know your audience and relate directly to them, their town, or this event, today. Make them feel special—why comedians are forever saying, "You've been a great audience," as they exit stage left.
5. *Develop a few appropriate one-liners that work anywhere.* Old standby one-liners—with which you are comfortable—are always there for you, like a good friend. They reduce your anxiety, help you convey confidence and connect with the audience, and assist in engaging the audience and helping them relax. One of my favorites goes something like this: "I've always wanted to speak at XYZ"—short pause—"Guess now I can die happy." That one never fails to get a laugh.
6. *Never read your speech.* It may be appropriate to read a short formal announcement or a reference to someone else's statement. But reading your content is the fastest way to lose your audience's attention, put them to sleep, or literally lose them as they vote with their feet going out the back door.

I once sat in the Michigan Legislature's gallery listening to Governor John Engler deliver his State of the State address. While I appreciated him and most of his ideas, I struggled to stay focused as he ponderously read line after line. You can guess what the opposition party was doing. To the Governor's credit he got better with time and, I was told by a few of his intimates, with professional help and practice. Good for him. Good for his constituency.

7. *Be brief.* FDR's "Be sincere; be brief; be seated" is a good rule of thumb for any speaker. In November 1863, Edward Everett gave the principal speech at the dedication ceremony for a new military cemetery at Gettysburg, followed by President Abraham Lincoln's "Gettysburg Address." Everett later wrote to Lincoln, "I should be glad if I could flatter myself that I came as near to the central idea of the occasion, in two hours, as you did in two minutes."[176]

8. *Tell stories.* Jesus generally spoke to crowds of followers in parables, short stories from everyday life with an application of deeper spiritual truths. While more than thirty parables are recorded in the Gospels, in the book of Mark it says Jesus used many other parables in his public speaking ministry. Indeed, "He did not speak to them without a parable" (Mark 4:34). People are interested in people and that's what a leader's best stories should be about.

9. *List core values and/or state goals clearly.* "It's impossible to affirm (your values) too much. Put them on everything."[177] Why goals? An important way to motivate people is to assure that they know where they are going.[178] Values and goals are part and parcel of a vision speech. Share them, or better yet, as leader embody them. Lead by example.

10. *Be positive.* "Negative campaigning" has long since become commonplace in American life. But a leader is better served

taking the high road. Ronald Reagan gave us a version of this, his eleventh commandment: "Thou shalt not speak ill of any fellow Republican."[179] This one has long since been discarded by both parties. In the last decade or so, national political discourse has coarsened considerably. It's sad, ugly, demeaning to the speaker as much to the opposition, and does not further understanding. Describe who you and your organization *are,* not who others or competitor organizations *are not.* Being quoted in media with a sound-bite attack on others is more about ego or vengeance than it is about advancing your organization's vision. Nobody follows a flamethrower for long. The heat is too intense.

11. *Use props to reinforce not replace your speech.* PowerPoints, video shorts, pictures, audio, other technology can be enormously effective tools for engaging an audience. But you're still the speaker and, for my money, you need to speak. No media has yet been developed that is as compelling as a passionate person who truly believes what he or she is saying. Use props wisely, but don't forget the natural power of going "unplugged."

12. *Use your same (best) vision speech repeatedly.* Remember Barry Z. Posner's formula for good vision communication: "Repetition, repetition, repetition!"[180] Richard Nixon makes the point most colorfully, "About the time you are writing a line you have written so often that you want to throw up, that is the time the American people will hear it."[181] Communicate the vision persuasively and persistently at every possible occasion.[182] And don't worry if you're sharing the vision too often. Management consultants Thomas Werner and Robert Lynch recommend leaders communicate their vision seven times in seven different ways.[183] I'd say a lot more often than that.

These items are suggestions born of experience, not rules. Some will apply all the time. Some will apply sometimes. It's your judgment call.

You are the leader. Lead with your words.

Say It Like a Leader

Even now, some readers, who would be unlikely leaders, are thinking, "But I'm not a speaker." To you I say, "You only need to become better than yourself, not someone else. Set a speaking goal and work toward it."

Winston Churchill is one of the best examples of all time, along with Moses, of a person who persevered, who overcame a speaking challenge and leveraged his success in leadership. Churchill had a speech impediment, a slight lisp for which he took diction lessons and even considered oral surgery. He possessed a prodigious memory, but he never gave a speech from memory because early in his parliamentary career he went blank in the middle of a speech and sat down in embarrassment. Thereafter, he diligently prepared for every speech. One of his friends, Lord Birkenhead, once said, "Winston has spent the best years of his life writing impromptu speeches."

Lead with your words.

Churchill used extensive, detailed notes when he spoke, employed short words where possible (He said, "Long, fancy words interrupt rhythm and are the crutch of the under-confident"), practiced his diction and the rhythm of his delivery, appealed to the everyday knowledge of the listener, and always argued or made a point. In time, Churchill became one of the twentieth century's most impressive orators.

Remember his speech in 1940? He helped engineer Britain's "finest hour" when he said, "I have nothing to offer but blood, toil, tears, and sweat."

Or his salute to the Royal Air Force? "Never in the field of human conflict was so much owed by so many to so few."

Churchill sincerely believed that "of all the talents bestowed upon man, none is so precious as the gift of oratory. . . . Abandoned by his party, betrayed by his friends, stripped of his offices, whoever can command this power is still formidable."[184]

Learn to communicate effectively, and you'll learn to lead effectively.

LEADERSHIP LESSONS

1. Godly, effective leadership is in short supply.
2. Passion is contagious.
3. Effective leaders don't demand but enthuse.
4. Leaders inspire others to aspire.
5. Leaders help followers think the impossible is possible.
6. Use symbolism more often than statistics.
7. Leaders who teach make things happen.
8. The central importance of telling an organization's story cannot be overstated.
9. Communicate vision clearly, concisely, practically, passionately, repeatedly.
10. Lead with your words.

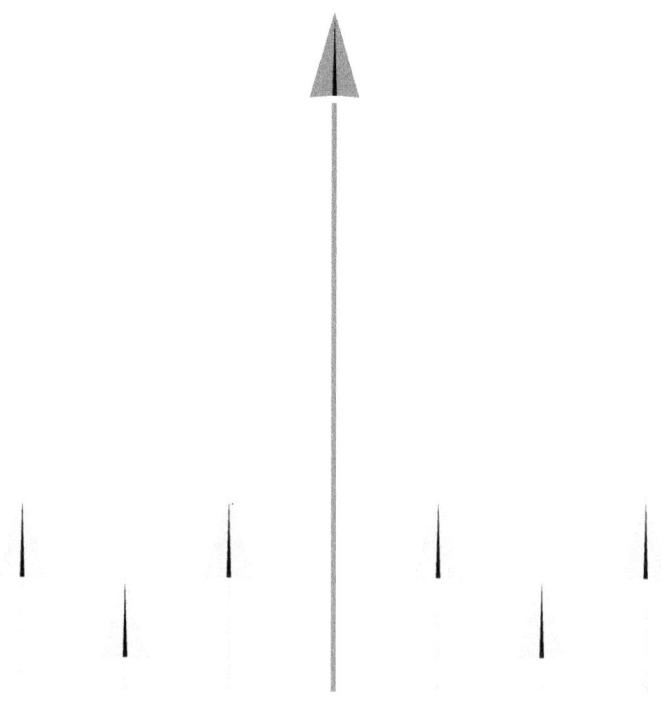

CHAPTER 7

COMMITMENT

What A Leader *Does*

DANIEL

Daniel was captured as a teenage youth in Jerusalem. Then he was deported, became an involuntary immigrant, and spent his entire life in exile. Still later he became a prophet known for prayer, counseling some of the greatest monarchs the world has ever known: Nebuchadnezzar, Cyrus, Darius.[185]

These kings were not like Democrats or Republicans. They held the power of life and death over their subjects. Yet Daniel lived for God and thrived in pagan Babylonian and Persian cultures that dominated the known world in his day.

Though Daniel never embraced the worldview of his surrounding culture he became a prominent leader. By God's enablement Daniel became a trusted interpreter of dreams, most notably assisting Nebuchadnezzar in his personal turmoil. Later, Daniel counseled Belshazzar who witnessed the "handwriting on the wall" during one of his state-sponsored orgies. Daniel was an efficient and effective administrator, a wise counselor, and a man recognized for his "excellent spirit" who was "faithful, and no error or fault was found in him" (Dan. 6:3–4).

Daniel turned his daily prayers into a lifelong practice. He even continued his prayers when jealous administrative rivals conspired to make prayer a capital crime. The resulting story of "Daniel in the Lions' Den" has become one of the most beloved in Scripture. It is not an allegory. In this historical account God shut the mouths of the lions, thus demonstrating to Darius and through his decree to the known world—and to us today—that "the God of Daniel . . . is the living God, enduring forever." (Dan. 6:26).

Though Daniel continued in prayer for his people's release from captivity he never returned home (Daniel 9). He lived into the third year of Cyrus the Great and in all probability influenced Cyrus's decree allowing the Jewish people to return to Jerusalem to begin rebuilding the temple. Through more than eighty years of statesmanship in a foreign land Daniel faithfully and visibly lived his faith.

Don't Just Stand There; Do Something

Daniel's life was a perfect illustration of the maxim that leadership is not academic; it's action. Leaders aren't really leaders until they lead, meaning they must do something. Who follows a leader who's standing still? Going nowhere? From the time he was a teenager Daniel led by example. He even led in the face of palace intrigue. His words mattered, but he empowered his statements with actions.

> **Leaders lead by example.**

Winston Churchill liked to say, "Ponder, and then act." Another of his favorite, pithy comments made a similar point: "Half-measures are vain." Churchill's character was resolute, unflinching, and decisive, and he abhorred procrastination, equivocation, and crass interest-group calculation. He was a man of force and clarity. He believed that "good ideas are not sufficient: drive, decision, and follow-through are equally important yet often insufficiently appreciated." About World War II he said, "I never worry about action, but only about inaction."[186] Churchill's comrade in arms,

FDR, agreed, "There are many ways of going forward, but only one way of standing still."[187]

Churchill and FDR both would have seconded Barry Z. Posner's observation: "Those who try are more successful than those who don't."[188] Real leaders, effective leaders, *do*. They make things happen.

In 1994, William Bratton was appointed police commissioner of New York City. The NYPD, with a budget of $2 billion and a workforce of 35,000 police officers, was rife with turf wars, relatively lower pay, politics, and a seeming inability to thwart an ever-rising city crime rate. In two years, without a budget increase, he helped turn New York into the safest large city in the nation at that time. He accomplished this feat, one of five successful turnarounds in his career, by fundamentally changing the department's organizational culture and by concentrating existing resources on areas most needing change and offering the biggest payoff. He was featured on the cover of *Time* magazine, but more importantly, the changes he made outlasted his tenure as leader of the NYPD.[189]

Rebecca McDonald is the founder and president of Women At Risk, International. As a child of medical missionaries in Bangladesh she saw some ugly things she never forgot. God used these experiences to plant a seed that took decades to germinate. In his timing God enabled McDonald to develop a ministry that helps rescue, redeem, restore, and empower thousands of women and children caught up in global human trafficking. Her experience, preparation, vision, and passion turned to action that inspires and sustains volunteers and supporters. Without that final step, action—execute, perform, produce—the vision and its potential would have remained unfulfilled.

What a leader *does* is "do." Leaders who don't do don't lead. Remember, "*holding authority* is not the same as *exercising leadership*."[190] Theodore Roosevelt said, "In any moment of decision the best thing you can do is the right thing. The next best thing is the wrong thing, and the worst thing you can do is nothing."[191]

Creativity

Leaders lead best when they demonstrate a penchant for looking for a better way. They do, but they do creatively.

Abraham Lincoln is rightly remembered and revered for effective leadership in the fierce crucible of the Civil War. But he was an equally shrewd thinker. He once famously said, "If I had eight hours to chop down a tree, I'd spend six sharpening my ax."[192]

Leaders look for a better way.

Effective leaders must evidence the discipline and drive to get things done. But you won't lead long if you repeatedly lead your followers over a cliff. Ronald Reagan, for example, was resolute in principle but creative in putting ideas into practice.[193] He *held his principles tightly but his ideas loosely*, with a willingness to drop them and move on, what Peter Drucker called "abandonment." A leader must be willing periodically to challenge everything and start over. On behalf of his or her organization, a leader must be willing to think the unthinkable.[194]

In the early 1990s, a few men living in the Middle East, including Dr. Terrence Ascott, held long discussions about how to take the message of Christ and Christianity to the vast and rapidly growing Arabic speaking population of the region. Traditional methods, including sending missionaries into local cultures, while not impossible, were nevertheless severely hampered by safety and security concerns, steep financial hurdles, and logistic challenges presented by the region's religion, rulers, and regimes. What to do?

At the time, Ascott was living in Egypt working in Christian print journalism when he experienced something of an epiphany. He'd just read a report suggesting the Arabic language population simply didn't read or at least did so at extremely minimal rates. Not good news for a print journalist. Walking home that day he espied children watching a small, old television propped on a box outdoors and connected via a long cord to a power source on an adjacent property. That's when it hit him. Television access was expanding significantly in the region, offering a means of communicating Christian teaching to the masses that far outstripped the capacity of print or any other methodology. The only question was how would he and his friends do this?

Leaders hold principles tightly, ideas loosely.

By 1995 they'd found their answer: satellite television, an emerging technology that had only recently become financially viable for nonprofit organizations. Ascott and company founded SAT-7, the first Christian satellite television effort in the region, and one year later began broadcasting with one hour of programming.[195] It was a humble but pioneering beginning.

SAT-7 now broadcasts Christian programming 24/7 in Arabic, Farsi (the language of Iran, parts of Afghanistan), and Turkish. SAT-7's footprint covers twenty-four countries in the Middle East and North Africa and several time zones. So, every day, every hour God's Word is shared with people living within some of the most closed countries in the world.

Still today, no technology exists permitting satellite channels to be selectively blocked. In other words, if a person has access to a television (98 percent today) and a satellite (average over 60 percent and much higher in some countries), he or she can receive uncensored programming from around the world.

Terrence Ascott and his friends practiced Drucker's abandonment. They discarded old means for new, even as they maintained their core values and their laser focus on the ends they wanted to achieve. They were creative. They looked for a better way.

Competence

All of us have been given talents by God, some at physical birth and some at our spiritual rebirth. Most of us are either multitalented or maxi-talented. Actually, I don't think I've ever met any truly one-talent people. This is too limited for God's abundant blessing.

Remember the old Christian saying, "God doesn't call the qualified, he qualifies the called"? (see 1 Cor. 1:27–29). Or another similar observation, "We have this treasure in jars of clay, to show that the surpassing power belongs to God and not to us" (2 Cor. 4:7). So, for sure, God gives us talents.

Attitude enables ability.

So, we have talents, but do we use them? "Peanuts" cartoonist Charles M. Schulz once said, "There is no heavier burden than an untapped potential."

Perhaps most of us are too risk-averse, too limited in our vision, too small in our view of God, too insecure in our sense of what God has given us, or maybe too lazy. So, we don't reach high enough to test our talents. If this is true than many people don't attain the level of achievement and thus fulfillment God intended for them.

This is a sad commentary on the human condition. It's a story of opportunity lost and a tale of "what might have been." Think of the undiscovered discoveries, the uninvented inventions, or the unexpressed artistry. A list like this is infinite.

I don't want to get to heaven and discover I had unused talents. I'd much rather reach for the next level and see what God might do. Aiming high shouldn't scare us. God is up there.

Don't be hung up on your presumed lack of talent. Use what you have. A lot of high-impact organizations were founded by one person with more vision and heart than evident talent.

Competence might be considered "polished talent," the idea that God gave us basic ability and it's our task to hone it. This is something I used to teach our children when they were young, especially while we watched the Olympics. All the athletes in an Olympic Village have world-class talents, but some have polished, honed, developed, or fine-tuned their talent to a level of competence, nay excellence, that sets them apart.

> **Competence is polished talent.**

This should be our approach. Don't bury your talent as some men did in the well-known parable of the talents in Scripture (Matt. 25:14–30; Luke 19:12–28). Use them. Steward them on behalf of the Master who granted them to you. Move your talent into competence, your capacity to complete successfully, effectively, and excellently the task God's given you. Because we're accountable to him, everything we do should be done as well as we can possibly do it. Certainly, this is true in leadership.

You'll always be able to look around and see people more talented that you are. But it doesn't matter. You're you.

There may only be one Teddy Roosevelt or only one Mother Teresa—but she had it right when she said, "Can't feed a hundred? Feed one." Remember, there's only one, just one-and-only you.

Energy and Work Ethic

President Jed Bartlett, the central character on NBC's television hit *West Wing*, frequently asked his staff, "What's next?" His question conveyed something about how his face-forward, proactive orientation, his frenetic schedule, and his energy and work ethic. While his team was wrapping up the last challenge, he was on to the next one. It's what leaders do. Dynamic and effective leaders are always ready to move on to what's next.

People joke they're "get-up-and-go got up and went," and of course age and less-than-perfect health eventually slow us down. This comes to us all, which is why the late Dr. Wilbert Welch,

Cornerstone University's Chancellor, used to ask me: "Are you taking care of your health? You know, whatever you do for the Lord you do it in a body. If you burn up the body, you won't be able to serve the Lord as long or as well." At the time, a man in his eighties who says something like this has a lot of credibility to put behind his words. Dr. Welch lived his faith and shared his leadership wisdom into his mid-nineties.

But beyond basic balance in our healthcare, leadership is by definition a racetrack. Leaders who lead well must run in front of the pack and "running" is an apt description.

Our energy level, aside from the Dr. Welch–type decisions we make, is pretty much determined by our DNA. Yes, we can protect and preserve our energy, but for the most part what we bring to the race is in our genes.

And that's okay. Lower energy people are not excluded from leadership. But they may need to address the typical demands of leadership in different ways. One way is via their leadership style, something we'll address later.

What you can directly control, I believe, is work ethic. While drawing on energy I believe work ethic is not so much biology as it is philosophy. It's learned behavior and a choice. Work ethic is more emotional than physical. Winston Churchill said, "Success is going from failure to failure without loss of enthusiasm." There's that thing again we call attitude.

Leaders must be more than warm bodies in the executive suite. One reason is that there's not a staff member in any organization who cannot tell you something about their leader's work ethic. They know, and your work ethic becomes their local gold standard.

A leader's work ethic becomes the staff's gold standard.

One evening during my first year as university president a senior professor came by the office about 6:30 p.m. He knocked and said, "What are you doing here at this hour?" When I responded that I didn't know what time it was and that I just wrapping up my work, he said, "You know, everyone on campus knows your car is still here." That was one of my early lessons in how the so-called leadership fishbowl is not just a periodic personal annoyance. It's something that can be used to great professional advantage if you're modeling attitudes and actions, you hope will be multiplied.

Let me repeat myself. Energy is a gift from God and should be the focus of proper stewardship. Work ethic is a learned behavior or a choice, an attitude you employ in fueling action. If you love leadership tackle it with gusto. It'll be part of your recognizable style. Leaders who demonstrate a "can do" spirit inspire confidence.

Styles of Leadership

We know that different circumstances seem to demand or produce different leaders. Not every leader, even good ones it seems, is able to lead well in any or all differing circumstances or conditions.

This is writ large each year in professional sports. Coaches or managers that until now enjoyed a good run, winning and maybe winning it all, can reach a point where their leadership simply isn't working. They get fired. Then they turn up at another team and start winning all over again. This happens in all kinds of leadership environments, politics, business, nonprofits, education, and more.

We also know that given leaders have been known to lead effectively in and through a wide variety of different circumstances, as well as in challenges associated with one organization or perhaps several over time. They learn to be flexible and versatile. They may even alter leadership styles as needed from directive to coaching to facilitator, etc.[196] These rare leaders seem to go with the flow. They seem to be able to change colors like a chameleon and fit into the new landscape around them.

In 1961 Johns Gardner, who was then head of the Carnegie Corporation and subsequently moved on to prominent leadership in the Department of Health, Education, and Welfare and then Common Cause, wrote a book with the simple title, *Excellence*. The book was subtitled, "Can We Be Equal and Excellent Too?" In this book, Gardner attacked the idea that it is almost undemocratic to excel at something over your fellow man.[197]

John Gardner passed away in 2002 just a few months shy of his ninetieth birthday. At one time or another, he had been a Marine, a noted scholar and student of leadership, president of one of the nation's most influential foundations, a Cabinet secretary, founder of civic groups, and a mentor to innumerable young people who went on to become leaders themselves. He was a model of purpose, a person who set out to "do good" rather than just to "feel good."[198] Gardner modeled effective leadership no matter what circumstances confronted him. He was always in every way a leader.

But not every leader, including good ones, can alter his or her approach to leadership so flexibly. It's not that easy to do. Some leaders simply become accomplished in one style versus another. It's their way of achieving their leadership objectives.

> **Great leaders set out to "do good" rather than just to "feel good."**

And leaders' personalities are different. President Richard M. Nixon was an austere, brooding personality, while Jimmy Carter was a hardworking micromanager who kept to himself, a somewhat aloof and highly focused leader. Ronald Reagan was forever optimistic about the country and left with a higher level of popularity than when he was first elected. He was always "up." Bill Clinton ran at a frenetic pace, yet was habitually late.[199] Each, so to speak, made the presidency his own.

So, it's possible to become a top-notch leader who migrates from one position to the next. It's also possible to become a top-notch leader capable of changing one's leadership "style." And it's possible for top-notch leaders to change the circumstances.

In each case leaders respond to inevitable marketplace and organizational change but in different ways. They can choose—or someone chooses for them:

1. to move to a new challenge that better fits their skills and style,
2. to change their style, or
3. to work to change the circumstances.

None of these actions are especially easy, but they're all possible. And they all get us back to leadership style.

Transactional and Transformational Leaders

Two of the best-known leadership styles have long since been called "transactional" and "transformational," thanks to the groundbreaking work of James MacGregor Burns in *Leadership*.[200] Both styles may exist within an organization. And while it's rare, it's possible a given leader may employ a transactional style at one time in his or her career and a transformational style in another.

"Transactional leaders approach followers with an eye to exchanging one thing for another."[201] Transactional leaders broker change. The type of change they encourage is minor, almost automatic, a kind of change that substitutes one thing for another or one place or another.[202]

Transformational leaders, on the other hand, change the very nature of their organizations. Transformational leadership works "to cause a metamorphosis in form or structure, a change in the very condition or nature of a thing, a change into another substance, a radical change in outward form or inner character."[203]

"Transforming leadership, while more complex, is more potent. The transforming leader recognizes and exploits an existing need or demand of a potential follower. . . .The result of transforming leadership is a relationship of mutual stimulation and elevation that converts followers into leaders and may convert leaders into moral agents."[204] In this way, "transforming leadership is elevating."[205] It occurs when people "raise one another to higher levels of motivation and morality."[206]

Transactional leaders work with followers to get things done in an evolutionary fashion. Transformational leaders work with followers to develop new leaders who get things done in what at times is a revolutionary fashion.[207]

Florence Nightingale was a transformational leader. Born in 1820, she lived most of her ninety years in the nineteenth century when culture pointed women toward home and family and not much else. Yet she worked as a nurse behind the battle lines of the Crimean War where she won acclaim as "The Lady with the Lamp," became a reformer and leading advocate for improved medical care in infirmaries, led extensive statistical studies, founded the Nightingale School for Nurses, which opened in 1860, wrote its early curriculum, did pioneering work in hospital planning, and much more.

Eventually, the Queen of England honored Nightingale for her transformational work in nursing and medicine. Written in 1893 for new nurses, as an adaptation of the "Hippocratic Oath" taken by doctors, the Nightingale Pledge is named in honor of Florence Nightingale's contributions as the founder of the modern nursing profession. Florence Nightingale was a transformational leader in the best sense and best model of the term.

Transformational leadership is especially important during times of increasingly rapid social and economic change, which tends to pressure transactional styles to the breaking point. To survive in this environment, organizations need leaders who look to the future, develop a vision for where they believe the organization should go, and then inspire their followers toward that vision. In short, rapid change puts a premium on transformational leadership.

> **Rapid change puts a premium on transformational leadership.**

Transformational leaders like Florence Nightingale give themselves wholly to the cause. They live it, so to speak, and they enthuse others to live it too.

Jesus was the ultimate transformational leader. He communicated his vision by embodying it.[208] He focused on twelve disciples whom he inspired to change the world one heart at a time. He kept his eye on the end game.

I admire transformational leaders and believe in the value of this style of leading. But it would be unfair and unwise to discount transactional leadership. Transactional leaders sometimes last longer, remain faithful in the long pull, and model perseverance, a leadership trait no one should underestimate.

Transactional leaders may not gain as many headlines or create brave new worlds, but competent ones leave lasting legacies of jobs well done. Often, one of the reasons transformational leaders can conquer new territory is because transactional leaders are coming along behind and solidifying the gains.

Making Decisions

Making decisions is more of a problem for some leaders than people might think. But there's nothing more demoralizing to a staff than a leader who won't or can't or doesn't make decisions in a timely fashion.

On Sunday evening, June 4, 1944, "no new weather reports would be available for hours. The ships were sailing into the (English) Channel. If they were to be called back, it had to done now. The Supreme Commander was the only man who could do it. Eisenhower thought for a moment, then said quietly but clearly, 'Okay., let's go.' And again, cheers rang through Southwick House."

"Then the commanders rushed from their chairs and dashed outside to get to their command posts. Within thirty seconds the mess room was empty, except for Eisenhower. The outflow of others and his sudden isolation were symbolic. A minute earlier he had been the most powerful man in the world. Upon his word the fate of thousands of men depended, and the future of great nations. The moment he uttered the word, however, he was powerless. For the next two or three days there was almost nothing he could do that would in any way change anything. The mission could not be stopped, not by him, not by anyone. A captain leading his company onto Omaha, or a platoon sergeant at Utah, would for the immediate future play a greater role than Eisenhower. He could now only sit and wait."[209]

Making decisions, even being decisive, isn't the same as being brash. Eisenhower and his senior staff had planned for months. Making decisions in a decisive manner is simply a function of knowing your principles and your goals and being confident in them.

Margaret Thatcher was decisive, once saying, "Standing in the middle of the road is very dangerous; you get knocked down by the traffic from both sides."

General Colin Powell said, "Good leadership involves responsibility to the welfare of the group, which means that some people will get angry at your actions and decisions. It's inevitable—if you're honorable. Trying to get everyone to like you is a sign of mediocrity: you'll avoid the tough decisions, you'll avoid confronting the people who need to be confronted, and you'll avoid offering differential rewards based on differential performance because some people might get upset. Ironically, by procrastinating on the difficult choices, by trying not to get anyone mad, and by treating everyone equally 'nicely' regardless of their contributions, you'll simply ensure that the only people you'll wind up angering are the most creative and productive people in the organization."[210]

One of the most important decisions leaders make is who sits in the seats nearest to them. These people will have his or her ear or should. Their leadership skills and potential are as vital in the long run as the leader's.

> **One of the most important decisions leaders make is who sits in the seats nearest to them.**

Leaders should make certain decisions themselves and should learn that there's an art to determining how or when a decision is made:

- Leaders should reserve for themselves the hiring and handling of key staff.
- Leaders should make decisions that have the greatest potential for impact on the organization or movement.[211]
- Steve B. Sample, former president of USC, said, "Never make decisions yourself that can reasonably be delegated to a lieutenant."
- Sample also said, "Never make a decision today that can reasonably be put off to tomorrow."[212] Maybe he learned this from Harry Truman who always asked, "How much time do I have?" Truman understood the importance of timing in a decision, and knowing things change, he put off the decision until he had more information and until the decision had to be made.
- Leaders at times need a do-over. President George W. Bush said, "Sometimes the best decision is to overrule an earlier one."[213] Winston Churchill said it differently and, as usual, eloquently, "I'd rather be right than consistent."[214]

"Command is lonely. Harry Truman was right. Whether you're a CEO or the temporary head of a project team, the buck stops here. You can encourage participative management and bottom-up employee involvement but ultimately, the essence of leadership is the willingness to make the tough, unambiguous choices that will have an impact on the fate of the organization."[215] That's what a leader *does*.

The Ironies of Leadership

Leadership involves perplexing ironies. Effective leaders recognize these ironies and apply the principles they teach in their own leadership.

First, *while leaders must lead and are necessarily in the "spotlight," effective leaders are humble enablers.* Moses's example of meekness is enough evidence to dispel the contemporary notion that leadership is *machismo*. Followers who are affirmed, appreciated, and assisted express more commitment to the organization's mission. It is the leader's responsibility to assure that followers are reinforced.

Second, *while leaders must know their followers, effective leaders must develop some social distance from them.* Christ's love for his disciples was great, but he declined James and John's request they assume a place at Christ's side in glory (Matt. 10:35–45). This delicate irony must be monitored carefully. It is not helpful to foster elitism. Effective leaders recognize that too-close friendships or ties can lead to misperception, rumor, and charges of favoritism. Leaders must maintain an appropriate objectivity in making personnel and resource decisions. Close relationships can make these decisions more difficult and even biased.

Third, *the wiser the leader, the more frequent the admission that he or she does not have all the answers.* Leaders must make informed judgments, but they do not speak *ex cathedra* or with *vox Dei*. This point is illustrated in Proverbs 15:22, "Without counsel plans fail, but with many advisers they succeed," and in Ecclesiastes 4:13, "Better was a poor and wise youth than an old and foolish king who no longer knew how to take advice."

Fourth, *the more emotional the times, the more rational must be the leader, the more rational the times, the more emotional must be the leader.* More emotional times are generally characterized by crisis. Leaders must be able to think clearly and render judgments based upon facts and identified alternatives, not feelings, sentimentality, or peer pressure. More rational times are those in which organizations forget their original purpose and yield to bureaucratic tendencies. Personnel begin to consider means more important than ends, and rules and regulations become more important than client interests and needs. Leaders in such times must be emotional. They must recall the organization to this *raison d'être* and clear impassioned leadership is one of the best ways to do this.

Fifth, *the more complex the organization and its future, the more focused, and even simple, leadership must be.* As organizations grow, they diversify, fragment, and multiply their parts. Leaders are hard-pressed to maintain coordination and continuity. Effective leaders use metaphors and easily understood goal statements. Joshua reminded the people that their task was to possess the land which the Lord their God had given them. Clear, concise leadership is all too rare in this day of circumvention and "doublespeak."

Sixth, *effective leaders are optimists at the same time they are realists.* They should have their heads in the clouds while their feet remain planted firmly upon the ground. Christian leaders must be optimistic realists, optimists because they affirm God's sovereignty and realists because they acknowledge the temporal presence and power of sin.

Seventh, *the busier the leader and the less time to pray and plan, the greater the necessity to take time to pray and plan.* Crisis management is sometimes required but leaders cannot long remain effective using this approach. Both prayer and planning help the leader and the organization to focus on identifiable, meaningful goals. Samson's career is a case in point. Although he periodically accomplished great feats for God, he neither prayed nor planned consistently. Consequently, except for the final hours of his life, Samson's ministry was a disappointment. While he contributed to God's service, he could have contributed much more. Leaders who pray and plan effectively apply an integrated faith and reason to God's world.

Eighth, *the "higher up the ladder" a leader climbs, thus the more specialized in leadership he or she becomes, the more of a generalist the leader must be.* Perhaps Nehemiah is the best scriptural example of this irony of leadership. He was promoted from cupbearer to leader of a reconstruction expedition. He became *the* leader, but his wisdom was taxed as a spiritual guide, organizer, builder, and more. Effective leaders develop a personality with a wisdom born of perspective and cultivate an eclectic understanding of their organization and the world.

Ninth, *the more effective the leadership, the greater the likelihood that the leader recruited people more intelligent, dynamic, capable, or credentialed than the leader.* "Threatened" leaders are not effective. They appoint individuals who are nonthreatening and who, by definition, weaken the organization. King Saul failed to understand this irony in his relationship with young David, but Pharoah avoided similar pitfalls by appointing Joseph to direct Egypt through years of plenty and famine. Someone observed that one measure of great teachers is the number of students who surpass them. Another way of expressing it is a paraphrase of Andrew Carnegie's epitaph: "I always had the good sense to hire people better than myself." Effective leaders do not allow their own egos to undermine their leadership.

Tenth, *the more dynamic, exciting, and even effective the leader's ideas, the more criticism he or she is likely to receive.* This irony is so much a part of the human condition that we can state with reasonable assurance that if leaders are not being criticized, they are probably not leading. If leading and changing go hand in hand, leading and criticism must be hand in glove. Great ideas change things. People don't like change. Ergo, change agents (leaders) attract criticism. Abraham lived with a family critic in his nephew Lot. Moses had to answer his critics before he could do great things for God. Paul responded to critics in the early church. The great man Job even had to deal with critics on his sick bed. Effective leaders fix their thoughts on Jesus, attempt to live peaceably with all people, and keep pressing toward the mark of the high calling of God.

Eleventh, *leaders turn their followers into leaders*. John C. Maxwell has nearly cornered the market making this point, and rightly so.[216] James M. Kouzes and Barry Z. Posner say good leaders create good leaders because leaders give people the courage to do things they've never done before. Leaders encourage the follower's heart.[217]

> **Leaders turn their followers into leaders.**

Twelfth, *leaders are always accountable to someone*. Leaders answer to the Lord, whether they ever understand or acknowledge this fact of life. Leaders are always responsible for their organizations and thus answer to someone, owners, constituents, personnel, clientele.

"Nothing much happens without a dream. And for something *great* to happen, there must be a *great* dream. Behind every *great* achievement is a dreamer of *great* dreams."[218] In the end, what leaders do, certainly what good, effective, or great leaders do, is dream . . . then they lead.

What do leaders do? They think about the better future of their organization and the well-being of the people they serve. Then they work with their people to make things happen.

LEADERSHIP LESSONS

1. Leaders lead by example.
2. Leaders look for a better way.
3. Leaders hold principles tightly, ideas loosely.
4. Attitude enables ability.
5. Competence is polished talent.
6. A leader's work ethic becomes the staff's gold standard.
7. Great leaders set out to "do good" not just to "feel good."
8. Rapid change puts a premium on transformational leadership.
9. One of the most important decisions leaders make is who sits in the seats nearest to them.
10. Leaders turn their followers into leaders.

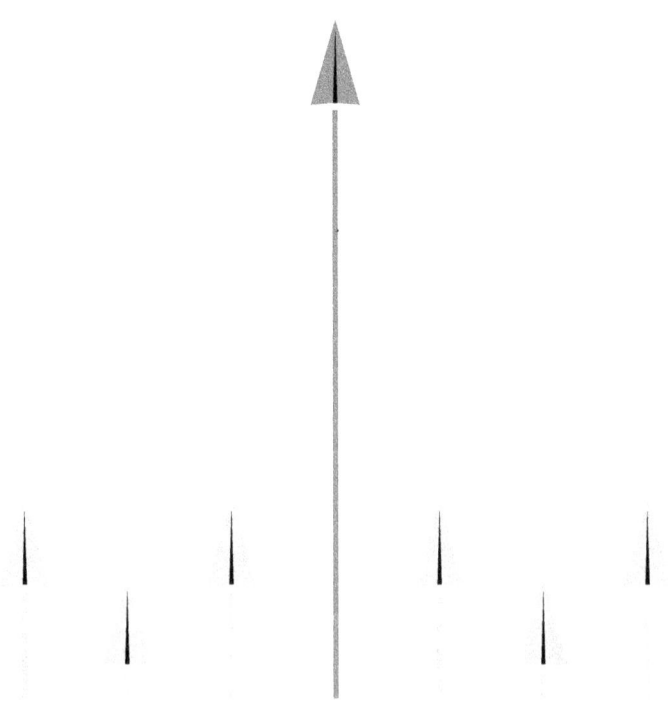

CHAPTER 8

COMMUNITY

Who Follows A Leader

DAVID

David's early life was an experience of pastoral simplicity. He was a shepherd, poet, and musician or psalmist—nobody around but sheep. Yet David became a champion, soldier, and king, living his entire adult life in the public eye.

No poet has been quoted so continuously through history.[219] And though David eventually committed some of the most grievous sins a human being can commit, God incredibly, and encouragingly, calls him "a man after his own heart" (1 Sam. 13:14; see Acts 13:22).

Be a person after God's own heart.

David's first test of character and courage came early in the form of a bear and a lion. He fought and killed both predators to protect his sheep. Later, David faced the giant form and persona of a Philistine enemy named Goliath. David demonstrated not only character and courage but leadership.

Israel's King Saul and his soldiers could have fought Goliath and his men, but they stayed in camp, overwhelmed by fear and humiliation. At this point, young David-the-shepherd arrived on the scene, assessed the situation, and volunteered to challenge Goliath.

The king could have provided leadership, but he had not, so God sent a boy to do what men should have done. Not just any boy but one spiritually mature beyond his years. While King Saul anxiously envisioned himself standing alone before Goliath, David confidently saw himself standing before Goliath knowing God would be with him.

Faith empowers leadership.

Someone said, "The heart is where leadership takes place; it is born there and there it dies as well."[220] This is the core of the striking difference between Saul and David. "Through faith David found courage, and through courage, much in contrast to Saul and his followers, he found freedom instead of fear."[221] Saul's lack of faith hijacked his leadership while David's faith empowered his leadership.

God therefore enabled David to slay the giant and become an instant hero in his native land. He was but a lad, but God was preparing him for greater things yet to come.

Yet David—like all of us—was far from a perfect person. Later in life this incredible servant of God, astoundingly, committed both murder and adultery (2 Samuel 11–24). To make matters worse, if they could be worse, he repented only after being confronted by the prophet Nathan (2 Sam. 12:1–14; Psalms 32, 51). And while David had been a faithful shepherd of his flocks and his people (Ps. 78:70–72) he failed miserably in shepherding his family, beginning with his immorality with Bathsheba and following with poor parenting of his children.

David's daughter, Tamar, was raped by her brother Amon, who was, in turn, killed by his brother Absalom. Later, Absalom rebelled against David and was killed. Then David's son Adonijah was killed by the order of Solomon, David's son by Bathsheba.[222]

> **Never fail to return to the Lord.**

To say David's family was a mess is an understatement. Yet through it all David never failed, eventually, to return to the Lord, to seek his forgiveness, and to live again in obedience.

Meanwhile David successfully united the kingdoms of Judah and Israel, solidifying the nation. He continued to write psalms. He built a palace, and he made plans and collected materials to build a temple. When God denied David this privilege because of the warrior's blood on his hands, King David encouraged his son Solomon to finish the work on God's house. David's work made possible Solomon's leadership during Israel's golden age.

Though David was a flawed man he was a faithful follower of God who became a fearless leader, meaning God knew what he was doing. "He chose David his servant and took him from the sheepfolds; from following the nursing ewes he brought him to shepherd Jacob his people, Israel his inheritance. With upright heart he shepherded them and guided them with his skillful hand" (Ps. 78:70–72).

> **Flawed person, faithful follower of God, fearless leader.**

The "secret" to David's spiritual resilience and therefore leadership effectiveness was his recognition that "God is our refuge and strength, a very present help in trouble" (Ps. 46:1).

Unlikely Leaders Need Help

Iconic images of David often show him as the boy-shepherd standing alone before Goliath. It's a great picture, if incomplete. David wasn't really alone, for the Lord was with him. Nor was David a loner in leadership. Most of his later work as a leader involved a host of counselors and colaborers around him. He became a strong leader among followers.

I believe in strong leadership—but always with two corollaries, *accountable leadership*, and *strong leadership at all levels.*

Unaccountable leaders too often fall victim to their own humanity, which is to say vanity. They can be captured by arrogance, which almost inevitably leads to upheaval in their professional and personal lives. On the other hand, good effective leaders don't mind being accountable to people with the right values. Being comfortable with accountability is a sign of competence and maturity in a leader.

Strong leaders need (and should want) help, because "none of us is as smart as all of us." Leaders don't know everything.[223] Weak leaders don't understand this.

It's always a precursor to trouble when leaders surround themselves with courtiers or sycophants whose warped sense of loyalty or selfish ambition disable their conscience and thus their ability to truly help the leader and the organization.[224] "Leadership does not emerge from blind obedience to anyone. Xerox's Barry Rand was right on target when he warned his people that if you have a yes-man working for you, one of you is redundant." [225]

Along the way, American evangelicalism has fallen victim to celebrity pastors who have been elevated or who have exalted themselves far above what wisdom or necessity requires. Their eventual falls from grace have been precipitous, sad, and spiritually devastating to the ministries (kingdoms?) they administered.[226] Unfortunately, Christian people and ministry organizations don't seem to have learned from the now multiple examples of this phenomenon. Yet with proper leadership accountability, this is an avoidable problem.

Some American presidents have been accused of leadership hubris. One who wasn't is Abraham Lincoln, whose approach to advisers and decision-making was heralded in Pulitzer Prize–winning historian Doris Kearns Goodwin's book, *Team of Rivals: The Political Genius of Abraham Lincoln.*[227] Lincoln was shrewd enough, and comfortable enough in his own skin, to invite inside counsel from a few leaders he knew did not generally agree with him politically. They were the opposite of yes-men.

Of course, a team-of-rivals approach may not work for everyone. The flip side is threatening. Seconds-in-command or members of a leadership staff who work surreptitiously to undermine the duly appointed leader can sink the leader, the ship, and themselves. In any event, if undetected, their weaknesses can become the leader's weakness.

I've experienced this in my career. It hurts most when you get stabbed by someone you know. Remember Caesar and Brutus? Because none of us are omniscient or even prescient, betrayal isn't always predictable. But it happens, so it's something we'll consider in a later chapter.

On another level, strong leaders who are confident in their talent and their assignment are not threatened, for example, by strong board members. Strong leaders do not want board members who check their brains and their backbones at the boardroom door. Strong leaders with the right values and perspective want strong leaders around them, including people to whom they report, people who may be hard to please *for the right reasons*, like excellence, fidelity to the organizational mission, integrity, and so forth.

Strong leaders need—want—help.

God built accountability into the fabric of human life, for he knew that sin would otherwise destroy us. I always admired Charles Colson, whose organization, Prison Fellowship, exists because of him. In other words, he was not just appointed an executive but was the founder of this organization. Yet he wisely created a board and voluntarily submitted himself to this board, allowing the board to establish policy and act as adviser. Years later "his" organization continues after he has gone to heaven, in part because he made room for other leaders. Such humility protects both the leader and the organization.

I've witnessed the opposite too. More times than I can count I have known or at least watched from afar as "big name" pastors or ministry leaders transition from their organizations, sometimes not by their choice, leaving behind an organization in disarray. Whatever the reason, when these dominant figures depart, a huge vacuum is left behind with few or sometimes no other leaders to fill it. Why? Because the big-name leader did not develop leaders within the organization. There is no bench. No one to step up. Sometimes this happens because the big name wanted it to happen—consciously or not, they wanted the organization to flounder without him or her.

Corporations experience this phenomenon too, but businesses governed by the bottom line generally are motivated to find new leadership talent rapidly. This does not always happen, at least not smoothly or without organizational damage, in nonprofit organizations where sentiment, emotion, misplaced loyalty, and other influences can muddy the transition.

I believe in accountability, but I also believe organizations are best served when strong leaders exist at all levels of the organization. Why? Because the stronger the links of the chain the stronger the chain. If leaders make things happen, it's logical to conclude that leaders working in a coordinated effort at all levels of the organization can make even more things happen.

Organizations that are "built to last" know how to incubate leaders. In fact, in the very best organizations "there are many leaders, not just one. Leadership is distributed. It resides not solely in the individual at the top, but in every person at every level who, in one way or another, acts as a leader to a group of followers—wherever in the organization that a person is, whether shop steward, team head, CEO."[228]

Strong leaders at all levels help balance the organization. "You don't have to be *the* leader to be *a* leader on your team."[229] Team-oriented leadership reinforces the entire organization. "No matter how clever or spiritually gifted you are, nothing in this world happens without teamwork."[230] Lincoln understood this, even with a team of rivals.

The fact that strong leaders exist on a board and strong leaders exist within the organization chart allows the person in the top executive position to be a strong leader. If strong leaders exist on the board, the top executive enjoys *the liberty of accountability*. If strong leaders exist within the organization, the top executive may exercise strong leadership without overpowering his or her coworkers. The same is true up and down the organization chart or links of the chain.

> **Strong leaders should be developed at *all* levels of the organization.**

"Great leadership is not a zero-sum game. What is given to the leader is not taken from the follower. Both get by giving."[231]

Political strategist, Lee Atwater, told President George H. W. Bush, "Access is power." His son, President George W. Bush said it worked the other way too: "It makes my job a heck of a lot easier to be able to have access to a lot of people, to get their feedback and reactions."[232]

As always, the key to balance is a right relationship with the Lord. Christians understand "you can never be *over* people in authority until you place yourself *under* the authority of God and the Word."[233] Strong leaders don't have to be narcissistic autocrats. Such people craft their own downfall. Strong leaders can get things done because they know, trust, and follow the God who gave them their talent in the first place. They're strong in leadership not to aggrandize themselves but to serve the Lord and others.

The "Right" People

"Teddy Roosevelt once observed, 'The best executive is the one who recruits the most competent men around, tells them what he wants done, and then gets out of their way so they can do it.'"[234] We should add women to this equation today,[235] but otherwise T.R.'s point is well taken. For T.R., one of those men was William Howard Taft, whose personality and talents were a perfect complement to T.R.'s. Though later in their political lives they went head-to-head in a presidential campaign, they ended with a personal fealty not often matched in politics.[236]

Finding, recruiting, enabling, and inspiring *the right people* is a huge and hugely important part of any leader's task. Simply put, without the right people the probability of genuine achievement is significantly reduced if not eliminated.

"In the workplace of the new millennium, one of the leader's most important roles is to retain the necessary talent and unleash it."[237] Once leaders understand they cannot and should not go or do it alone then the next task is to identify, recruit, empower, and work alongside *the right people*. Just who these right people are and how they are found and developed is the trick.

One definition of the right people is "people with different gifts than the leader." The point is leaders cannot and certainly should not attempt to appoint people who are in most ways clones of the leaders. Organizational leaders need to surround themselves with people whose skills make up for or complement the leader's shortcomings.[238]

Identify the right people with the right stuff.

For example, organizational presidents have vice presidents for at least three reasons:

1. Presidents cannot do everything—there's not enough time for one person to physically pull it off.

2. Presidents cannot do everything—they don't know how to do everything.
3. Presidents cannot do everything—some things they should not do.

The same is true for all leaders, whatever their title. The objective should be to get smart, energized people into the right places so they will make the right decisions.[239] It's a need and a process that never ends, lasting the length of a leader's tenure in office. Finding the best or right people, enabling and empowering them, then letting them do what they know to do is the core of an organization's work to fulfill its mission.

So, in Jim Collins's terms, do you, the leader, have the *right* people on the bus?

- When in doubt, don't hire—keep looking.
- When you know you need to make a personnel change, act. "People" are not your biggest asset as is commonly stated; rather the *right* people are your biggest asset. If you have the right people, you won't have to spend time motivating them; they'll be self-motivated.
- Put your best people on your biggest opportunities, not your biggest problems.
- And if you have the right people on the bus, are they in the right seats?[240]

"Surround yourself with great people. Have beliefs and communicate them. See things for yourself. Stand up to bullies. Deal with first things first. Loyalty is the vital virtue. Prepare relentlessly. Underpromise and overdeliver."[241]

Remember, there are "right people" who are unlikely leaders and don't know it yet.

Making the Hard Decision

Sometimes—sadly, more often than you'd think—some people just won't do their work, can't do their work, will not or cannot grow into new demands upon their position as the organization grows, refuse to support colleagues as a member of the team, will not support the leader's vision (especially if it's new or a change of direction), evidence character flaws like dishonesty, and even, believe it or not, actually work within the organization against the organization's mission, promoting their own agenda.

With some people, no matter how much a leader wants them to succeed, helps them, winks at shortcomings, or otherwise extends opportunities, certain individuals cannot or do not do what they're assigned to do. Equally true, some people will not or cannot respond to clearly stated goals and expectations, professional development counsel, or warnings. By not performing their jobs they hurt colleagues, the organization's mission, and possibly those who the organization serves. These situations are not always malicious but nevertheless exist.

Consequently, the leader(s) have a choice: maintain an unproductive staff member or make what I call a "hard decision" and discontinue the unproductive staff member's employment.

I've been told at various times on my administrative leadership journey that Christian organizations should never dismiss an employee for any reason, Christian leaders should not offer criticism or redirection in their oversight, and Christian compassion demands that Christian organizations make provision to assist their employees in everyday life. I am not sure where in the Scripture these good-intentioned people based their ideas, but I have never found such mandates. Of course, I agree Christian organizations and Christian leaders cannot justify (and should never try) treating employees harshly.

But the Christian organization, and certainly other organizations not defined by a specifically Christian mission, are not the church.

We understood this at the Christian university where I served. In a few sad cases we needed to let someone go. Why? Because a person misused, several times over three months, a corporate credit card for personal expenses, had been warned but did not change. Because the staff member had engaged in immoral sexual activity, was again counseled, but did not alter behavior. Or because they simply did not do the job for which they were hired and, though assisted and directed, did not change. And so it goes. There are myriad reasons why individuals might not fit or might not deserve to continue to receive compensation from an organization because their actions do not fulfill or might even undermine the mission of the organization.

For some leaders, this decision is one they avoid if not at all costs in terms of themselves, then certainly at great cost to the organization, their leadership, and even the unproductive staff member.

Sometimes leaders delay making hard decisions because they want to be liked. But it's been said, "There is an inverse relationship between people's leadership potential and their need to be liked."[242] If a leader thinks about decisions in terms of his or her likability, leadership effectiveness is going, going, gone.

Leaders who do not want to be unpopular often falter if not fail before they've started. But leadership is not a popularity contest. Many leaders who fail at transforming their organizations do so because they are unwilling to be disliked. They muddle through, kick the can down the road, ignore organizational or staff deficiencies, or give in to the bureaucracy. Most of all, they do not make the hard decisions regarding personnel.

Now make no mistake. *There is no pleasant or easy way to tell someone he or she has lost a job, any more than there is a pleasant or easy way to learn you've lost your own job.* So, in one sense it's understandable why some leaders avoid the hard decision like the plague. But avoidance doesn't make the problem go away.

Make the "hard decision" about struggling personnel.

And if leaders maintain unproductive (unable, unwilling, or willfully subversive) staff members, what message does this send to other productive employees? What does this say about the quality of the organization or the value of the leader's vision? How does this affect the probability or potential of even achieving the vision? To be blunt about it, "any business or industry that pays equal rewards to its goof-offs and its eager-beavers sooner or later will find itself with more goof-offs than eager-beavers."[243]

No, in the calling or career of every leader, hard decisions—uneasy and unpleasant—must be made. *The key is to make hard decisions correctly, professionally, compassionately, and maybe courageously, while treating the departing colleague with dignity . . . but still, to make the decision.*

Yet some Christian leaders duck hard decisions, arguing this action lacks compassion. I was once told that "Christian organizations should never fire anyone." The underlying message self-righteously implies that any organization or individual involved in a personnel termination is obviously outside God's will.

This approach, however, creates its own problems making it easy for Christian leaders or organizations to "hug" people too long. It sounds harsh, but it happens. Leaders "hug" by making up rationales to avoid the problem, for instance, "The guy loves his wife and does not kick his dog." Hopefully that's true, but it doesn't change the fact that he cannot do or is not doing what the organization is paying him to do. Personnel who are clearly struggling are maintained well past the time when their ability to help the organization ceased, because, well, they are nice people. Meanwhile their coworkers must take up the slack, and they know it.

I knew a Christian leader who put off hard decisions as long as possible, then disappeared while some other manager was left to deal with the problem. This approach not only lacked courage but seemed to me to lack conviction, to undermine the credibility of that leader's vision and work.

Again, it is not pleasant or easy to make or implement hard decisions. We're talking about other human beings, colleagues, and maybe longtime friends. Many if not most of them are indeed "nice people." Nothing I've said here should be read as trivializing or making light of people's feelings or somehow dismissing the fact that leaders should treat all people with respect. But think like a coach. Winning teams don't just happen. The coach recruits the "right people," and then makes tough decisions putting the best lineup together.

Another way of looking at this is to think about the struggling staff member in terms of the question, would you hire this person if he or she applied today? No? Then why do you keep him or her in the organization?

One last thought: while no one wants to lose his or her job, and it could create short-term challenges for the individuals involved, it's not necessarily the worst thing that can happen to them. I've had individuals circle back a year or even three or four years later and admit they'd been considering leaving but didn't have the courage, or that the Lord had taught them new things and opened new doors, or that this experience finally got their attention about some attitudes and behaviors that needed to change in their lives. I don't share this as some gloss to make leaders feel better about how losing a job can affect people (it's still a hard decision), but to report objectively the perspective that while one organizational assignment might not fit, others will, and God has not forgotten the one walking out the door.

And remember this. If leaders and organizations recruit well, hard decisions can typically be minimized.

That said, leaders need to understand that no one bats a thousand, so even with the best recruiting, periodic hard decisions will still be a fact of organizational life.

Relationships

Kouzes and Posner said, "Leadership is a dialogue."[244] In other words, leaders and followers or employers or staff are or should be communicating, which is to say some kind of relationship needs to be maintained to allow this interchange to happen. Kouzes and Posner go so far as to say that a leader's number one success factor is his or her relationship with subordinates.[245]

To accomplish anything of value, leaders need followers. Remember the old proverb, "He who thinks he leads, but has no followers, is only taking a walk."

Leadership ultimately is just a relationship, a connection between two or more people, one of whom steps forward with an idea about what could be better in their environment. The Lone Ranger is not a good leadership model, at least not his title. But think about it, even the Lone Ranger wasn't alone. He had his trusted sidekick Tonto who went through every adventure with him. Leaders-as-loners is not a workable formula, and insofar as it exists, it lends itself to lack of leader accountability and lack of strong leadership at all levels.

Leaders work with others. "People who are unable to build solid, lasting relationships will soon discover that they are unable to sustain long, effective leadership. Needless to say, you can love people without leading them, but you cannot lead people without loving them."[246]

In this sense the maxim "'They don't care how much you know until they know how much you care' is not an empty cliché." It is important to "watch over each sheep, not just 'the flock.'"[247] Shepherds "know the names of their sheep; a good leader leads, feeds, and cares for his sheep, but not necessarily in that order."[248]

"Great leaders, including 'little' people, may have gruff, demanding, uncompromising exteriors. But deep down inside the great ones have empathy and an unqualified acceptance of the persons who go with their leadership. Acceptance of the person, though, requires tolerance of imperfection. Anybody could lead perfect people—if there were any."[249]

Leader-follower or leader-staff relationships come in many forms, but there's always a difference in that one is charged with certain responsibilities and making decisions for the whole and others are not. This can result in a psychological if not social distance, that if properly managed can benefit all concerned. The distance should not be about the leader's hubris or entitlement but about a continual focus on how most effectively to accomplish the organization's mission.

Christ's love for his disciples was great, but he declined James and John's desire to assume a place at his side in glory (Mark 10:35–45). This delicate irony must be monitored carefully. Effective leaders recognize that "too close" friendships or ties can lead to misperceptions, rumors, and charges of favoritism. Leaders must maintain an appropriate objectivity in making personnel and resource decisions. Close relationships can make these decisions more difficult, even biased.

Caveats acknowledged, relationship with those in the organization can be among leaders' most enjoyable and fulfilling aspects of their position. God created and he loves people, not simply vision, organizations, goals, or accomplishments.

Developing More Unlikely Leaders

Developing more leaders, including those considered unlikely, is one of the most important things leaders can do for their organizations. After all, in one way or another, there will eventually come a tomorrow in which today's leader no longer leads. Consequently, "the most significant contributions leaders make are not to today's bottom line: they are to the long-term development of people and institutions who adapt, prosper, grow."[250]

Very few leaders or organizations, it seems, understand this. If they did, there would not be so many reports of organizations floundering or failing after a leader moves on. Leaders need to produce more leaders, not followers.[251] The very future of the organization can at times depend upon it. Neither Joshua nor David developed future leaders for the nation of Israel, and the nation suffered.

The fundamental paradox about leadership is that good leaders turn their followers into leaders—leaders in some ways make followers become better persons than they want to be.[252]

"Successful corporations don't wait for leaders to come along. They actively seek out people with leadership potential and expose them to career experiences designed to develop that potential."[253]

I benefited from this philosophy early in my professional experience. I had worked throughout the year at the university on what we called the Academic Computing Committee, a name that now sounds antiquated. Our work concluded with a recommendation to the administration that a Director of Academic Computer Services be appointed, someone from a liberal arts background who could help faculty embrace the newfangled tools to the best advantage in their respective disciplines. Working in my office shortly thereafter, I was visited by a faculty colleague who'd served with me on this committee. In due course, he said, "You know that new position we recommended?" "Sure," I said. He smiled and said, "You're the man for the job." To say I was surprised is an understatement. But long story short, that's what happened, and in the providence of God it launched my administrative leadership career in higher education. Someone else saw leadership potential in me and a university president gave me the opportunity.

That's what excellent leaders do. They develop the people closest to them and then allow them to develop others within the organization. John Maxwell recommends that leaders pour themselves into the top 20 percent of their staff, working to develop their leadership skills, because "the greatest potential for growth of a company is growth of its people."[254]

The problem is, sometimes people know the language, but they don't know how to lead.[255] But leaders can teach others to lead. Zig Ziglar says that the difference between good and excellent companies is training.[256] "Great companies are not made up of employees of average ability and acceptable performance but of employees committed to and living out lives of superior achievement and the highest ethical standards." These kinds of people refuse to let "the work of our hands destroy the example of our lives." They model and teach excellence because this is a higher calling that comes alive in the mission and vision of the organization.[257]

Leaders motivating leaders is an everyday calling. "The more that change characterizes the business environment, the more that leaders must motivate people to provide leadership as well. When this works, it tends to reproduce leadership across the entire organization, with people occupying multiple leadership roles throughout the hierarchy."[258]

Recruit people with leadership potential and then help them achieve it. People need significant challenge early in their career, then later they may have a chance to grow beyond the narrow base that characterizes most managerial careers—lateral career moves, special task force assignments, early promotions, and so forth.[259]

One of the best ways to develop the unlikely leaders around you is to give them opportunities, just like that university president did for me long ago. Recognize good and improved performance.

Develop unlikely leaders by giving them opportunities.

"Don't overlook people who quietly and effectively do their jobs."[260]

Everyone, up and down the organization, can and should be given the opportunity to develop their leadership skills and contributions. "Organization charts and fancy titles count for next to nothing. Organization charts are frozen, anachronistic photos in a workplace that ought to be as dynamic as the external environment around you. . . . Titles mean little in terms of real power, which is the capacity to influence and inspire. Have you ever noticed that people will personally commit to certain individuals who on paper (or on the organization chart) possess little authority—but instead possess pizzazz, drive, expertise, and genuine caring for teammates and products?"[261]

Leaders need to learn what most motivates people and fill their arsenal with these inducements, which are not what most people think. "One of the greatest weaknesses in any recruiting effort is leading with a list of benefits. We have been conditioned to believe that the lure of gold is what will help us build the best and brightest teams. Yet history proves that people work for more than gold, and in fact will often work their hardest and best when they aren't getting paid at all—at least not in money."[262]

Men and women do not live by bread alone.

Creating a Leadership Culture

If you have become an unlikely leader, one of your greatest joys will be helping to develop other unlikely leaders, particularly in your own organization. "Winning companies win because they have good leaders who nurture the development of other leaders at all levels of the organization. The ultimate test of success for an organization is not whether it can win today but whether it can keep winning tomorrow and the day after. Therefore, the ultimate test for a leader is not whether he or she can make smart decisions and takes decisive action, but whether he or she teaches others to be leaders and builds an organization that can sustain its success even when he or she is not around. The key ability of winning organizations and winning leaders is creating leaders."[263]

Leadership scholar John P. Kotter said it this way, "Just as we need more people to provide leadership in the complex organizations that dominate our world today, we also need people to develop the cultures that will create that leadership. Institutionalizing a leadership-centered culture is the ultimate act of leadership."[264]

The best leaders create high-performance cultures, set demanding goals, measure results, hold people accountable, are change agents, and are passionate. "Great institutions are not managed, they are led."[265] Certainly one key component of this kind of culture is leadership development in the ranks. This involves not one new leader but potentially many. It involves the organizational culture.

Leaders not only think "big" but long-term. "The most far-sweeping act of a transformational leader is revamping the organizational culture. This means that the values, attitudes, and entire atmosphere of the organization changes. The most typical change is to convert the culture from a low-risk, stiff, bureaucratic one to a culture in which people are more adventuresome and less constrained by rules and regulations."[266]

> **Leaders not only think "big" but long-term.**

Many things conspire to prevent a leader from changing the organization's culture or from developing unlikely leaders. Indeed, the presumably urgent can be the enemy of the important, as are day-to-day "normal" activities. Bennis's First Law of Academic Pseudo Dynamics applies to more than academia: "Routine work drives out non-routine work and smothers to death all creative planning, all fundamental change in the university—or any institution."[267] Leaders who transform an organization's culture, who develop leadership cultures, must find ways to be proactive and strategic even while they get necessary basics done each day.

"Never neglect details. All great ideas and visions in the world are worthless if they can't be implemented rapidly and efficiently.

Good leaders delegate and empower others liberally, but they pay attention to details, every day. . . . Paradoxically, good leaders understand something else: An obsessive routine in carrying out the details begets conformity and complacency, which in turn dulls everyone's mind. That is why even as they pay attention to details, they continually encourage people to challenge the process. They implicitly understand the sentiment of CEO-leaders like Quad Graphic's Harry Quadracchi, Oticon's Lars Kolind and the late Bill McGowan of MCI, who all independently asserted that the job of a leader is not to be the chief organizer, but the chief disorganizer."[268]

Transformative leaders delegate. They push decisions down to where they should be made. In an empowered organization, four things happen: people feel significant, learning and competence matter, people are part of a community, and work is exciting.[269]

Effective delegation and vision casting is more challenging than it sounds. Winston Churchill said, "The difficulty is not winning the war; it's persuading people to let you win it."[270] The best leaders connect their delegation to the greater purpose.

Transformative leaders create a culture where the brutal facts of reality may be confronted, where truth can be heard. Everyone wants to be the best, but most organizations lack the discipline to turn it into reality.[271]

Transformative leaders create a culture of continuous improvement. "Don't think best; think better. How can it be done better the next time?"[272]

Transformative leaders inspire staff to build an organization better today than it was yesterday. Such leaders build unity around a guiding purpose. In a divided organization, there is no shortness of vision but a problem of no shared vision, no shared purpose for which hearts and minds can unite to face challenges.[273]

Sometimes, as a leader, it feels like you must be everywhere at once—and sometimes that's exactly what you need to do. You must get out of the office, look for things to improve. You need to interact with personnel in any way and place that you can, especially if they did not expect to see you there. Listen to what frustrates personnel, especially the "little things" like irritating redundant processes. These are low hanging fruit. Change the process on the spot. Show personnel what matters to them matters to you the leader, then invite them to care about your vision. These are precious teachable moments when you can share your vision anew.

Paradoxically, people long for "strong leaders" even as they rebel against anyone who dares to tell them what to do.[274] This is a characteristic of American culture. We admire great leaders but grumble about the leaders in place now—just be sure, as a leader, that you don't give staff something legitimate to grumble about.

To be effective over the long-term, leaders must recreate the organization in their own image. Otherwise, the changes they wrought last only for the lifetime of their leadership, if that long. This sounds like aggrandizement or arrogance, and it can be if a self-centered person occupies the leadership position. But with an others-centered focus on what's good for the organization, a dynamic leader can indeed instill dynamism into the organization.

Louis Gerstner noted that IBM was known as much for its culture as for its product. But when he took the reins of a struggling company in the early 1990s this was not necessarily a good thing. A while later he said, "I came to see, in my time at IBM, that culture isn't just one aspect of the game—it *is* the game. In the end, an organization is nothing more than the collective capacity of its people to create value. Vision, strategy, marketing, financial management—any management system in fact—can set you on the right path and can carry you for a while. But no enterprise— . . . or *any* area of human endeavor—will succeed over the long haul if those elements aren't part of its DNA."[275]

Gerstner thought it would take at least five years to change the culture at IBM, a challenge that he later admitted he had underestimated. To make this corporate culture change happen, Gerstner knew that he had to lead it, that the CEO had to commit thousands of hours of personal activity to pull off this change, had to be up-front and outspoken about what he was doing, had to get his leadership team to join him, and had to talk openly and directly about culture, behavior, and beliefs. Most of all, to change the corporate culture, he could not be subtle.[276] His methods worked. When Gerstner became CEO in 1993, IBM had an entrenched bureaucracy out of touch with customers and had lost $16 billion in three years. In the previous eight years 175,000 employees had lost their jobs. Both the media and IBM's competitors were calling it a dinosaur. When Gerstner stepped down in 2002, IBM had become number one in the world in information technology services, hardware, enterprise software, and customer-designed, high-performance computer chips.[277]

Leaders who stand for something, who stand up for something, inspire followers, and when the goals are worthy, people are eager to participate. They want to help make changes.

"In the end, management doesn't change culture. Management invites the workforce itself to change the culture." It does not work well to force it. "At the same time I was working to get employees to listen to me, to understand where we needed to go, to follow me there," Gerstner said, "I needed to get them to stop being followers. This wasn't a logical, linear challenge. It was counterintuitive, centered around social issues and emotion rather than reason."[278]

Leadership is not for the faint of heart nor the lazy. It takes resolve and hard work. But the rewards are great, for transformative leaders, including the unlikely ones, are privileged to be in the action, to help people help themselves and to accomplish great things together.

Giving Credit Where Credit Is Due

Leaders should never forget that "together" part. Remember, leaders are not leaders without followers and leaders cannot nor should not attempt to accomplish great goals alone. Others matter, and they must be regularly appreciated.

Max DePree said, "The first responsibility of a leader is to define reality. The last is to say thank you."[279] Navy Admiral D. Michael Abrashoff said it this way, "As a manager, the one signal you need to steadily send to your people is how important they are to you. In fact, nothing is more important to you. Realize your influence and use it wisely. . . . Communicate purpose and meaning."[280]

My friend Gene Goulooze, former CEO of Sonneveldt-Ameriserve Company, said, "It's not conflict or confrontation that holds people accountable. It's giving them a word of encouragement."[281] Leaders encourage the heart.

Since the first month of my upper-level leadership experience, I've had Proverbs 3:27, inscribed in calligraphy and framed, hanging on my office wall. "Do not withhold good from those to whom it is due, when it is in your power to do it." This reminded me every day that as leader I was in a position to recognize people. I could thank them. I could share good with those to whom it was due, because it was in my power to act. And the corollary to this is, you cannot thank people too much.

By thanking others, especially staff members, leaders signal not only gratitude but graciousness. They don't soak up all the good will in the room. They spread it around. Leaders are better off if they "take the blame but share the credit."[282]

Ronald Reagan kept this quote on his desk in the Oval Office: "There is no limit to what a man can do or where he can go if he doesn't mind who gets the credit."

Leaders who share credit where it is due never lose or diminish their authority or stature. Expressing gratitude enables leaders to release untapped potential.

LEADERSHIP LESSONS

1. Be a person after God's own heart.
2. Faith empowers leadership.
3. Never fail to return to the Lord.
4. Flawed person, faithful follower of God, fearless leader.
5. Strong leaders need—want—help.
6. Strong leaders should be developed at *all* levels of the organization.
7. Identify the right people with the right stuff.
8. Make the "hard decision" about struggling personnel.
9. Develop unlikely leaders by giving them opportunity.
10. Leaders not only think "big" but long-term.

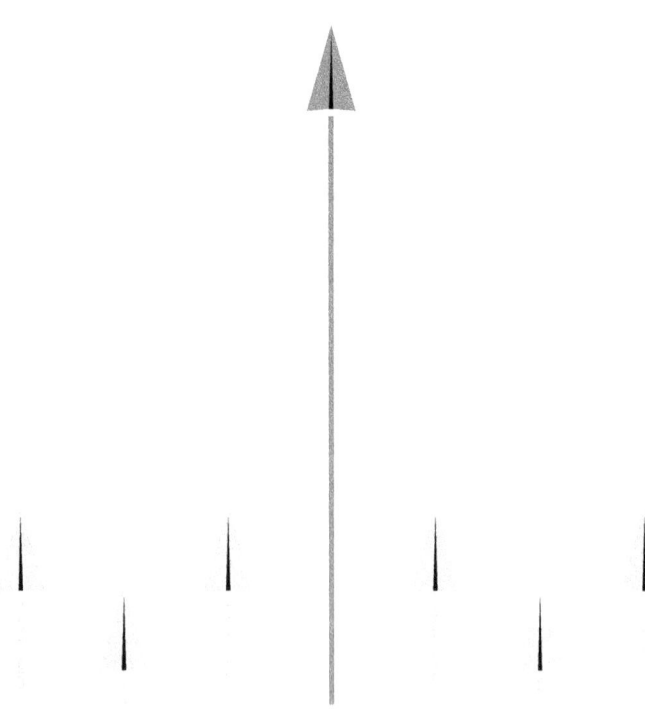

CHAPTER 9

CRISES

When A Leader Is *Challenged*

NEHEMIAH

Nehemiah was born in exile and worked in the responsible but uncelebrated job of being cupbearer to the king. Once Nehemiah understood the great challenge before him to rebuild the wall of Jerusalem, in a matter of months, he became a leader, patriot, soldier, builder, and statesman.

Nehemiah got involved. He was a man of action but also a man of prayer. Eleven incidents of prayer are recorded in his book. He lived the truth that "the leader who knows how to pray will know what God wants him to do."[283]

Nehemiah's strength came from an inspiring purpose and definite aim, all while he was humbly dependent upon God.[284] He needed to be. Nehemiah experienced ridicule (2:19, 42), fear (4:7–23), guile (6:2–4), false accusations (6:5–9), and corrupt friends or associates (6:17–19). While he was repeatedly beset by the slanderous criticisms of Sanballat, Tobiah, and Geshem, "he saw the greatness of his God and the greatness of the work, and he refused to budge."[285]

Nehemiah had vision rooted in his burden to rebuild the wall because he cared about his people. He remained resolute because he remained spiritually strong, and he inspired his people accordingly.

"Nehemiah knew how to work with people and how to get people to work for the Lord. Every true leader begets leaders. He doesn't use others to build his authority; he uses his authority to build others."[286]

Nehemiah was a leader in every sense of the word. He lived with focus, and he got things done. His book ends with the prayer of perspective: "Remember me, O my God, for good" (Neh. 13:31).

Welcome to Leadership

You can't be in leadership longer than about ten minutes without taking criticism. In this sense at least, like in Nehemiah's day, we all act like Israelites.

> **Criticized? Welcome to leadership.**

To lead is to invite criticism because leaders are involved in change and people often do not like change or fear change. Or they consider change too much work.

Criticism is a given because it arises from human nature. Leaders can react defensively, or they can maintain an even keel, look for what they can learn, carefully considering whether the criticism is warranted, and then respond with grace and gravitas.

Why do people criticize? The reasons probably are infinite but here are a few:

- People have different personalities and backgrounds.
- People don't possess all information relevant to the issue at hand.
- People are nearly infinitely creative.
- People make different judgment calls.
- People have competing agendas.
- People get tired, disengaged, or unenthused.
- People are creatures of habit and don't like change.
- People do not want the leader to succeed (competitors, "enemies").

- People don't like the leader (they don't have "chemistry" or are "frenemies").
- People "know" the leader is wrong and needs corrected.
- People have better information than the leader and the criticism may be correct or warranted.

Criticism will likely always be there. So, to borrow from President Harry S. Truman, "If you can't stand the heat, get out of the kitchen." Seriously, it's not a sin to be sensitive and if indeed you find as a leader that criticism paralyzes or otherwise brings you down to ineffectiveness, you will likely be better off to pursue a different professional endeavor. This isn't weakness. It's wisdom.

On the other hand, there are myriad ways a leader can learn to handle and respond properly to criticism. Perhaps remembering these principles—hard won from the school of hard knocks—will lend you some perspective:

1. As a leader, if you're not experiencing criticism, you're probably not doing much.
2. Even the best and most highly regarded leaders receive criticism.
3. Criticism seems to come as often from within as from without.
4. Criticism hurts most when it comes from your own.
5. Critics attack leaders personally because the critic's argument about policy or direction lacks merit, because individuals are easier to isolate than issues, or because the leader simply isn't well regarded.
6. Some online criticism is designed to provoke a response, for example, "trolling."

Receiving and Interpreting Criticism

Criticism can come from within or without the organization. Sometimes the source helps a leader understand best how to respond. But leaders do not necessarily need to know the source. Leaders can and should respond not to critics per se but respond in principle to the criticism. Who offers the criticism might be irrelevant. The point is leaders can learn from the criticism and respond for the good of the organization.

What if the criticism is correct? Even Churchill could change his mind, saying, "I'd rather be right than consistent."[287]

Critics, sometimes intentionally, sometimes unintentionally, tend to criticize using what might be labeled "techniques."

1. Criticism often shifts from the *organization* to the *individual* or from the idea/initiative/incident to the individual. In other words, criticism tends to get both personal and intense rather quickly. Critics tend to focus upon concrete things they and their supporters can swiftly grasp, and a given person's leadership role, persona, or personality become fair game.
2. Or criticism shifts from the *idea/initiative/incident* to the *organization*. This phenomenon seems to contradict the shift just noted, but both come into play. Both can move the arguments of the criticism from the actual trigger point, which can be debated and perhaps resolved, to the more complex individual or organization, which may be less easily debated or resolved.

Experienced leaders will recognize, even anticipate, these typical techniques of criticism and, if response is called for, do so in a winsome manner. Leaders that let their own emotions take control, or worse be expressed, and then react to the intensity or personal nature of the criticism, will soon find themselves in a defensive, less effective posture.

Leaders must know the facts before they act.

Since we live in a media age, criticism also sometimes comes from those in media who consider it their calling not only to report what we used to call "the news," but also anything with which they might disagree, anything that does not fit their worldview or agenda. They may do this with a significant bias. Then again, simply because they are media does not mean they are wrong or the enemy, so it is the leader's responsibility to test the criticism to discover if there is anything valid there, anything that requires his or her attention for the good of the organization's mission.

Remember what Jim C. Collins observed in *Good to Great*, "You absolutely cannot make a series of good decisions without first confronting the brutal facts."[288] It might not be easy to admit, but the brutal fact may be that some of the criticism is justified. Know the facts before you act.

Communication is a two-way street. As we noted earlier in this work, effective leaders must learn to be good listeners. If a leader is truly engaged, respecting his or her people enough to *hear them*, the leader will learn more, find more pressure points that can be eased, and get the facts on the ground, which will help people move more quickly toward the vision than anything else a leader might do. "No great idea ever enters the mind through an open mouth."[289] St. Francis said, "Lord, grant that I may not seek so much to be understood as to understand."

Leaders lead best when they master the fine art of listening, especially to criticism.

Leadership is about developing the art of active listening so that you can learn from others, glean their best ideas, and test the accuracy of your understanding of reality. But beware, "unsolicited advice confronts the leader at every turn." Leaders should be attentive but hold their own counsel. Attentive listening, though important, can nevertheless unintentionally signal acceptance of an idea. FDR suffered from this problem because he was a good listener. Ultimately, a leader must know when to stop listening and when to make a decision, delegate, or move on.[290]

Leaders lead best when they listen.

Then there are those who lean toward nonlistening. They want to act, and maybe have a quick trigger, meaning their capacity to respond immediately can be an asset. There may be times when this kind of talent or personality reinforces leaders, especially facing strenuous criticism. But just as often, this penchant in a leader's personal wiring can get him or her into trouble.

A couple of Churchill's favorite maxims were "Ponder, then *act*" and "Half-measures are vain."[291] Responding to criticism is not an old west gunfight. The leader does not have to be the first on the draw.

Responding to Criticism

In a media age, "being able to take a public whipping from the media when you deserve it, and to do so without whining, gives you more credibility when you subsequently complain about coverage which is patently unfair."[292] Turn the other cheek, keep a stiff upper lip, be ten feet tall and bulletproof.

But leaders have more to think about than the media. Responding to criticism can say a lot about a leader's character or mettle and in some cases a response can make or break a leader's career, no matter how and when the response is reported.

How leaders respond to critics can say more about the leader than *what* is said.

First, *determine what, if any, response is appropriate*. Because someone offers a criticism does not mean he or she is owed a response. The leader must decide when to respond and, just as importantly, when not to respond, at least in a direct personal manner.

"Not all criticism is valuable and meant for our good. Criticism that is anonymous, vague, mean spirited, or couched in 'other people are saying' language often says more about the critic than it does us. We can often reject this kind of criticism. But even when people deliver it the wrong way, there may still be a grain of truth in what they say. We don't want to get into a habit of reflexively rejecting all criticism without evaluating it. Even painful criticism may still have content we need to hear."[293]

How leaders respond is as important as what they say.

Sometimes responding can lend unearned credence to an otherwise superfluous criticism. Or responding can unintentionally escalate a perceived conflict. On the other hand, when a leader does respond, he or she must never overreact, remembering, "This too shall pass."

And "it goes without saying that some leaders deserve the criticism they get. They act in unbiblical ways; they are unrepentant when confronted for sin; they scandalize the gospel and defame the name of Christ with their behavior; they teach falsehood—these kinds of leaders should be censured."[294]

Need we say, don't be one of these kinds of leaders. In fact, they aren't leaders. They are autocrats.

Second, *leaders can almost always respond to criticism by beginning with a positive, saying "Thank you."* This does not mean you agree with everything in the criticism, but you can sincerely thank the disgruntled or concerned persons for taking the time to share their insights with you directly, as opposed to blasting their opinions across social media, finding the leader guilty even before he or she has a chance to respond.

And leaders can always exercise grace, forgiving critics, even if they believe the critics are 100 percent wrong. Again, this does not mean the leader is agreeing with, much less endorsing, everything the critic said, just that criticisms conceivably leveled harshly or harmfully can be left in the Lord's hands.

Third, *leaders must never respond with ego, revenge, self-righteousness, or "overwhelming force."* Remember proportionality. Leaders who take a big stick approach right out of the gate each time they face criticism usually develop a reputation for autocratic or belligerent behavior, or worse, ineffective leadership.

Fourth, *leaders should never respond in-kind.* This generally means avoid escalating the confrontation by using emotionally loaded words. "Losing it" is not a trait of good leadership. Emotions, especially anger or pique, produce more heat than light.

Fifth, *leaders should never put in print what would embarrass them if published online or otherwise circulated—ten years later.* Early in my career, I got exercised by something that—tellingly—I cannot remember, but I do remember being upset. I remember writing a scathing letter with phrases like "voice crying in the wilderness." Yes, I was that far off the deep end. Once finished, I sealed this diatribe in an envelope, gave it to my department chair, and asked him to hand it to the appropriate committee person the next afternoon. Then I went home and thought about what I'd done. I will forever be grateful to the Lord for the attack of conscience he gave me—that disquieting of the spirit—along with the strength to go the next morning to the department chair and request my unopened letter be returned to me. I then destroyed it.

This lesson has stayed with me to this day. In later years during some administrative leadership turbulence, I remember writing a few letters just to get my thoughts organized and sort of "out of my heart." Then I always destroyed the letter. It was a great way to "cool off" and I provided no lasting evidence of ill will. This does not mean I never spoke to the individuals with whom I disagreed or who were upset with me, but speaking directly, if done in a respectful manner, is far better than denouncing people with emotional language in print.

> **What leaders say in cyberspace never goes away.**

Now with the power of social media, in seconds, emotional responses can be published for readers' immediate access literally around the world. And even if these statements are taken down or deleted, they are never really erased because invariably someone captured them with a screenshot. The number of celebrities, athletes, entertainers, academics, and political leaders who have learned this the hard way are too many to count. What you say in cyberspace never, never goes away. So leaders especially should avoid "shooting off their mouth," in print so to speak, emoting via social media. It will not end well for leaders who ignore this advice.

Sixth, *no matter how off-the-wall or egregious the criticism, look for kernels of truth you need to hear.* Check it out. This gives the critic a certain honor, protects the leader from inadvertently defending the indefensible, and demonstrates wisdom and perspective. For no organization and no leader are without flaws. If there is truth in the criticism, then the leader can acknowledge this, own the problem, and as appropriate, apologize. If you are wrong or the organization made a mistake, say so; thank the concerned critic, and work to rectify the situation for the good of the organization.

> **Leaders who were wrong should say so.**

"One of the greatest arrows in any leader's quiver is the ability to say these words: 'I was wrong.' 'Forgive me.' 'Thank you for challenging my decision.'" Be wary of resenting people who tell the real story. We should look for them.[295] In this sense, critics can be a leader's friend.

Seventh, *avoid responding to criticism with long, point-by-point rebuttals or explanations of how you, the leader, or the organization have been wrongly accused.* You won't persuade most critics, and this sort of response is both defensive and a waste of the leader's time.

Just say, "Thank you for writing. We take your concerns seriously," and as appropriate, state what you will do. Then, let it go.

Engaging in long rebuttals also provides others with more they can, if they wish, use to your or the organization's detriment. It's a bit like defense attorneys advising their clients, "Just say yes or no. Don't volunteer information." Except in the rarest of circumstances, long rebuttals are an ego trip for an overly sensitive leader.

Eighth, *contact the concerned person directly by phone.* This response is surprisingly effective, almost always unexpected, and *may* be useful. As appropriate, meet with concerned people personally. The value of this approach is that it sends that always helpful message of respect to those who are distressed, it provides an opportunity to listen and clarify, and unless you commission a stenographer, avoids creating any record in print. You are free to say things one-on-one—perhaps private matters, concerns—that you would never put in an email, text, letter, or other preservable response.

I used this approach several times in my university leadership days, always to good results, in part because I found the concerned person was generally less agitated and more amenable to finding solutions in person than he or she might have been exchanging communiqués.

Person-to-person contact de-escalates the tension and makes it more difficult for false allegations to be made. It's why marriage counselors usually start by trying to get the couple together in the same room, or why foreign policy summits convene international leaders at some beautiful resort. Talking is better than shooting at one another.

Ninth, *always take the opportunity to restate the leader's or the organization's vision, values, distinctives, and goals.* Use this as a teaching, reinforcing moment. Remind the concerned persons and the public of what's good about the organization and what its tomorrow could be.

Tenth, and finally, *be sincere, be brief, and be gone.*

"Great leaders and their organizations are often criticized. As the saying goes, 'It's difficult to get to the top, but even harder to stay there.' Why is it harder to stay on top? Because it's easy to grow complacent—and it's difficult to endure the critics that don't believe you've earned the right to be there in the first place. Staying focused is critical when you are a leader, and diffusing the noise by staying focused on the next level of evolution in your business will help you shut down your critics."[296]

This happens in sports. Losing teams fuss much more than winning teams.

Criticism That Hurts

I can tell you from personal experience that criticism that comes from within hurts more than criticism that comes from without. This doesn't mean one is more or less accurate, just that criticism from those close to us is more emotional, thus more difficult to process and to resolve.

I find it interesting as I reflect on more than sixteen years as the president of a Christian university that while we periodically received concerns from without—the public—we received far more from within—our constituency. This may not be every leader's experience, but it was ours.

> **Criticism hurts most when it comes from our own.**

Criticism from "frenemies," like Nehemiah's Sanballat, Tobia, and Geshem, is one form of challenge. But this suggests a principle: *spiritual opposition always follows spiritual opportunity* (see 1 Thess. 2:18). You can see this in ancient Berea where people wanted to learn more about God's grace, "But when the Jews from Thessalonica learned that the word of God was proclaimed by Paul at Berea also, they came there too, agitating and stirring up the crowds" (Acts 17:13; see vv. 10–15). Even among Jesus's disciples, there was Judas.

Criticism from one's own can also be rooted in envy or lack of understanding, for a "prophet is not without honor except in his hometown and in his own household," the Scripture tells us (Matt. 13:57).

But not all criticism from within, hurtful though it may be, should be regarded as an attack or as some means of undermining the leader. Maybe the criticism is well taken. Maybe it needs to be heard. Maybe the leader needs to pause and listen, like Moses did when his father-in-law Jethro told him he was heading toward ineffectiveness and burn out as a leader, one mired in minutia.

"Moses's father-in-law said to him, "What you are doing is not good. You and the people with you will certainly wear yourselves out, for the thing is too heavy for you. You are not able to do it alone. Now obey my voice; I will give you advice, and God be with you!" (Ex. 18:17–19). Moses did listen, and he thereafter delegated. "Any hard case they brought to Moses, but any small matter they decided themselves" (Ex. 18:26).

Or maybe like King Hezekiah, the criticism is rather harsh and threatening. In this instance, Hezekiah's and the nation of Israel's survival were directly and credibly put at risk by the king of Assyria who mocked Hezekiah's worship of the one true God. King Hezekiah laid the issue before the Lord and prayed, and the Lord responded with a miracle, that night sending angels against the Assyrians, killing their army of one hundred and eighty-five thousand men (2 Kings 18–19).

Spiritual opposition always follows spiritual opportunity.

Perhaps God will not always respond in this dramatic and miraculous fashion, but he can. He is God, and the point of the biblical record is to remind us of this very fact. Our Sovereign God omnisciently and omnipotently oversees even our worst leadership challenges, our most ominous criticism, our greatest perceived enemies. God does hear and does answer prayer. Leaders who lead well know this and take momentous steps for the Lord.

Finally, the likelihood of criticism that hurts makes it imperative that leaders are committed to their calling and their vision. The more clearly these ports in the storm are understood, the more the leader will be able to sail the organizational ship safely through the storm.

Giving Criticism

Aristotle once said, "Anyone can become angry. That is easy. But to be angry with the right person, to the right degree, at the right time, for the right purpose, and in the right way—that is not easy."

Two thoughts on this quote: leaders who become angry are not acting like Christian leaders and are in danger of losing their effectiveness, but responding "for the right purpose, and in the right way," that aligns with a Christian perspective.

Leaders lead people, often called followers, and since these followers are human beings, inevitably, from time to time some will need redirection, correction, or appropriate criticism. The critical point about a leader giving criticism is what Aristotle mentioned, communicating for the right purpose and in the right way.

Several practical considerations:

- Never criticize staff members publicly in front of others.
- Focus upon the incident at hand, not a litany of past mistakes.
- Never throw one staff member under the bus while ignoring the underperformance of others.
- Consider whether you, as leader, are the right person to share the redirection, because the correction might be better received if shared by the staff member's immediate report.
- Begin with what's good about the staff member's contributions, then identify any need for improvement.

- As appropriate, a leader may reference a mistake he or she once made and how this reinforced growth, thus offering the staff member encouragement rather than discipline.
- Recognize that, though you as leader may be correct, sharing truth with someone is not always going to be well received because it means admitting one's faults or failures or missteps, and some find this difficult to do.
- In today's litigious environment and out of due consideration for Human Resources protocols, plan what you are going to say, treat the staff member with dignity while saying it, and always post a record of the interaction in Human Resources.

Some additional issues worth considering:

- If the staff member is a different sex than the leader, the leader should take care to plan the interaction in a private but accountable location, like a conference room with windows, an office with glass or windowed doors, a room where another appropriate staff leader, especially one of the same sex as the staff member, can join the session. This may seem like overkill, but there is no better illustration of the old saw, "an ounce of prevention is worth a pound of cure."
- Plan exactly how you want the meeting to proceed and conclude, and if this is a second or third strike offense that will result in dismissal, know exactly what your organization's Human Resources protocols require and follow these to the letter.
- As noted above, post a record of the interaction in Human Resources, but in addition to this, consider whether a brief, personal letter will be beneficial, written to the staff member and summarizing concerns and steps forward.

Sharing criticism is not easy or fun. Leaders who share criticism with the right motives in the right way at the right time, can reap great dividends. I remember two staff members whose mode of dress were not considered appropriate by the organization or others around them. The woman consistently dressed immodestly. The man dressed in an unprofessional manner.

Regarding the woman, we asked another mature woman staff member who had worked with this younger staff member if she had noticed and felt that the younger person's apparel was inappropriate. She agreed on both counts, so we asked her privately if she would quietly speak with the young staff member about her attire. The mature staff member agreed, did so, and the perceived problem disappeared because the young woman received the counsel well and responded. I often wondered, though, if that young staff member had been brought into H.R. and officially reprimanded, whether the organization might have lost her as an employee and maybe not helped her grow in the process.

Regarding the man, since he often worked alongside me, I took the step of talking to him myself. His response was unanticipated. He said his father had died young and he never had the influence or guidance of a father on a variety of key matters including dress, so he appreciated the input. Immediately thereafter he worked with his spouse to correct the problem (affordability was not the issue) and began to dress as well and as professionally appropriate as any man in the organization.

So, there are success stories for "criticism" rightly delivered. Much of it tracks back to treating the staff member with dignity and with a goal to help them rather than chastise them.

"Leading people is rarely a joyride. God's leaders—yes, even those called by Him—endure incredible amounts of heartache, controversy, and animosity. The end-product—the outcomes of leadership—is what makes it worthwhile for leaders."[297] Surely, working toward a worthy vision alongside credentialed, competent, committed staff members is one of a leader's most fulfilling experiences.

Hard Times

In addition to criticism, leaders must deal with crises, unanticipated developments that can rock the organizational ship at any given time: high-profile personnel moral failures or sexual-harassment allegations, financial shortfalls, accidents, cyber breaches, terrorist attacks, an active shooter, natural disasters, social unrest, personnel embezzlement or other dishonesty, public health emergencies, interventionist health protocols, new post-pandemic virus variants, recession, supply chain delays, inflation, labor market shortages, childcare and safety issues, international political instability, human resources challenges emerging from SOGI (sexual orientation gender identity) issues, government regulations regarding climate change politics, health care costs, crime surges, immigration and refugees, or for churches, constituency splits.

The seemingly impossible *can* happen. We live in a fallen world, so every leader who leads long enough will, sooner or later, experience hard times.

This happens in the US presidency too. The tenure of President George W. Bush will forever be associated with Hurricane Katrina, 9/11, and the Iraq War. For President Barack Obama, there was the Deepwater Horizon oil spill off the coast of Louisiana, considered to be the largest marine environmental disaster in the history of the petroleum industry, and the social unrest of the Arab Spring. For President Donald Trump's first term, the worldwide COVID-19 pandemic, and for this second, war in the Middle East and Ukraine.

Crises come in all shapes and sizes, day or night. No leader and no organization are invulnerable to crises.

No leader is invulnerable to crises.

Handled improperly, crises can contribute to the decline of the organization or downfall of the leader. Handled well, crises can define a leader's tenure if not his or her legacy.

Nothing tests leaders and nothing proves the quality of their leadership like hard times. Such times require great leaders. Speaking of Elijah, Chuck Swindoll said, "God looks for special people at difficult times."[298]

Rita El-Mounayer served with the Middle East and North Africa Christian satellite media ministry almost from its launch on air in 1996. In a twenty-five plus year career she worked as a writer, on-air host, channel director, chief channels officer, and deputy CEO. Finally, in April 2019, she was appointed SAT-7 International CEO.

Soon after her early days in office the COVID-19 pandemic captured the world's attention with certain countries in the Middle East and North Africa particularly hard hit. For the region, it was an experience of layered crises, one on top of the other, rampant inflation, unstable currencies, unemployment, grinding poverty, corrupt governments, the multiyear ongoing Syrian civil war and proxy war in Yemen, the usual saber rattling of Iran, Turkey, and other countries like Russia or the United States positioning for regional hegemony.

SAT-7 personnel, working in upward of twenty-seven countries, faced a significant challenge, how to continue to function with travel restrictions and government mandated stay-at-home orders, how to function with the possibility of declining revenues from ministry supporters, and how to encourage viewers on air, most of them from non-Christian backgrounds. Along with this, some personnel themselves could be anxious, struggling with family economic survival or worries about family health.

In the face of these challenges, as CEO, Rita emerged as the port in the storm, the steady voice, the long-term view with perspective, the gravitas, the depth of theological knowledge, the experience as a child growing up during the Lebanese Civil War, and the expressed faith in God who she knew was faithful and strong.

Rita was able to communicate these qualities via a weekly international all-personnel Zoom prayer time she established early on. In just thirty minutes, these online gatherings of colleagues from across the Middle East, North Africa, Europe, Canada, United States, and Brazil proved invaluable to the faith, confidence, camaraderie, and hope for all who participated. Rita shared most of the early short devotionals, giving her an unplanned opportunity to draw on her childhood experience with serious crises, to demonstrate her knowledge and her faith, and to encourage others.

One blessing and benefit of this experience was that God clearly used this time to solidify Rita's position as CEO, not that staff did not know or trust her, but now, through this, they saw her in action. For the first time, they saw her *act* as a leader. And they heard her time and again remind everyone of the big picture, SAT-7's mission to make God's love visible, about which they were motivated to find new ways to communicate to Middle East and North Africa viewers.

The lesson from this story is that crisis is not only a threat but an opportunity for leaders who lead. Effective leaders anticipate and prepare their people for hard times, not by constantly sharing doom and gloom but by realistically evaluating the volatile marketplace in which every organization now exists and by working to build an organizational culture that is open, sound, and productive.

> Crisis is not only a threat but an opportunity
> for leaders who lead.

Crises develop from several sources, including this illustrative but not exhaustive list:

1. Leader and/or personnel faults or limitations, including conduct unbecoming.
2. Unexpected offshoots of change working toward the vision.
3. Economic or marketplace fluctuations.
4. Significant criticism, even attack, by those who disagree with the vision or simply see themselves as competitors.
5. Spiritual opposition.

6. Social upheaval, natural disasters, or other outside marketplace developments.

It may seem surprising to learn that some 80–90 percent of organizational problems involve internal considerations that the leader or organizational personnel alone cause, and they alone can solve. "Satan, the most powerful source of evil on earth, was not what stood between the disciples and progress. It was always and only *their* lack of faith. . . . If you really want to get down to business, as a team, recognize there is only God and you. And then watch what happens."[299]

Progress, or change, toward the vision almost inevitably generates unexpected challenges. "While many long for a roseate leadership style that can rally institutions and persons without the threat of pain or burden, . . . there is always a likelihood of casualties and that a great leader must be willing to count up the cost of any noble vision or bold action."[300]

Some personnel, for example, who start the journey toward a new organizational vision will not, cannot, or perhaps choose to not be there when the organization reaches the next level of professionalism and excellence. Maybe for positive reasons they choose to seek employment elsewhere, and that's OK. Or maybe, to put it bluntly, they don't have the talent or the work ethic or the desire, and either they make the decision to go elsewhere, or the leader is forced to make this decision for them. You can find this observation in both Jim Collins and John Maxwell's works on leadership. It may not be pleasant, but it is a nearly universal phenomenon and in terms of progress toward the vision a necessary one.

Crises involving spiritual opposition are perhaps a special category. Moses, Nehemiah, King David, the apostle Paul all faced this.

In hard times like these, it is essential for the leader to repeat his or her commitment to right values and a worthy mission. Keep the focus on the long term and stand firm, not becoming weary in doing good.

Social disruption can strike an organization, if not directly then as a ripple effect, at any time: unrest or rioting, conflict, domestic terrorism, racial tension, and more. The leader's responsibility at this point is to know the facts, communicate openly with well-defined terms, and, to quote football's Vince Lombardi, to model "quitters never win but winners never quit."[301]

Hard times are when leaders must lead, whether president of the United States or a key person among friends or family. It's a time that may very well separate those who can and will lead effectively from those who can but won't or those who can't and don't try.

"Challenge provides the opportunity for greatness. Most of us are like tea bags. We'll never know how strong we are until we get into hot water."[302]

So, "if you are in charge, take charge. Be proactive; take initiative. Do something even if it might be wrong; paralysis or over-analyzing is riskier. As you make decisions and take action when leading through a crisis, communicate those actions truthfully and honestly."[303]

One of the most effective ways leaders lead during hard times is to communicate, to tap into the insatiable desire of both personnel and much of the public to know what the leader thinks and to understand where the organization is going. This reduces fear and encourages hope because "people can handle just about anything except the unknown."[304]

"Perhaps the most essential element of crisis leadership is clear and trustworthy communication."[305]

Speaking credibly and speaking often gives the leader a chance not only to calm fears but once again to convey his or her vision for the future of the organization. Leaders remind staff why it's important their organization not only survives but thrives in crisis.

"How we respond to a crisis is more crucial than the crisis itself.... Our response to any crisis is an opportunity."[306] Hard times offer an opportunity to rally the faithful and attract new support. Hard times are a golden chance for leaders to repeat, and repeat again, the vision, what he or she believes is possible and essential.

"Adversity can quickly stop a leader who lacks purpose, but it only 'fans the flames' of leaders with a strong purpose."[307] Leaders should never be caught without a sense of purpose. Remind people, especially during hard times, they are "building a cathedral" not just "cutting stone."

Keep the Faith

It is important for leaders to keep the faith, "not only when filled with the zeal of the Lord of Hosts, but when one is fed up, under attack, alone and in the depths, when faith is low and the darkness is all around.... In those times when the call is muted or the spirit weak, it may help to remind us that the call is still there, but so also is God's sustaining grace."[308]

Leaders who keep the faith are now ports in the storm as never before. We live in a time when American culture tends to reinforce anti-authority attitudes. American culture is awash in contrarian views, dissent, rejection of timeless verities like God, truth, morality, and responsibility. We've created a culture more interested in what divides us than in *E pluribus unum*. This has been the case at least since the 1960s and it has intensified in the 2000s. Sad to say, America is polarized.

Younger employees are especially susceptible to the influences of this culture. While they do not all share the same values or personalities, they have come of age in a time when saluting authority, loyalty even, are not widely promoted or embraced. Rather, for them it is a culture about uncertainty and pushback and one that argues for rights more than responsibilities.

Social anxieties get in young as well as older people's heads, and they bring this to the workplace.

"The realities of a distracted workforce have been well-documented. According to a survey by Udemy, 70 percent of workers admit they feel distracted when they're on the job, and about one in five admit to feeling 'almost always distracted.' The problem appears even greater when we look at results from surveyed Millennials and Gen Zers, who admit to feeling distracted 75 percent of the time."[309]

Through social media, in seconds young people can share their point of view about virtually everything with virtually everyone. There are no limits on what is said, how it is said, when it is said, or to whom it is said. And there are no governors or fail-safes that act to instill caution or words to the wise on social media. If you think it, you can share it, immediately.

Younger American employees are also often more concerned about social justice, about whether the climate is changing, about sexual expression, than about what their organization wishes to achieve. As a cohort, they are at times hypersensitive to any authority questioning their values, and they are quick to label as intolerant or even bigoted any expression of traditional moral views with which they disagree.

All this makes the leadership environment even more complex and challenging. So, now more than ever leaders are needed who live in a manner that upholds personal and professional integrity—authenticity—and who base their attitudes and actions upon faith and vision—knowing what they believe, why, and how it contributes to a better world.

Leaders in the early twenty-first century must evidence resilience in the face of criticism and crises. The best leaders "create a pathway of Hope going forward."[310] They know their purpose, and they remain resolute and stand firm. They fight the good fight, they finish the race, they keep the faith (2 Tim. 4:7). They stay the course.

Unlikely leaders, great leaders, learn to review each criticism and regard each crisis as an opportunity to fulfill the organization's mission.

LEADERSHIP LESSONS

1. Criticized? Welcome to leadership.
2. Leaders must know the facts before they act.
3. Leaders lead best when they listen.
4. *How* leaders respond is as important as *what* they say.
5. What leaders say in cyberspace never goes away.
6. Leaders who were wrong should say so.
7. Criticism hurts most when it comes from our own.
8. Spiritual opposition always follows spiritual opportunity.
9. No leader is invulnerable to crises.
10. Crisis is not only a threat but an opportunity for leaders who lead.

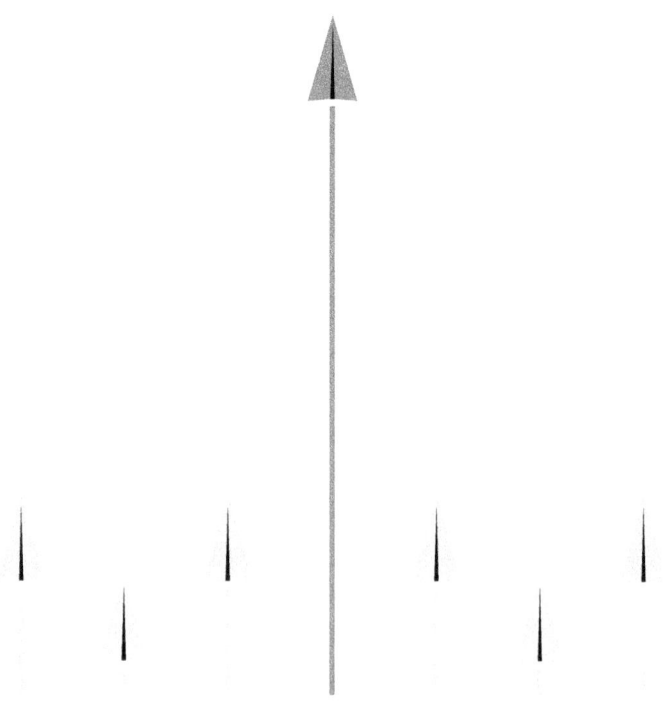

CHAPTER 10

CONDUCT UNBECOMING

When A Leader *Fails* or *Falls*

SAMSON

Samson began life with considerable advantages. An angel of the Lord announced his birth. His parents were godly, and his home was what today we'd call a "Christian home." He became a Nazarite, set apart to God from birth. He was specially gifted with a great strength he used against the enemies of the Israelites whenever the Spirit of God came upon him. For twenty years he acted as a judge in Israel during the days of Philistine occupation and harassment.

But Samson somehow missed learning a key spiritual lesson: bad choices and bad character trump great ability and great advantages. Samson was a spiritual Jekyll and Hyde. Time and again throughout Samson's relatively short life he demonstrated he was as spiritually weak as he was physically strong. His problem was not "money, sex, and power." His problem was just sex.

Bible teacher Warren Wiersbe had a great line when he said, "Samson not only had "I" trouble but also "eye" trouble.[311] Samson's MO was raging narcissism. He lived to fulfill selfish desires, most notably in terms of the lust of the eyes and the lust of the flesh—first for the Philistine woman of Timnah, then for a prostitute in Gaza, and finally and fatefully, for Delilah.

It isn't too difficult to believe Samson had other dalliances in his life, but these three are the ones the Scripture records. Samson's sexual misadventures are a lasting example of what immoral relationships can do to leaders who fail to heed God's command to "drink water from your own cistern" and avoid sexual immorality (Prov. 5:15; see vv.15–23; 6:23–7:27).

> **Bad choices and bad character trump great ability and advantages.**

Delilah betrayed Samson's love more for the promise of a large reward than any interest in her Philistine heritage. Her nagging for the source of Samson's strength wore him down. Eventually, he violated his Nazarite vows by telling her all. Delilah's seductive disloyalty was treacherous indeed. But unlike Joseph who ran from temptation, Samson succumbed. His fall resulted in the loss of his strength (for the Lord had departed from him) and his sight (for his enemies cruelly gouged his eyes). It's a tragic picture, but by the grace of God, not the end.

Samson repented, asked God for his Spirit one last time, and brought down the house—literally. Samson collapsed the pillars of the temple of Dagon, killing more enemies of God's people than he had during the whole of his life as a judge. Samson died in his second chance. His rejuvenated faith earned him a place in the faith hall of honor of Hebrews 11. Still, Samson's life is a story of "what might have been."

When Leaders Fail or Fall

Leaders are role models. People watch them, know what they do, where they go, what they wear, who they are with, how long their car is in the company parking lot—or if it's spotted in a questionable place.

Such visibility is part of leadership, which raises the bar of expectation for leaders. They can't fake it. Who they are shines through.

No one is or was perfect, except Jesus. Not Moses, not David, certainly not Samson. Leaders, like everyone else, make mistakes, maybe make ethically wrong choices. And leaders' choices have consequences.

James MacGregor Burns cataloged three types of standards or norms by which leaders are judged, and leadership is evaluated:

- *Virtue*, norms of conduct or habits of action such as chastity, sobriety, honesty in personal relationships, or self-control
- *Ethics*, modes of formal and transactional conduct like integrity, promise-keeping, trustworthiness, reciprocity, or accountability, as seen in the Golden Rule
- *Public values*, lofty public principles of order, liberty, equality, justice, and pursuit of happiness.

It is possible, Burns contends, to measure well on public values yet fail in either virtue or ethics, as seen in FDR and Bill Clinton's marital infidelities.[312]

Leaders are role models.

Failing or falling in leadership are distinct if at times overlapping in real-life experience.

1. *Failing in leadership* usually refers to not meeting organizational or operational goals or not getting along with employees. This can happen for many reasons including the fact all of us live in a fallen world and none of us are omniscient. We see through a glass darkly. Moral considerations—virtue, ethics—may be involved but often are not.
2. *Falling in leadership* refers to willful, sinful choices breaking fellowship with God and yielding to temptation. Moral

considerations—virtue, ethics—are most definitely involved. When leaders make sinful choices, like Samsom, they start down a broad road to deceit, prevarication, dishonesty, immorality, and destruction of their career, their relationships, or even their life.

Failing, depending upon the nature and extent of the leadership fail, is not usually fatal to leadership. But falling frequently spells the end of the road because it invariably results in loss of credibility, trust, and reputation.

Celebrity athletes, while not organizational leaders per se, have too often demonstrated what not to do.

Football great O. J. Simpson "had it all" yet he fell dramatically from the public's good graces. While he was controversially acquitted in what was called "the trial of the century" and legally avoided life in prison for the 1994 murder of his wife, Nicole Brown, and a friend Ron Goldman, he later did nearly nine years of time for theft. He then lived out his life ignominiously.

Golfing titan Tiger Woods's moral free fall pursuing illicit sex with allegedly 120 women cost him his marriage and, arguably, negatively affected his world-class career wherein he failed to reach his oft-stated goal of winning more professional golf majors than Jack Nicklaus.[313]

Politicians in this category of moral bankruptcy are legion: Bill Clinton, Andrew Cuomo, John Edwards, Gary Hart, David Petraeus, Arnold Schwarzenegger, Eliot Spitzer, and others.

Notice this illustrative list is all men. This does not mean women leaders never make poor moral choices, but the occurrence is rare, and sex is less often involved. Business tycoon Martha Stewart spent five months in jail, convicted for lying to federal investigators, conspiracy, and obstruction of justice in relation to her stock sales.[314]

Failing is not fatal to leadership; falling frequently spells the end.

Even religious leaders have too often joined the list of the fallen, some who repented and revived their ministries, many who never again wielded spiritual influence publicly, for example: Jimmy Swaggart, Bill Hybels, Jim Bakker, Ravi Zacharias, Jerry Falwell Jr., James MacDonald, Carl Lentz, Bill Gothard, Mark Driscoll, Robert Morris, and numerous Catholic priests in a worldwide sex scandal that cost the Roman Catholic Church billions of dollars.[315]

When Leaders Fail

King Saul, the first Old Testament Israelite king, is a scriptural example of a man who began his public life with all the advantages. He looked like a leader—right out of central casting (1 Sam. 9:2). In the early days, he was popularly acclaimed. He was in every sense of the phrase "a likely leader."

But for all this, he turned out to be a spiritually weak and arrogant king who disobeyed God's commands on a series of occasions, including his command to destroy everyone and everything in the Amalek kingdom. In this battle, King Saul directly disobeyed God by sparing the Amalekite king and by selecting the best livestock for what the king said would be sacrifices to the Lord. But the prophet Samuel later reminded King Saul that God had said to destroy everything. Then Samuel uttered that telling biblical statement: "To obey is better than sacrifice," meaning God desires a pure heart of submission more than ritualistic sacrifice (1 Sam. 15:22).

"Saul (did) not, on his own, possess a sense of purpose for his people, a vision for the direction he would lead them. . . . From the start, Saul's great concern was his own prestige, his own popularity, his own grip on the reins of power. . . . Though frightened at first to be king, and for good reason, Saul got used to the executive mantle soon enough. But it was the trappings of power and not the calling that fueled his imagination.

"Saul does not inspire, he demands; he does not lead; he dictates, and he cajoles; he does not build for the future but reacts to the crises of the day. . . . He had authority, but little influence. *Saul was a king, but he was not a leader.*"[316]

Saul saw only himself standing alone before Goliath, rather than as the shepherd-musician David saw God with him. "This is what makes a champion. Not strength of arms, not wizardry at spearheads, not a charismatic speaking style, but strength of heart, conviction, and passionate faith."[317]

King Saul failed in leadership repeatedly. He disobeyed God, he struggled with fear, and he chose self-aggrandizement over selfless service time and again.[318] And in later years, King Saul developed a jealous paranoia toward the young David, so much so that today we would say, "David lived rent free in Saul's head." Yes, at first the king looked upon David as a beloved armor-bearer and musician. But then the insecure king began regarding David as a rival and tried to kill him. King Saul's leadership had long since lost its divine purpose.

The prophet Samuel admonished King Saul repeatedly. The king could have altered his own future by confessing his sins and seeking to avoid moral deterioration going forward. If he had, his legacy would be different.

"The heart is where leadership takes place; it is born there and there it dies as well."[319] This is where King Saul failed before he started. His heart did not align with God's heart such that God could not say of King Saul what he said of King David, "a man after his own heart" (1 Sam. 13:14).

> "Man looks on the outward appearance, but the Lord looks at the heart."

Coach John Wooden noted that "failure is not fatal, but failure to change might be."[320] This was King Saul's lifelong error. Because

God is longsuffering, the king's failures were never catastrophic or fatal . . . until the end (1 Samuel 31).

It's a lesson leaders would do well to learn. It's not the failure but the response that matters most. If there's no change or a poor response, leadership failure can be costly.

"Even before the pandemic, unanticipated leadership failure was a widespread issue among organizations, with an estimated 50 percent of leaders failing (meaning that half those who are initially successful will eventually be fired). Leadership failure has long posed a significant financial risk to organizations, given the costs of recruiting, selecting, onboarding, and training replacement leaders—costs that can add up to three times an executive's salary, in some cases. Leadership failure can also have negative spillover effects on the productivity of other members of the organization, as well as on the company's morale and reputation. This is especially true when leaders were successful early on and were expected to continue performing at a high level."[321]

What factors cause or contribute to failure in leadership?

1. Mistakes.
"Because leaders are human, leaders make mistakes. How they handle those mistakes reveals their true character. Do they blame others? Do they try to cover things up? Do they make excuses? When Joshua made a mistake, he turned to the Lord for forgiveness and wisdom, and then he made his mistakes work for him. . . . People who don't make mistakes usually don't make anything. People who make mistakes and give up are quitters, but people who make the best of their mistakes are overcomers."[322]

Mistakes are unavoidable and inevitable. Leaders fail when they try to cover up their mistakes and they do well when they identify, own, apologize as appropriate, and learn from their mistakes.

2. Micromanagement.
Leaders, usually through insecurity—or the flip side, ego—sometimes overmanage or micromanage their staff. When this happens, the bottom line is the leader does not trust his or her staff to fulfill their assignments, and after a short time, the staff knows this, leading them to not trust the leader.

Trusting employees or followers as such is a statement of respect, and it is empowering. It not only releases the leader from micromanaging, liberating his or her time, it also releases the staff to work productively and proactively.

3. Inability to lead.
This can be rooted in a host of sources—distraction; boredom; inexperience; poor communication skills; disorganization; negative attitudes; inarticulate visions, goals, or expectations; or personal problems. Leaders who fail because of an inability to lead may need more leadership development. This book argues leadership can be learned and leadership capacity developed. The trick is to identify this problem and its source quickly and act. That alone demonstrates leadership.

4. Mis-leading.
This means leading with wrong decisions or leading in the wrong direction. Shooting from the hip or the lip, poor research or misidentification of challenges, inflexibility—all these variables contribute to mis-leading.

Or it could be a mismatch, the "wrong" leader or the "wrong" time for his or her style of leadership in terms of the organization's needs and potential. This happens when an heir apparent, like a family member or long-term employee, is elevated to a position of leadership without proper preparation, or it can happen when a leader refuses to recognize how his or her own leadership style should be changed.

5. Dissension between leader and staff.
Dissension is a human problem because we are all sinners at birth and remain so as sinners saved by grace or sinners in need of grace. In nontheological terms this means "we fuss." Leaders can get sideways with their staff when they do not listen, do not share credit, do not express gratitude, make unrealistic demands that amount to "more bricks, less straw," lack empathy, care only for the bottom line or personal accolades, are gone from the organization more than the task and opportunities warrant, and maintain a deficit-spending approach.[323]

Dissension can be addressed with more and better leader-generated communication and a leader-demonstrated willingness to hear what's being said. This does not mean that staff are always right and leaders much kowtow to whatever wind is blowing, but it does mean that hearing concerns can allow leaders to respond with facts, explanation, vision, and initiatives.

Failure is not forever and it's not, or need not be, fatal. Henry Ford once said, "Failure is simply the opportunity to begin again; this time more intelligently."[324]

Leadership guru Barry Z. Posner echoed Henry Ford when he said, "If you're not making mistakes, you aren't learning. You have a flat learning curve. Most innovations are failures in the middle—need to stick with it. Just remember the African proverb: 'Never test the depth of the water with both feet.'"[325]

So, leaders who succeed learn how to fail forward.

"Every successful leader must fail at some point. Whether or not the leader has the necessary skills for his or her position, leadership effectiveness can depend on external factors such as organizational culture, company size, and work environment. Leadership failure is inevitable. It's difficult to avoid it in any organization at any time. You can be the most competent leader and occasionally be perceived as an intemperate leader."[326]

But "when failure is reframed as a tool for progress, leaders can move the organization forward."[327]

Leaders who succeed learn how to fail forward.

"Failure is the key to success. Failure not only assists leaders in developing character and resilience but also enables them to enhance their flexibility and adaptability. This is primarily because the mindset that contributed to the failure is unlikely to yield success in the future, necessitating a shift in thinking and approach. So, how does failure lead to success? By being more flexible and adaptable in their thinking, the leader opens the door to creative and innovative thought by demonstrating intellectual humility."[328]

Correction is open to anyone. The American people have long since demonstrated they are a forgiving bunch, often willing to give people a second chance. Leaders who humble themselves before God and as needed before those around them, can regroup and go on to good, productive, and successful leadership careers.

Disney's Michael Eisner said, "Failing is good, as long as it doesn't become a habit. Guts: Must take risks. Clearly, no risk, no reward. Survive success by continuing to risk failure."[329]

Then there is Winston Churchill who said, "Success is going from failure to failure without loss of enthusiasm."[330]

Correction is open to anyone.

But failure is not fun. This was one of my early lessons in leadership. I was not handling the challenge well, and in fact had worked myself into a level of stress that caused abdominal and back pain. I can remember a given weekend when I literally bent double with that pain. That's when I became convicted by how I was handling, or rather mishandling, the challenge and the experience. I thought, *Lord, I'm carrying this alone, acting like you are not there or do not care, and I'm assuming I'll somehow figure my way out of this.*

Not so. I needed the Lord's help first in my person, my inner being, and second in my leadership.

I immediately began a process—meaning multiple and continuing prayers—of giving this challenge and experience to the Lord. I prayed, *Lord, I've hit the wall, and I cannot do this. I ask you to forgive me for presumptuously thinking I could do this in my own strength. I ask you to forgive me for working myself into this level of stress. I know I've been wrong in how I've reacted to this challenge thus far. I need your wisdom, discernment, engagement, and peace. Lord, I give this to you. I submit to you my attitude and abilities, this challenge, and whatever response you wish me to make.*

Now the Lord did not need this prayer. But I did.

Since that time, I have often prayed this prayer in the face of significant leadership challenges, including my own mistakes, missteps, and failures. I know from experience this submission of the heart is both personally liberating and professionally energizing. The challenges still lay before me, but I was able to proceed (almost) stress-free, trusting the Lord for the outcome. I strongly recommend this prayer to you. God be praised that he walks beside us in the face of trials, including ones that involve our failure.

So, not all failure is bad, and great leaders learn how to fail forward by owning and learning from their mistakes and those of others.

But falling in leadership is different, dangerous, and perhaps morally deadly. Great leaders who care about the Lord, their family, and their organizations must be alert for Satan's attack. Leaders must "be sober-minded; be watchful. Your adversary the devil prowls around like a roaring lion, seeking someone to devour" (1 Peter 5:8). Leaders must avoid Satan's manifold and relentless temptations to fall.

Even the Savior was tempted in this manner when Jesus was in the wilderness, fasting and physically weakened, a state of vulnerability that set the stage for moral and spiritual testing (Matt. 4:1–11). Satan chose this seemingly optimal time to tempt Jesus:

- to turn the stones to bread, a misuse of divine power for personal comfort.
- to throw himself from the pinnacle of the temple, a temptation to test God or seek public validation through spectacle; and
- to worship Satan in exchange for all the kingdoms of the world, to achieve power without suffering, by compromising spiritual allegiance.

In each case, Jesus responded by quoting Scripture, affirming obedience to God over selfish gain or shortcuts to power. Jesus is a model for how leaders with the Spirit's help can resist temptation and remain morally steadfast.

When Leaders Fall

Samson's youthful indiscretions amounted to more than failing. He squandered his spiritual heritage, and he fell morally—repeatedly—losing his influence and probably years off his life.

As we referenced in an earlier chapter, King David fell morally—spectacularly. He lusted for Bathsheba, sent for her and committed adultery with her from which she became pregnant, arranged for her soldier husband to come home, figuring Uriah would sleep with his wife and thus cover up the pregnancy—but Uriah refused this opportunity out of loyalty to his fellow soldiers—so King David arranged for Uriah to be placed in the front lines where he was soon killed. Only by God's grace, and because David responded to the prophet Nathan's spiritual comeuppance and repented, did David remain in power (2 Samuel 11–12). And not only this, but his family also remained in the lineage of the Savior Jesus Christ.

> **Submitting the heart is personally liberating and professionally energizing.**

Falling morally, no matter the type of sin, is no small potatoes for leaders at any level in any organization. It brings emotional and spiritual pain; damage to the organization, its personnel, clients, and constituency; destruction of a legacy; and grievous defilement of the testimony of any Christians involved. Quite often, the reputation of the leader is ruined permanently and irretrievably.

But organizations try to avoid this, right? Yes, over 90 percent of Fortune 500 companies have a statement of ethics but for many it's just a document on the wall.[331] So in American society not a year goes by without various kinds of leaders falling morally, damaging if not destroying their honor and public esteem, wrecking their credibility, and often losing their position of influence.

Leaders who fall make willful, sinful choices. They do wrong at a level that is incredibly risky, and indeed almost never escape accountability because the Bible says, "Be sure your sin will find you out" (Num. 32:23).

> **Leaders who fall make willful, sinful choices.**

This biblical statement was carried into culture by none other than William Shakespeare. "The truth will out" is a proverbial expression, meaning the truth will eventually be revealed, no matter how much someone tries to hide or suppress it. The phrase dates to at least the fifteenth century and is famously used by William Shakespeare in *The Merchant of Venice* (Act 2, Scene 2): "Truth will come to light; murder cannot be hid long; a man's son may, but at the length truth will out."[332]

Lies, deception, or hidden truths are temporary; in time, reality asserts itself. "What's done in the dark will come to light." Leaders who risk all for momentary pleasures soon discover how unwise they chose to be, and how painful it is when they have "to come clean."

Falling in leadership can involve:

1. Moral transgression
- Illicit sex or sexual harassment
- Lies
- Theft (e.g., absconding with funds, Ponzi schemes, gambling debt)
- Substance abuse or selling illegal drugs
- Violence (e.g., maybe verbal or psychological, but also physical)

This list is probably what most people think when they hear the term "moral failure," using that word *failure* here but defined in this usage not as mistakes but as immorality leading to accountability and often dismissal. In practical experience, leaders who get in trouble morally, frequently engage in not just one of the behaviors in this list of wrongdoing but in several simultaneously, especially lying, which is inevitably the foundation of cover-ups.

2. Arrogance, self-aggrandizement
- Leader believes his or her own press
- Leader "leads for me not for thee"

Egomaniacal leaders exist but are at first sometimes difficult to detect. In time, the sad reality becomes apparent. In modern organizations, narcissistic leaders usually do not last long but, unfortunately, they can hurt a lot of people before their character becomes evident. Warning signs include leaders who talk more about themselves than the organization or its staff, leaders who pad their day-to-day corporate lifestyle if not their pockets by spending money on lavish offices or taking junkets to conferences in luxurious locations for purposes that do not advance the organization.

Arrogant or self-aggrandizing leaders use their influence to advance themselves. They are not about excellence or service or duty, honor, and country, but about me, myself, and I.

3. Rejection of the Christian faith

People rejecting their Christian faith is a sad reality we periodically witness living in a fallen world. This spiritual backsliding has been around since the first families in ancient times. It's still a problem now and when it happens, the hurts are broad and deep. Entire organizations, especially ministries, have been forced to close their doors when leaders "suddenly" reject the Christian faith. Churches sometimes struggle for years after a prodigal leader left them to go into "a far country," usually meaning they fell into (chose) moral sin.

Our postmodern culture rejects truth and accountability while promoting new ideologies like LGBTQ+ or "God wants us to be happy" or "I have to be true to myself." Leaders in Christian music and entertainment or mega churches have succumbed to these heresies, or they have been forced out of the ministry due to their immoral behavior. Others have attempted to maintain their positions of Christian leadership and influence even while promoting apostate teaching at odds with the Scripture, like "love is love." Proponents of this unbiblical mantra often argue, for example, same-sex marriage is blessed of God and should be embraced by the church.

If we define leader broadly, meaning a person of influence whether he or she runs an organization, then examples of fallen leaders are easy to identify.

"In October 2012, the International Cycling Union confirmed seven-time Tour de France winner Lance Armstrong had been doping for thirteen out of the nineteen years he'd been professionally cycling. Armstrong was stripped of his titles, including a bronze

Olympic medal. Armstrong, who created the Livestrong brand, lost an estimated $75 million in sponsorship deals, and had to pay $15 million in legal fees and $21 million in settlements.

In 2013, one of celebrity chef Paula Deen's employees sued her, accusing her of racist comments and racial discrimination. The lawsuit was ultimately dismissed, but not before Deen was dropped by the Food Network and lost her endorsements. Similarly, Papa John's pizza founder, CEO, and public face in advertising, John Schnatter, resigned as the pizza chain's chairman in 2018 after a Forbes report detailed a conference call where he used the N-word.

Elizabeth Holmes was the youngest self-made female billionaire in the world. In October 2015, a Wall Street Journal investigation revealed her blood testing company Theranos wasn't providing accurate results. By 2018, she and her cofounders were charged with 'massive fraud,' which could put her in prison for twenty years. She pleaded not guilty. In 2019, her lawyers dropped her because she couldn't afford to pay the fees.

In November 2017, anchor Matt Lauer was fired from NBC for 'inappropriate sexual behavior.' He had been earning $25 million a year. In October 2019, Ronan Farrow's book *Catch and Kill* reported that Brooke Nevils, Lauer's former colleague, accused Lauer of rape. He has denied this claim."[333]

"Unethical and amoral behavior can take many forms. It can involve lying, cheating, stealing, or engaging in other forms of misconduct. When leaders engage in such behavior, they undermine the trust and respect of their followers, colleagues and other stakeholders."[334]

Leaders who are Christian believers must always remember that they are anything but invulnerable. In fact, leaders saying publicly they are Christian may make them even greater targets of Satan's intention to weaken their testimony and impact.

Think about Samson again. Samson was apparently always "looking." He repeatedly put himself in the way of temptation, the wrong place at the wrong time with the wrong woman.

Abraham's nephew Lot lacked spiritual discernment, Christian critical thinking, if you will, wherein one applies biblical knowledge to cultural issues (Rom. 12:1–2, Heb. 5:12–14) so, like the Men of Issachar, one will know what one ought to do (1 Chron. 12:32).

No one is invulnerable to sexual temptation or immorality. Christian counselors say from professional experience that many Christian leaders get into moral trouble not because they're "looking" but because they "fell" into it unexpectedly. It begins with an *encounter* (meeting someone intriguing), proceeds from *encouragement* (some flirtation or openness, subtle or not so subtle), results in some kind of *expression* (a statement of interest or proposition, maybe a touch), and all too often ends with *experience* (by this point the near irresistible desire to sexually engage).[335]

> **No one is invulnerable to sexual temptation or immorality.**

Years ago, at the Christian university where I served as president, our seminary dean, the late, wise, and eloquent Dr. James Grier, and I talked about a pastor who had gotten involved with a woman not his wife and of course had been discovered. The dean counseled the man, as he had counseled many others before who'd "fallen morally."

Dean Grier then shared an observation that confirms the sequence in the earlier paragraph about "how this can happen." The dean said, "These men are not usually on the prowl. They did not wake up one morning and think, 'I should have an affair.' Such an idea would have shocked them. No, many in small churches work alone for long hours. They do not have sufficient fellowship or accountability. They become overstressed, beaten down, physically and emotionally weary. Often, they've allowed emotional distance between them and their wife to grow in their marriage, and their tank is all but empty. Then some new development occurs that is just too much. The burden is overwhelming. And at that point, Satan brings temptation."

That temptation might be a woman with whom the pastor works at the church, who saw his distress and expressed caring concern, to which he responds, or the woman expressing concern touches his shoulder or arm and it ignites a spark they did not know was there, or a woman comes for counseling and tells a story involving emotional need and a door is opened.

The examples of temptation are endless, but the point is the same. And this sequence can be applied not just to pastors but to any leaders. Satan attacks at a time of the leaders' greatest vulnerability.

Leaders fall when they have allowed their relationship with the Lord and with their spouse to die a slow death from lack of interaction and nurture.

Of course, men and women must be able to work together for organizations to function and thrive. So, separating the sexes is not viable or even necessary. But there are a few important things leaders can do to protect themselves, and if shared properly through Human Resources, their employees:

Develop the relationship and fellowship with one's spouse.
Keep no secrets. Periodically retreat together. Invest in him or her. The Lord does not want broken marriages (Mal. 2:13–16).

Avoid flirtation, physical contact, sensual or sexual nonverbal interaction, sexual jokes (see 1 Cor. 7:1).
Leaders should avoid this kind of behavior but also outlaw this kind of interaction among their staff. This is not prudery but common sense and respect for others.

There is another thing to avoid here. Adults did not fall off the truck yesterday, meaning we know when certain signals are being sent. For years I've called this sort of availability signaling "advertising." In my leadership career I had to work through Human Resources on a few occasions to help employees, both male and female, to understand how they dressed, how they carried themselves, and the way they interacted with the opposite sex, for instance, touching them needlessly, sent wrong and dangerous messages—perhaps subconsciously, but usually they knew what they were doing—inviting sexually charged responses. Beware of those who are advertising and never engage in this way with them as a person and as a leader.

Avoid pornography.
"Research reveals that 70% of Internet pornography happens during work hours, between 9 a.m. and 5 p.m. There is a link between viewing pornography and unethical behavior. Dehumanization of coworkers may lead to sexual harassment or contribute to a hostile work environment."[336] This can happen not simply with employees but leaders, including leaders in Christian ministries.[337]

Pornography is addictive, eventually, in the mind of the one consuming it, making every interaction somehow about sex. Such a destructive mindset inevitably produces a desire for action or experience, thus enhancing our temptation to physical immorality or sexual harassment.

If necessary, change the architecture or arrangement of an office.
To reinforce appropriate male/female interaction it is sometimes wise to reconfigure how offices are constructed and therefore how men and women participate in daily workflow. Close quarters can be altered. This may seem mundane or inconsequential, but in certain settings, like small church offices or even large corporations where office arrangements were set up without consideration of male/female interaction, such changes can be liberating and safer for all involved.

If approached or propositioned by a person at work or anywhere, immediately inform your spouse.
This maintains transparency and trust and involves your spouse in helping determine how to avoid this problem going forward. Informing one's spouse does not necessarily mean immediately talking to Human Resources—though this may be warranted in given situations to protect, for example, a woman staff member who has been approached with unwanted sexual attention—but it does mean you are protecting yourself by trusting this information with your spouse. Such an "approach or proposition" can be sexual harassment, which entails considerable legal and professional, as well as personal, liability.

Live a life of impeccable, unimpeachable, unassailable, irreproachable morality.
This is the best defense against the day you are falsely accused. In the 1990s when Bill Clinton was accused of womanizing, what Betsey Wright, Clinton's 1992 deputy campaign chair, dismissed as "bimbo eruptions," the women's sexual incriminations hit the public as all too plausible.[338] Whether they had a ring of truth or seemed fanciful, the accusations from a series of women just fit because people by then had learned something about Clinton's character.[339] Clinton's womanizing was simply believable. Leaders who want to avoid this predicament should live their lives in such a way that moral accusations simply don't make sense and don't stick.

The pitfalls of leadership:
- Money—the lust of the eyes
- Sex—lust of the flesh
- Power—pride of life

Life is a whole cloth (1 Tim. 3:1–12). Corporations are now recognizing that a person's family life affects his or her work productivity. Successful leadership begins with a commitment to "keep your heart with all vigilance, for from it flow the springs of life" (Prov. 4:23).

Leadership is a privilege. "Great leaders truly care about those they are privileged to lead and understand that the true cost of the leadership privilege comes at the expense of self-interest."[340]

The Scripture acknowledges this by saying, "Not many of you should become teachers, my brothers, for you know that we who teach will be judged with greater strictness" (James 3:1).

We need leaders with the moral fortitude to embrace this high bar of expectation, who can become leaders (with the Lord's enablement) in all sectors of the economy, and whose lives are examples of character, integrity, courage, resilience, honesty, and a vigorous work ethic.

Leadership is a privilege.

Leaders who think they are ten feet tall and bulletproof and charge ahead without regard for nurturing their spiritual life will not, I am sorry to say, end well.

Burned Out, Bummed Out, Bounced Out

The fictional heroes we love best show us their tender side. Even Superman was vulnerable. He had his kryptonite.

Real people in positions of leadership are human beings. They're not invulnerable. Chuck Swindoll noted that Elijah suffered from discouragement, despondency, and depression. Moses once became so blue and discouraged that he asked God to take his life. Jonah, after the revival in Nineveh, did the very same thing. Paul even "despaired for his life."[341]

Leaders are people too and dare not forget it.

General Eisenhower once said, "There are no victories at bargain prices." Sometimes what we do in leadership exacts a greater return from some of us than we are able to give. Leaders sometimes buckle. Some of them break.

Leaders who live life in the fast lane while ignoring basic principles of virtue, ethics, and public values will end their leadership days:

1. burned out—unable to go on; or
2. bummed out—disillusioned about leadership and life and thus ineffective; or
3. bounced out—forced to leave their position in the wake of a personal meltdown resulting in conduct unbecoming.

Burned out leaders reach a point where they can't go on. This is spiritual, emotional, and mental, but it can also be physical. Sometimes leaders convince themselves that "giving their all" is the path to success, but we're all human beings who need balance. The Cornerstone University Chancellor, Dr. W. Wilbert Welch, a man then in his 80s once told me, "Everything you do for the Lord, you do it in a body, and if you burn up your body, you can't serve the Lord." His caveat encouraged personal stewardship, rest and recreation, and exercise. He lived to his mid-90s.

Bummed out leaders may also reach a point where they can't go on, but this stems from inner turmoil rather than emotional or physical exhaustion. Leaders who've lost their vision, who are spiritually adrift, who've allowed challenges and circumstances rather than the Lord to define and limit their confidence can get so discouraged they don't know what to do or don't want to do it. Preventatives for being bummed out include fellowship with the Lord, family, friends, perhaps colleagues, retreats with a focus on rejuvenation, the perspective visiting other organizations or traveling usually provide, and a focus on others not oneself.

Elijah may have been burned out and bummed out but certainly the latter. He was so at wit's end he wanted to die. But the angel of the Lord told him, "Arise and eat, for the journey is too great for you" (1 Kings 19:7). There was no rebuke for being human, so to speak; there was a remedy that focused upon physical restoration, then spiritual.

Bounced out is when leaders reach a point where they can't go on because the owners or the board or some authority prevents them. Logically, leaders want to avoid being bounced out. It can happen for operational reasons, for sure, but often also for conduct unbecoming. Clearly, it's one thing to not reach operational or organizational goals and it's another thing entirely to behave in a manner that brings opprobrium or forced resignation.

One way leaders can protect themselves and their organizations from this dead-end street is accountability partners, a few trusted confidants, perhaps other leaders, who can check in from time to time, caring and sharing to help the leader avoid blind spots. Another way is what we've mentioned earlier, live a life of principle and biblical morality. "A little leaven leavens the whole lump," so beware (Gal. 5:9).

Leadership guru Noel Tichy once observed, "The scale, it seems to me, is tipped in the direction of more failed leaders than great ones."[342] As we've illustrated thus far, it's not difficult to find examples.

I think back to my early years in leadership. In 1989, Jim Bakker fell precipitously from the nationally known leader and televangelist of *The PTL Club* and Heritage USA to a convicted felon serving a forty-five-year prison sentence. In his later published biography, sadly, honestly, and I thought admirably entitled *I Was Wrong*, Bakker lists six ingredients leading to his personal and professional destruction:

1. No real accountability—"Yes men" on his board, a ministry personified by him
2. Belief in his own importance—adulation of the masses; believing his own press

3. Loss of the ministry goal and focus—working to develop/operate the organization becoming bigger than the ministry
4. Vulnerability to temptation—being overworked, stressed-out, spiritually debilitated, having poor personal stewardship
5. Failure to heed spiritual warning signs—joking about a struggling marriage or having affairs
6. Wrong theology—espousing a "prosperity gospel."[343]

In the mid-1990s, I remember discussing Jim Bakker's moral plunge with my leadership team at Cornerstone University. We noted with amazement how Bakker's team joked openly about spouses and marriage, and about having affairs, and that his team apparently made other indecent remarks about women.

Now our team members were not angels, including me, but we noted then that we had never under any circumstances—not once—made jokes about each other's marriages or spouses. We never hinted at or made thinly veiled comments that tiptoed on the edge of moral impropriety and certainly did not engage in repartee that went over this line. We simply did not conduct discussions of any kind that explored the idea of sexual adventurism or made chauvinist or sexual observations about women.

For us the contrast was instructive. Bakker and his team got into trouble because they allowed small steps that led to larger ones making light of sexual fantasies, evidencing carnal curiosity, or alluding to hedonistic behavior.

Song of Solomon 2:15 warns of "the little foxes that spoil the vineyards." Small, seemingly insignificant issues—bad habits, unchecked emotions, undisciplined thoughts and conversations including jokes and "innocent" flirtations, and temptations—can gradually undermine a leader's spiritual life, his or her relationships, and ultimately his or her leadership.

Wise leaders protect themselves and those whom they lead by laying "aside every weight, and sin which clings so closely, and . . . [running] with endurance the race that is set before us" (Heb. 12:1).

"The Modesto Manifesto"

In November 1948, after a crusade sermon in Modesto, California, a youthful Billy Graham was devastated to hear of the moral collapse of one of his fellow Christian evangelists. That evening, he directed his equally young staff—Grady Wilson, Cliff Barrows, and George Beverly Shea—to go to their rooms, pray, write down everything they could think of that caused men to fall in ministry, and then return to his room for a discussion. That humble but momentous occasion produced what staff members in the Billy Graham Evangelistic Association later came to call "The Modesto Manifesto."[344]

They discussed ethical pitfalls in ministry. From that November meeting, they crafted a set of four guiding principles covering finances, sexual conduct, local church relations, and publicity:

"We will avoid financial abuses, downplay offerings, and have financial accountability."
They would rely on local fundraising and a designated salary from their ministry—not love offerings at the event. This allowed Billy to answer reporters' questions honestly, that he had no idea how much money was given at a crusade, and no, he got a salary determined by the ministry board, not his hand in the till, so there was no incentive or thought given to preaching in a manner that might juice the giving.

"We will avoid any situation that would have even the appearance of compromise or suspicion of sexual immorality."
There would be no travel, meetings, or meals alone with any woman other than the man's own wife, to avoid even the appearance of impropriety.

As much as possible, they also booked their rooms alongside one another in hotel hallways, so comings and goings could be seen, thus reducing the possibility someone might sneak a woman into a room.

"We will partner with all who would cooperate in the public proclamation of the gospel. We will avoid any antichurch or anticlergy attitude, refusing to criticize local churches and pastors." They would always cooperate with local churches and avoid criticizing them publicly. This tended to reduce politics, favoritism, and jealousies that could undermine the crusade's spiritual impact, and it sought to engage as many as possible in the ministry's intent to share what "the Bible says."

"We will commit to integrity in our publicity and our reporting by avoiding the exaggeration of successes and attention to numbers." They would consistently provide media with honest attendance and publicity figures—no exaggeration.[345] This alone set the fledgling Billy Graham Evangelistic Association apart, for Christian leaders had long been known and still are for "elastically" or "evangelistically" stretching the numbers, so to speak.

Post–World War II, many corporations and trade associations began developing internal codes to address growing concerns about responsibility, integrity, and public trust. Rev. Billy Graham and his then rookie team were on the cutting edge of this movement. They set a high bar for themselves. Not an unreasonable bar, for what they listed simply details how to operationalize the Christian faith in life and work.

The Modesto Manifesto as the team later dubbed their standards is a noteworthy ministry milestone. What is more remarkable is the unassailable fact that in more than fifty years of ministry not one of this team violated their commitment to the Lord, their spouses, each other, or the people to whom they ministered. They were but men, not perfect, but by the grace of God they stewarded the leadership influence God gave them with unimpeachable integrity. They were blameless in word and deed, outstanding examples of what leadership can and should be.

LEADERSHIP LESSONS

1. Bad choices and bad character trump great ability and advantages.
2. Leaders are role models.
3. Failing is not fatal to leadership; falling frequently spells the end.
4. Man looks on the outward appearance, but the Lord looks at the heart.
5. Leaders who succeed learn how to fail forward.
6. Correction is open to anyone.
7. Submitting the heart is personally liberating and professionally energizing.
8. Leaders who fall make willful, sinful choices.
9. No one is invulnerable to sexual temptation or immorality.
10. Leadership is a privilege.

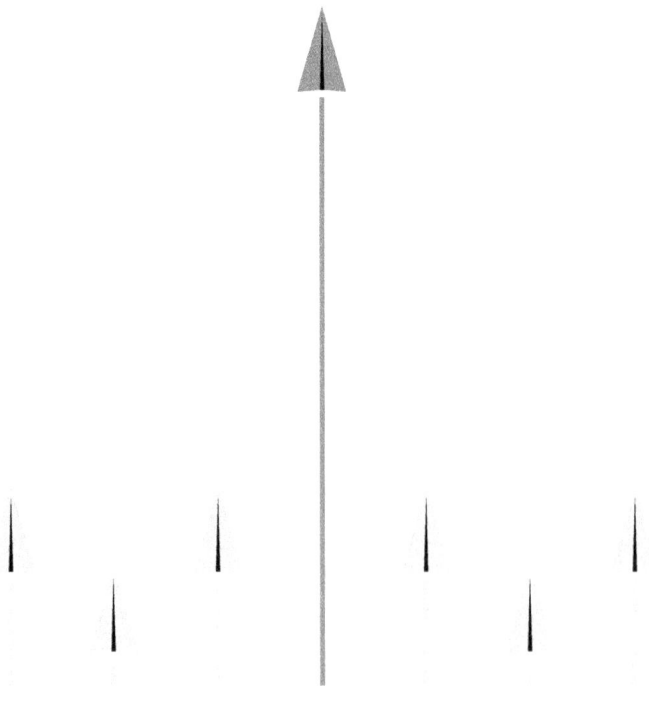

CHAPTER 11

CONTINUITY

What A Leader *Leaves Behind*

GIDEON

At the beginning of his life, Gideon looked at life from the bottom up. The most notable thing about Gideon was his obscurity and poverty. When an angel of the Lord—a theophany, a visible appearance of God to a human being—called him "mighty man of valor," Gideon wondered how this could be, for in his view his clan was the weakest in Manasseh, and he was the least in his family. Then the Lord said, "I will be with you" (Judg. 6:12, 15–16).

Gideon is well known for his seemingly faithless response in which he further tests his call by asking God for a sign. God obliges by first placing dew on a wool fleece but not the surrounding ground, then the next night placing dew on the ground while keeping the fleece dry (Judg. 6:36–40). Thereafter Gideon's army of just three hundred men followed the Lord to victories over the Midianite oppressors of God's people.

Later in life, Gideon became a judge, a leader whose initial direction steered Israel away from idols and whose military triumphs granted the land forty years of peace. He even turned down the people's offer to make him a king, saying, "I will not rule over you, and my son will not rule over you; the Lord will rule over you" (Judg. 8:23).

But Gideon allowed peace and prosperity to weaken him. He did not continue resisting idols, even making one himself from the gold spoils of war given to him by the people. So, the Israelites, including Gideon's family, spiritually prostituted themselves once again by worshiping false gods (Judg. 8:22–35).

Gideon's legacy is mixed. Amazingly, he's cited in Hebrews 11 for his faith, but his family and his people departed from honoring God while Gideon still lived. Once he died, the nation's spiritual decline was steep and rapid. Adding insult to injury, the people mistreated Gideon's family because they failed to remember the good things Gideon had done (Judg. 8:33–35).

Leaders Always Leave

We are all short-term stewards. We do not live forever, nor of course do we serve in leadership forever. Time marches on and we move on too, through promotion, transfer, downsizing, resignation, termination, retirement, or death.

No leader leads forever. Every leader will eventually be replaced and succeeded.

> **No leader leads forever.**

Some 1,181 leaders are named in Bible—1,073 in the Old Testament, 108 in the New Testament. Another 13,000 leaders are referenced without a name. But of all the named Bible leaders only one in three finished well.[346]

Part of being an effective, accomplished leader who finishes well is to think about what the organization would look like and how it would function without you. This is not morbid. It's just good stewardship, like caring for wills and family trusts to better protect your family when the time comes that God calls you home.

More than one organization, including especially those blessed with outstanding leaders, have found themselves in disarray after the leader was suddenly removed from the scene, because he or she had not developed the leadership capacities of reporting staff members. It's next man up, or in today's terms when women are key players too, next person up. Who will be the one who now leads the organization to boldly go where no one has gone before?

"The untimely death in 1997 of Coca-Cola Enterprises. CEO Roberto Goizueta reminded the world that no complex organization can afford to rely too heavily on a single leader, however gifted or charismatic. . . . In famed investor Warren Buffett's view, Goizueta's greatest legacy is the way he so carefully selected and then nurtured the future leadership of the company."[347]

Leaders who prepare the organization to thrive without them are remembered as selfless, perhaps great leaders. They create and communicate the vision, meaning they instill purpose, and build a culture that strives toward that vision and allows young, up-and-coming leaders to learn, contribute, and grow. So "in the best companies, the purpose continues even when the leadership changes, as it inevitably must."[348]

John C. Maxwell said of leaders (both men and women), "Success comes when he empowers followers to do great things *with* him. Significance comes when he develops leaders to do great things *for* him. But a legacy is created only when a person puts his organization into a position to do great things *without* him."[349]

Leaders Leave Legacies

Legacies are an imprint of the leader's vision. Something lasts. What is it?

In the movie, *Gladiator*, Maximus Decimus Meridius, commander of the Armies of the North, told his troops just before they ventured into battle, "What you do in life echoes in eternity." He was correct. But we could also say, "What you do in life echoes later in life."

Pepsico's executive development program asked executives not how high they wanted to rise but what legacy they would leave at the end of their careers.[350]

Legacies are an imprint of the leader's vision.

The final test of leadership is legacy, what a leader leaves behind. Joshua left Israel with an unparalleled record of God's fulfilled promises. As importantly, he left a generation of elders who served the Lord all the days of Joshua and all their days after Joshua died (Josh. 24:31; Judg. 2:7).

John C. Maxwell quoted a friend, "'Success is not measured by what you're leaving to, but by what you are leaving behind.' When all is said and done, your ability as a leader will not be judged by what you achieved personally or even by what your team accomplished during your tenure. You will be judged by how well your people and your organization did after you were gone. You will be gauged by the law of legacy, and your lasting value will be measured by succession."[351]

A leader's impact on the organization is often better understood after he or she leaves office than when the leader is in office. While Joshua left behind a body of elders capable of leading, these elders who outlived Joshua failed to develop the next generation of godly leaders. As a result, Israel suffered grievous spiritual and political decline.

The Bible tells us no one lives to himself or dies to himself. And whether we live or die we influence people around us and we belong to the Lord (Rom. 14:7–8). What we are inside, in our hearts, is our character. What we live before others day by day becomes our reputation. And our reputation, lived out over time, becomes our legacy.

The apostle Paul left spiritual legacies wherever he traveled. In one of his letters, Paul points out to the believers in Corinth that *they* were the *result* of his ministry.

"And you show that you are a letter from Christ delivered by us, written not with ink but with the Spirit of the living God, not on tablets of stone but on tablets of human hearts" (2 Cor. 3:3).

When Paul was in Corinth, he lived for the Lord and led others to Jesus Christ. When his ministry took him elsewhere, Paul left behind Christian people as living letters, living legacies of his testimony for Christ. Paul's life as "Paul" was as spiritually positive as his earlier life as "Saul" had been spiritually negative. He created spiritual legacies.

My family and I have lived in four states. In each location I've left behind friends, acquaintances, and impressions. I can go back, but I can never relive those periods of my life. For good or for ill, I've created a legacy in each place. If my name ever comes up, the only thing those old friends have is a recollection of my attitude and behavior *while I was with them*. My legacy there is established, permanently.

You and I are creating legacies right now with our families and our associates. Every day, we're influencing someone in a spiritually productive or unproductive way. God wants us to live for him.

Paul's ministry can be summarized with the word "results." In the providence of God and with the Spirit's help, Paul got results. With the passage of time his results became legacies. The best thing about Paul's legacies is that they were not buildings or empires or things but people—living, breathing legacies that could multiply his ministry to others for decades, even generations, to come.

Each time I read 2 Corinthians 3:1–3 I think of my Grandpa Lewis Davis, a man nearly everyone called "Bones" all his life. Grandpa lived what some might call a simple, working man's life. He did not collect great achievements or acclaim. What he did was touch peoples' lives. He was a man with an eighth-grade education who could and did read. He read his Bible, and he read organic gardening magazines. People used to joke about which flourished more, his spiritual life or his gardens. From the Word of God, Grandpa developed a wisdom strangely rare in this day of information technology, access to higher education, and notable scientific advancement.

When Grandpa Davis's church turned toward theological liberalism, he helped start and lead a Bible-believing church across town. Years later, that church became my home church, and it is still thriving today. Grandpa remained faithful in Christian service, not only as a deacon but also as an untrained song leader who began church services with "Greetings in the name of our Lord and Savior Jesus Christ." His favorite hymn was "Saved, Saved, Saved," and I can remember his tenor voice singing out with enthusiasm while I tried to match him and learn to sing bass.

People wanted to meet Bones Davis. Even more, they wanted to sit on his big back porch swing and talk to him about their lives. He counseled scores of people in this way, including me, and he always had something meaningful to say. He was known for his sense of humor, but that's not why people sought him out when they faced decisions or trials. What he gave them was a working knowledge of the Bible—real application to everyday life, something else that is all too rare today.

Through these people Grandpa multiplied his life's values. He, like the apostle Paul two thousand years before, helped people open their hearts to the Spirit of God's desire to write God's Word upon their hearts. By the grace of God, Grandpa created living letters of testimony, living legacies. Most, like me, continue that living legacy today.

Leaders leave legacies, one kind or another. Creating living legacies is what I believe a leader's life should be about. All of us touch lives. Typically, leaders touch even more lives than most, so they have greater opportunity and responsibility.

Creating living legacies is what a leader's life should be about.

By *being* living letters, leaders can be used of God to *create* living letters. Paul did. Grandpa did. We can too.

Sacred Cows

Sacred cows are a kind of "animal," so to speak, with which leaders coming and going need to become familiar.

Sacred cows are an organizational phenomenon that leaders can find when they arrive for their new assignment, and they can be something leaders leave behind as an unwanted legacy for their successors.

Sacred cows come in many forms but what they hold in common is their ability to hang on, be protected, or somehow attain an untouchable status in the organization. This is especially challenging when the sacred cow is not a policy or practice but a person: a star performer with toxic behavior, some notable's relative who marks time but does not produce, a "nice person" who has been there from the beginning (so long he or she is by far the senior employee, beloved, drawing a salary, but no longer contributing), or a staff member who operates by his or her own rules and flaunts the behavior (someone who seems to possess sacred cow status but no one really knows why).[352]

When I was a young academic vice president I met my first sacred cows. One was a dear lady who had served the longtime former president and now the new president who had recruited and appointed me. She was beloved but it didn't take long to realize the staff knew she was not able to keep up and that at times she was simply not able to provide the administrative support the president's office required. I wondered about this until I learned that she knew all the trustees and, out of a sense of politics and genuine compassion, the new president was reluctant to make the hard decision. He could be forgiven or admired for his compassion, but the problem was, her inability to fulfill her assignment negatively affected how people viewed his administration and therefore his leadership credibility.

The other sacred cow was a longtime finance vice president, at my positions' rank in the organization chart but exercising far and away more authority, beyond typical business office boundaries, simply because he'd always done it that way. Again, the new president knew this but had not taken steps to rectify this situation because the finance vice president seemed too difficult to replace. Not long into my assignment as the academic vice president, I discovered one of my administrative decisions had been countermanded down the hall. Since I'd previously discussed a similar matter with the finance vice president to no avail, I took this one to the president, saying, "If the finance vice president is going to act as executive vice president, then we need to announce it, and if that's not what you want, then would you please clarify this with me and him." The president to his credit stepped in to correct this circumstance, then over the next few months helped this gentleman move into his long-talked-about-retirement. It seemed to me that while the president knew what to do and had the authority to do it, what he needed was moral support, which I inadvertently provided.

"Poor" or "bad" employees, for example someone who shirks his or her duties or a person who steals or lies, create human resources problems that are relatively easy to solve. The leader who makes the hard decision in these instances will be well regarded. Staff will "rise up and call you blessed," or something like that, or at least they'll usually be grateful the leader took care of a problem they recognized affected them and the organization.

On the other hand, people, especially "good people" like the two examples I provided, create human resources problems that can be more challenging to administer. This is particularly the case if the individuals have achieved sacred cow status. "Nice" people—they love their spouses, they don't kick their dog—usually have a lot of friends in the organization even if they are no longer contributing or for some other reason are not supporting the vision.

One of the reasons they are sacred cows is no one wants to make a decision that causes them discomfort. But leaders, new or departing, who administer these challenges with professionalism and aplomb can reinforce the vision even as they help people move on. One key to successfully transitioning longtime sacred cows, or any staff member for that matter, is to treat them with dignity. They can always be thanked for their service, given proper severance, and wished the best in their future endeavors.

Sacred cows may also be traditions and rituals that no longer align with the vision, pet projects or legacy initiatives, or physical assets no one uses—"entire departments justified by tradition, outdated processes, compensation structures defended as 'industry standard,' and cultural norms considered core identity."[353]

"Sacred cows in the workplace can hinder innovation and growth."[354] So, one thing leaders can't do is ignore them. New leaders need to deal with them, and doing so relatively soon during the leaders' honeymoon period may be easier than later. Leaders planning their departure can do their organization and their successor an enormous favor by ushering the sacred cow out the door before the leader rides off into the sunset.

Ignoring sacred cows can create a culture of complacency, a sense within the organization that favoritism means more than fairness or politics means more than productivity. Ignoring sacred cows can mean money is expended for "we've always done it that way" rather than innovation or a key new hire.

> **Ignoring sacred cows can create a culture of complacency.**

Dealing with sacred cows can create leadership capital. "Your willingness to identify and eliminate your most sacred cow often determines whether your change initiative succeeds or joins the graveyard of expensive failures. As Steve Jobs said, 'We run Apple like a startup. We always let ideas win arguments, not hierarchies. Otherwise, your best employees won't stay. Collaboration, discipline and trust are critical.'"[355]

Frame changes with sacred cows as alignment with values and mission, not as rejection of them or the past. Keep looking to the future.

Closeted Skeletons

When people talk about an organization having "skeletons in the closet," they usually mean hidden facts, past actions, or ongoing practices that—if exposed—could damage its reputation, lead to legal trouble, or erode trust. Skeletons in the closet can be cover-ups, unethical or illegal action hidden in plain sight, or a collection of years of misconduct by one leader.

Skeletons in the closet can be relatively minor, like a forgotten unfinished initiative, or quite serious, like a founders' misconduct (racism, abuse, fraud, sexual misdeeds), financial irregularities, mismanagement, or aberrations (hidden debts, tax evasion, misuse or embezzlement of funds, undisclosed conflicts of interest or self-dealing), misleading practices (falsified reports, metrics, or research to attract funding or customers, concealing product flaws or safety hazards), systemic sexual harassment, bullying, or discrimination, poor treatment of whistleblowers, research or testing done unethically, pending legal issues, including bribery or corruption, secret settlements to hide wrongdoings, like nondisclosure agreements to silence victims or former employees, or examples ad infinitum.

These skeletons can remain hidden for years—or even decades—until investigative journalism, whistleblowers, lawsuits, audits, new personnel. or new leaders bring them to light. Current staff may not know about closeted skeletons, but then again, they often do and have kept their head down in a culture of fear or silence.

Examples of organizations trying to hide skeletons in a closet are many: Enron perpetrated massive accounting fraud hiding debt and inflating profits, leading to its collapse in 2001.

Lehman Brothers used "Repo 105" accounting tricks to temporarily hide billions in debt before the 2008 financial crisis.

WorldCom falsely inflated assets by $11 billion, leading to one of the largest bankruptcies in US history.

Volkswagen's "Dieselgate" resulted when the company installed software to cheat emissions tests while marketing cars as environmentally friendly.

Theranos promised revolutionary blood testing technology that didn't work; data and demos were faked.

Big Tobacco knew of the addictive and harmful effects of smoking but denied or suppressed the evidence for decades.

Fox News suffered because leaders did not deal wisely with multiple high profile sexual harassment scandals involving company executives and media stars, some scandals covered up with large settlements and nondisclosure agreements.

Uber perpetuated a culture of sexism and bullying under former CEO Travis Kalanick, practices which came to light through employee complaints.

One of the worst: the Tuskegee Syphilis Study sponsored by the federal government, 1932–1972, observed Black men with syphilis but unethically denied them treatment to study disease progression.

The American Red Cross was strongly criticized for mismanaging donations after major disasters (e.g., Haiti earthquake 2010), including unclear accounting for hundreds of millions of dollars.[356]

Skeletons in the closet can involve more than money, like sexual abuse and cover-ups.

The Southern Baptist Convention is a Christian denomination, the largest Baptist and Protestant body, and the second-largest

Christian body in the United States. In 2019, several convention churches were subject to widespread claims of sex abuse including accusations of rape, cover-ups, and gross mistreatment of women seeking justice. An independent investigation in 2022 revealed that SBC leaders kept a secret list (they tried to hide skeletons in a closet) of over seven hundred abusive ministers and workers while publicly denying problems and often intimidating victims.[357]

The Southern Baptist Convention, an association of 46,876 churches, has declined by over 1,500 churches since the sex scandals broke. But with this many churches operating independently, it remains a strong organization.[358]

Beginning in the 1990s, the Boy Scouts of America, long highly regarded and admired, fell far from grace when it was alleged the Scouts had kept "perversion files" for decades, documenting sexual abuse allegations against scout leaders without reporting to authorities, eventually leading to bankruptcy and thousands of lawsuits. In February 2025, the Boy Scouts of America officially changed its name to Scouting America to reflect its commitment to inclusivity. This move has been praised by some as a positive step toward a more diverse and welcoming organization but criticized by others who view it as a departure from traditional values.[359]

The Boy Scouts of America, new name and all, has suffered mightily from its sex scandals, declining in membership from its peak of 4.8 million in the 1970s to around 1 million in 2024. And with the addition of LGBTQ scouts and leaders and an influence of woke policies, Scouting America has lost its vision as well as its reputation.[360]

Leaders who allow skeletons to develop and hide them in a closet are duping the public, maybe destroying their organizations, and damaging their own reputations and legacies. Nothing good is served by hiding skeletons in a closet.

Nothing good is served by hiding skeletons in a closet.

Effective and ethical leaders do not allow skeletons in the closet, and when they are discovered, such leaders take action to expose, examine, and eradicate them. But remember, like sacred cows, sometimes closeted skeletons are there because personnel put them there and would just as soon keep them in the closet. Employee or even board resistance might result when the leader opens the closet.

But good stewardship of the organization and its mission demand a reckoning. Like with anything dead, it's best to proceed in a dignified manner and dispose of the matter properly.

New leaders should keep their antennae up looking for closeted skeletons, not as a matter of suspicion regarding those who've been in charge but simply as best practice. Identify closeted skeletons early, exhume them, then give them a transparent, ethical, and official burial.

And departing leaders concerned for their legacies don't leave closeted skeletons behind for their successors.

Historic Preservation—Structure

Organizations are sometimes burdened by structures that are no longer nimble, aren't set up to engage the now changed and current marketplace, don't enable employees to grow or contribute their best, or don't allow for new products or services the organization could develop and provide.

These structures might be sacred cows but can just as easily be historic frameworks that simply "always have been" and no one's had the "gumption," as my dad used to say, to change them.

One such structure is the organizational culture the leader finds upon arrival. "Organizational culture is the shared values, beliefs, behaviors, and norms that guide people's actions and decisions within a company."[361]

"Organizational cultures are created in part by leaders, and one of the most decisive functions of leadership is the creation, the

management, and sometimes even the destruction of culture."³⁶²
Why? Because bad cultures typically do not permit the organization to move forward and thrive.

This is both a challenge and an opportunity for new leaders. Changing the culture is the quickest way to get the organization moving toward the leader's vision.

Sometimes moribund organizational cultures just need new juice, something dynamic new leaders can provide. Point to the vision, encourage, and go.

> **Changing the culture is the quickest way to get the organization moving toward the leader's vision.**

Or sometimes cultures are out of sync with what the organization now needs to do or be to survive and thrive. Earlier in this book I mentioned the "4 Cs" speech I developed and shared what seemed like a few thousand times when I first arrived at Grand Rapids Baptist College and Seminary (GRBC&S). This speech embodied culture change. Remember, it focused on what I wanted listeners to understand: we were a Christian College, Conservative, Comprehensive. The "4 Cs" provided a snapshot of what our culture change would look like and where we were going—transforming, I hoped, from a fundamentalist liberal arts college and seminary to an evangelical Christian university.

The old organizational culture was rooted in a Bible college model and mentality. Nothing wrong with this, but that is not what the college was becoming or aspired to be. Insofar as high school students thought GRBC&S was "just a Bible college," many of them with liberal arts and professional studies goals did not consider GRBC&S an institution where they might enroll.

The old culture emphasized rules whereas the new culture emphasized spiritual discernment and critical thinking. The old culture was inward looking while the new culture wished to be outward looking. The old culture presented as "that little college on the East Beltline that wants to be left alone, and if you bother us, we'll bite you." The new culture wanted to proactively engage the world with a dynamic Christian worldview.

Not long after GRBC&S changed its name to Cornerstone University in 1999, the university marketing department contracted a local firm to publish billboards around the city. The billboards featured a beautiful, six-inch corn sprout standing alone in a furrowed brown dirt field. The caption read "Think big. . . . Think bigger. Cornerstone University." That campaign, simple though it was, got more reaction than any other thing we did, and I referenced it in presentations and speeches for some time thereafter. It helped convey that not only did the institution change its name, but a new wind was blowing, a new culture, and everything about the public response was positive.

Changing an organizational culture for the right reasons and in the right way is one of the more powerful early-on actions a new leader can take. Leaving behind a healthy, dynamic, open, forward-thinking, vision-focused organizational culture is one of the best legacies a departing leader can provide his or her successor. Strong organizational cultures that allow personnel to contribute ideas and productivity, know they are valued, and experience success is a gift that keeps on giving long after a leader departs.

Lame Ducks

To be, or not to be, or how to avoid being a lame duck. I've experienced this phenomenon a couple of times in my career. One of the things I've learned is that despite my intention to be otherwise (that is, I planned to keep working proactively and to not become a lame duck) staff members *make you* a lame duck. Whether a departing leader becomes a lame duck is more the personnel's determination than the leader's decision.

Now it is possible to do somethings that help reduce the time and the reality of becoming a lame duck:

- Clarify your intentions early, but not "too early." In my experience, both my key transitions were announced—at board request—a year in advance to the board and several months in advance to personnel. If I had it to do over again, I would ask the board to allow me to make this known maybe three months in advance, not six or more.
- Act like you're staying even when you're not. I don't mean lie or misrepresent. I'm referring to how you behave. Set expectations: "I will lead fully until the final day." This is still conditioned by personnel response, but you can stay active, relevant, and forward-looking until your very last day. Influence lasts longer than a title.
- Identify two to three key initiatives you will personally champion until your departure. Frame your legacy in terms of what will continue, not what ends. Stay engaged in results.
- Resolve lingering or politically sensitive issues your successor shouldn't inherit. Remember, deal transparently with sacred cows and skeletons in the closet.
- As appropriate, publicly recognize and empower high-potential individuals. But avoid overanointing a "favorite" successor so as not to tie the hands of the next leader.
- Tell the story of continuity, optimism, and tomorrow, not just the leader's departure.
- Champion the next leader even before his or her name is known and especially after the name is announced. Be supportive and gracious whenever you refer to or interact with the new leader. As needed or desired, help the new leader with his or her onboarding.
- Let everyone engaged with the organization know, "I'm not winding down—I'm winding forward."

Leadership transitions that are planned well, supported by the departing leader, and go well help remove the lame duck enigma.

Leadership Succession

"The king is dead. Long live the king!"

Beginning in fifteenth-century monarchies, this proclamation conveyed continuity and stability amid generational change. A traditional statement of fact, it is also a symbolic act solidifying the transition of power.[363]

All leaders are temporary. Every reign comes to an end. Leadership is borrowed, not owned, and time spares no leader. Or as basketball great Charles Barkley puts it, "Father time is undefeated."

So, the reality of changing leaders is not the problem. But changing leaders *badly* can destroy an organization. In fact, poor leaders and poor leadership transitions can ruin or even dismantle in a short time what took years to build.

What happens in and to your organization after you leave matters. It's a responsibility departing leaders should own. "Some of the world's leaders experienced great success, but because they failed miserably at succession, their life accomplishments collapsed shortly after their departure."[364]

The best and most successful leaders prepare for succession. "Max Dupree, author of *Leadership Is an Art*, declared, 'Succession is one of the key responsibilities of leadership.' Yet of all the laws of leadership, the law of legacy is the one that the fewest leaders seem to learn."[365]

"One of the biggest failings of any institution is the failure to develop bench strength. The lack of at least one strong internal candidate for succession is a clear sign of leadership failure. A leader who doesn't prepare for the future has flunked an essential test of leadership."[366]

Remember what we said earlier, think about what the organization will look like, and what you hope it will look like without you.

"At a convention of the National Association of Evangelicals, Ted Engstrom told an assembly of pastors and CEOs that 'one of the most important legacies a leader can give or leave the institution is a smooth transition in leadership where the organizational alliance can be quickly and readily given to the new leader.'"[367]

Think about what the organization will look like without you.

The old monarchies often worked with a built-in leadership transition process. Whenever father stepped aside, son, sometimes daughter, stepped in. It was simple . . . when it worked. But innumerable examples of palace intrigue, family infighting, power struggles, feuds, bloodline conflict, and protracted civil wars can be cited as examples of what happens when the human heart lusts for power. Forms of these breakdowns in leadership transition can happen in any organization.

The last thing a departing leader should want is a succession crisis that damages his or her organization, business, company, or ministry. Admittedly, especially in nonprofit organizations, the outgoing leader does not typically possess the authority or opportunity to direct succession, but the departing leader can still lay groundwork, assisting key players in preparing a succession plan and encouraging engagement of the right stakeholders in a professional and trusted process.

Leadership transition is a matter of stewardship. Boards or ownership groups that develop a leadership contingency and succession plan, a kind of "Leader's Will," greatly increase the chances of a smooth and successful leadership transition.

The longer the departing leader has held his or her position, the more important it is to prepare the organization for leadership transition. In long tenure leadership situations, it is especially important for leadership transition to be friendly, not hostile, prudently quick, not painfully long. Leaders "finish well" when they set aside their egos and invest their reputations into the fiber of the organization.

> **Leadership transition is a matter of stewardship.**

King David is a fine example. He made abundant preparations for the building of a magnificent temple that he never saw and that he charged Solomon to build for God. David was a man after God's own heart partly because he thought about how his peoples' spiritual needs would be met even long after he was gone.

So, how does the former leader and the organization prepare for transition? Most of us acknowledge that *who* we choose as the new leader can make or break our organization. But *how* we choose a new leader is also important. The *process* can either hinder or help the new *person*.

Formal search processes for new leaders are virtually inevitable and almost always desirable. Organizations do not always enjoy the comfort of an in-house "heir apparent," and even if they do, it is better for the "heir" and the organization if he or she wins or earns the new position rather than it being granted outright. A search helps validate the choice. Besides, a search may make it evident that an assumed heir is not so logical or capable after all. Remember Samuel? He wanted to choose several of Jesse's sons as the "logical" next king, but God said to keep searching. Young David was at first glance a very unlikely leader.

One of the best ways to prepare an organization for leadership transition is to develop potential leaders who can later be considered in the search. "Up-and-comers" should be targeted for mentoring, role modeling, networking, and special assignment opportunities. Failure to develop young staff can drive away a whole generation of prospective leaders, crippling the organization for years to come. Organizations are strengthened by plans that proactively identify and support leadership talent from all walks of life.

The apostle Paul is probably the best biblical example of a leader who mentored his successors: Timothy, Mark, Silas, Barnabas. Paul recognized, particularly in Timothy, not a rival but a future leader who would multiply the work of Paul's heart and life. The Scripture also offers a few examples where mentoring apparently did not take place. Gideon, Eli, and Samuel, great leaders for God, all failed to develop their sons' ability to serve the Lord.

Finally, remember that leadership transition is not successfully finished when the new leader is appointed. Some means of formal public endorsement is essential. If the former leader is a long-serving, popular individual, it is especially important that the outgoing leader bestows a public blessing. The organization's constituency must know that the mantle of leadership has been passed. Moses laid hands on Joshua. Elijah mentored and mantled Elisha.

Organizations should not underestimate the value of ritualized transfer of power. Ceremony creates credibility for the new leader. Every four years, the United States spends several million dollars to create an elaborate public spectacle featuring the newly elected president. While some instances of extravagance might be identified, the importance of the occasion is nevertheless indisputable, especially after a hard-fought, close race. Ceremony jump-starts a leader's service with conferred credibility, and credibility is one of a leader's (and therefore the organization's) most precious possessions.

> **Ceremony creates credibility for the new leader.**

So now the new leader is in place. Now what?

Leadership transition works best when leaders know when to leave. Perhaps ironically, an organization's potential for long-term viability is increased when it is affirmed that no one is irreplaceable.

It's the old maxim: put your finger in a bucket of water, remove your finger, and the hole fills immediately. The leadership position you held will be filled. Let's say it again. No one is irreplaceable. This includes founders, survivors, beloved leaders, "GOATs," everyone.

Lame duck leaders or "Emperors who have no clothes" are deadly to an organization's image, effectiveness, and health. Sometimes leaders stay too long because they've fallen victim to a human inclination General Colin Powell warned us about, "Never let your ego get so close to your position that when your position goes, your ego goes with it."[368]

King Saul is an illustration of a threatened leader who was mandated by God via Samuel to relinquish his throne. Rather than recognize his spiritual failings and step aside, Saul fought a protracted battle resulting in the loss of physical resources and human life. Saul's egoistic reaction hurt Israel morally, economically, militarily, and more.

In nonprofit or profit settings, boards or ownership groups must take responsibility. Weak boards produce weak organizations and nowhere is this more quickly evident than instances wherein departing leaders are permitted or sometimes begged to stay too long.

Or sometimes departing leaders just can't let go and don't depart. I've watched this sad development at least three times in my career, a leader helped build the organization, but then when it came time to, in these cases, retire, the leader couldn't let go. He hung around or demanded an office on-site or the board appointed him a trustee, etc.

In one case, the former leader was a longtime respected pastor who'd helped build a Christian college, yet when the board appointed a new president, the former president did not leave. I knew the new president, and I know the pain he experienced that was no fault of his own. On at least two occasions, the former president publicly countermanded the current president's statements. The former president's ill-advised attitudes and actions literally divided the constituency. In a matter of a year or so the former president helped tear down an institution he'd worked hard to build for forty years. The board was apparently too weak to protect the organization. The end of the story is that the college declined and closed.

In the other two instances, former nonprofit organization leaders did not leave after a new president was appointed, and worse, attempted to lure donors to support their new enterprises at the expense of the organization they had led. This is what's called "stealing sheep." It is highly unethical and a horrible testimony. Again, these now older, former leaders helped tear down ministries they had previously worked decades to build. Why? One cannot read hearts, but a good guess would be ego and a failure to remember the ministry belonged to the Lord, not them. Both destructive efforts continued for a time but eventually ended in the collapse of one of the ministries and bitter animosity in the other.

Another experience bears repeating. I worked with an associate who was an excellent leader, capable, trusted, and accomplished in what he did. Then it came time to retire, and he struggled. This emotional calculus regarding impending retirement is not rare but in this gentleman's case it caused him considerable anxiety and a kind of depression. I met with him in my office, and we discussed pending plans. Finally, he said to me, "You don't understand. I *am* the (and he named his title)." In other words, in his mind, he and his position were inseparable. His identity was his position. I said, "Okay, but you are also a husband, father, grandfather, highly respected speaker, theologian, philosopher, and sought-after counselor. All this can continue after you retire, and the Lord will open new doors for you." Our discussion continued from there, but it took him a while to disassociate his identity from his professional assignment.

This can happen to any leader. If we love what God has given us to do, it's easy to think of ourselves as "that's who I am." But God does not see titles and positions or accomplishments when he looks at us. Yes, he blesses our stewardship of these endeavors, but like King David, God wants us to be a man or woman after his heart. God is God in our leadership, and God is God in our after-leadership.

Sometimes boards, which consist of people after all, do not always make the best decisions. Boards sometimes let compassion overrule stewardship. However, boards that truly understand biblical stewardship will never be forced to choose between the current leader and the organization. Biblical stewardship advances God's priorities to everyone's benefit.

Allowing—at times by the board's urging—an outgoing leader to serve on the organization's board is problematic. Shepherding a smooth leadership transition reinforces continuity. But leadership transition is generally more successful when it is complete, not partial. Former leaders symbolize and sometimes actively continue to promote an earlier corporate culture. Change, progress, or "just doing things differently," are more challenging if the former leader is on board.

There are other less problematic ways former leaders can support their former organizations besides serving on the board. Former leaders should never publicly criticize the new leader's decisions or directions but can take opportunities to affirm, praise, and otherwise cheerlead for the organization, and as appropriate the new leader too. Former leaders can attend public events, not on the platform but as participants. As invited, former leaders can make themselves available privately to the new leader for whatever conversation the new leader wishes. Former leaders can privately send periodic congratulations or encouragement or praying-for-you or stand-firm notes to the new leader.

One last thought on former leaders leaving. I can say from experience that it is emotionally easier to leave the right way at the right time than it is to hang around and become a nuisance. A clean and total break does not mean that you don't care about the organization that previously occupied so much of your life and thoughts, or that you aren't interested in your friends back there. It just means that "letting go" can be emotionally liberating.

> **Better for a former leader to lead and leave than to lead and grieve.**

I agree with John Maxwell: "When it's a leader's time to leave the organization, he has got to be willing to walk away and let his successor do his own thing. Meddling only hurts him and the organization."[369]

So, if you are the departing leader, take a page from President George Washington's book, who after two terms, departed the presidency in 1797 and returned home to Mount Vernon. When you leave, *leave*.

LEADERSHIP LESSONS

1. No leader leads forever.
2. Legacies are an imprint of the leader's vision.
3. Creating living legacies is what a leader's life should be about.
4. Ignoring sacred cows can create a culture of complacency.
5. Nothing good is served by hiding skeletons in a closet.
6. Changing the culture is the quickest way to get the organization moving toward the leader's vision.
7. Think about what the organization will look like without you.
8. Leadership transition is a matter of stewardship.
9. Ceremony creates credibility for the new leader.
10. Better for a former leader to lead and leave than to lead and grieve.

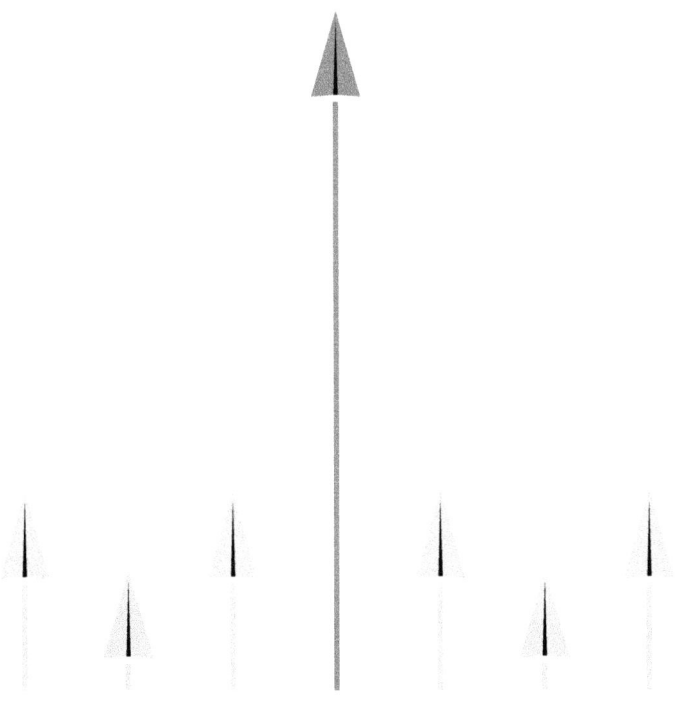

CHAPTER 12

CONCLUSION

Why Becoming A Leader Is Not *Option* But *Opportunity*

QUEEN ESTHER

Esther is the central figure in an Old Testament story of power, beauty, "ethnic cleansing," and courage. In a book in which God's name is never mentioned, the sovereignty of God is writ large.

Beginning life as an orphaned Jew in exile whose name is Hadassah, she becomes Queen Esther, one of the most significant women in Old Testament Israelite history. The turning point in her life was not her selection as queen but her decision to trust God in risking everything for her people.

Esther was a Jew, an orphan, a refugee, a woman, and poor. She was the most unlikely of leaders. But "Esther didn't allow her limits to limit her."[370]

Esther was in the right place at the right time, and she courageously responded to a divinely appointed opportunity to lead, saying, "I will go to the king, though it is against the law, and if I perish, I perish" (Est. 3:16).

Through two banquets with her husband, the king, and with Haman, the enemy of her people, Esther demonstrated courage, planning, patience, political skill, and wisdom. Later, after the king had learned of Haman's treachery against the Jews, Esther displayed organizational skills and an understanding of the legal landscape of her day. She worked with the king to assure his decrees protecting the Jews were not simply implemented during his lifetime but were written in the law of the Medes and the Persians. In other words, her leadership created a legacy. She became one of the Jewish peoples' greatest heroines.[371]

Esther's greatest asset was not her exceptional beauty, nor was it her love for her people or even her courage. It was her faith in the Almighty God. She demonstrated that outstanding leaders lead even when afraid, and that leaders can be effective through influence and collaboration rather than solely through authority.

"Esther's story is a reminder that there's no one image of a leader. If a leader is someone who effects change, then a lot of people have the ability to be leaders."[372]

Esther will be remembered with the highest esteem as an unlikely leader who, when her opportunity came, stepped up "for such a time as this" (Est. 4:14).

Leadership Maxims

Throughout this book I've been saying that anyone can be a leader. No matter how unlikely it may seem, you can learn to lead. You can stand up and step up, just like Esther, when the Lord gives you opportunity.

You can lead for such a time as this.

"Great leaders, the research shows, are made as they gradually acquire, in the course of their lives and careers, the competencies that make them so effective. The competencies can be learned by any leader at any point. The challenge of mastering leadership is a skill like any other, such as improving your golf game or learning to play slide guitar. Anyone who has the will and motivation can get better at leading, once he understands the steps."[373]

So, I will say it again. Anyone reading this book can become a leader. It only takes a willing heart, a teachable spirit, and an opportunity that God provides.

We need leaders who stand for something, leaders who try, who do, who take risks, who inspire others to aspire. Yet a crisis of leadership exists today in both church and culture. Our need for leaders is never ending, and demand exceeds supply. To steward this nation and our families in a way that allows both to flourish, America needs principled leaders, men and women, who use opportunity and influence wisely.

> **We need leaders who stand for something, leaders who try, who do, who take risks, who inspire others to aspire.**

The Bible is filled with stories of everyday people who learned to lead for the Lord. I've called them "God's unlikely leaders." If you are not already a leader, you can become one of these unlikely leaders. No matter your background you can learn to lead by making a choice to do so.

"Former Coca-Cola CEO Muhtar Kent described it this way: 'I learned that everyone has the innate capacity to lead. Leadership isn't just a trait found at the very top of an organization. I have seen truly extraordinary leadership at all levels of our organization and from all types of people.'"[374]

Years ago, I noticed what seemed to be a plethora of books published with the word "coping" in their titles. Most of these books at the time were aimed at women, specifically Christian women, so I asked my wife, why are so many authors encouraging women to "cope"? Is this the scope of their dreams or the reach of their goals? Is "coping," sort of "muddling through" in life, the best these women can experience?

My wife noted that a kind of malaise existed in the Christian church at the time, particularly among women who seemed overwhelmed by modern life's circumstances. These "coping" books were speaking into this context, trying to teach women how to get along. But she believed Christian women who put their faith in the power and presence of God should and could aspire not to "coping" but to being "more than conquerors through him who loved us" (Rom. 8:37; see vv. 31–39).

My wife believed this was not some warped "Pollyanna" theology but a genuine application of an authentic faith. This did not mean every woman would become a "Joan of Arc" charging about righting wrongs, but they nevertheless could proceed with the confidence that God is sovereign, that he would engage in their lives, and that he would give them direction and peace on how to be a God-fearing, capable woman in the Lord's service in her family, work, and community. They, too, could be an ordinary person who accomplished extraordinary things for God.

Men and women leaders "who are Christ-centered do not merely cope with the secular world; they thrive in it. They do not accept it as it is; they know they are commanded to change it."[375] These unlikely leaders reach beyond technique, themselves, today, and tomorrow. They don't just go *anywhere*; they go *somewhere*.

> **Leaders don't just go *anywhere*; they go *somewhere*.**

What then have we learned about being one of God's unlikely leaders?

1. *Godly, effective leadership is in short supply.* There are manifold opportunities for you.
2. *God's standard of leadership selection is different from ours.* The Lord can and will use you if you are obedient and willing.
3. *Men and women of God must be godly men and women, which goes double for leaders.* If you follow the Lord and allow him to work in your life, he will accomplish his will through you in ways you have probably never considered.

4. *Life is a whole cloth; bad people cannot in the eyes of God be good (or great) leaders.* How you live your life, your values, and your character matter, and who you really are will be evident to those around you, particularly if you step up to leadership.
5. *Leadership is always* about *something.* Leaders cast vision, painting a picture of what can be. Absence of a leader's vision is best described by Lewis Carroll, "If you don't know where you are going, any road will take you there."[376] Great leaders know this, clearly identify the vision, and move toward that vision even when it is not yet understood.
6. *Real leaders lead when others are not yet following.* This does not mean leaders ignore their followers, only that great leaders see things before others, see a possible future, aspire to it, and inspire others toward it as well. But remember what my academic dean, "Doc Johnson," (the late Dr. Clifford W. Johnson, Cedarville University) told me years ago, "Don't get so far out in front of your people they mistake you for the enemy and shoot you in the back."
7. *You can't be in leadership longer than ten minutes without being criticized.* Criticism is part of any leadership experience, especially if you are actively engaged in change. How we handle criticism is what matters.
8. *Spiritual opposition comes hand in hand with spiritual opportunity.* The apostle Paul and Silas faced spiritual harassment as they ministered in Berea and Thessalonica. "The brothers immediately sent Paul and Silas away by night to Berea, and when they arrived, they went into the Jewish synagogue. Now these Jews were more noble than those in Thessalonica; they received the word with all eagerness, examining the Scriptures daily to see if these things were so. Many of them therefore believed, with

not a few Greek women of high standing as well as men. But when the Jews from Thessalonica learned that the word of God was proclaimed by Paul at Berea also, they came there too, agitating and stirring up the crowds" (Acts 17:10–13).

The Thessalonica rabble rousers, the spiritual opposition, did not know it, but God used them. While Scripture says Silas and Timothy continued to work in Berea, the resistance caused the local Christian brothers to move Paul on to Athens where he soon spoke on Areopagus or Mars Hill to the most influential intellectuals of his day (Acts 17:16–34). The lesson is that God can use spiritual opposition to further spiritual opportunity.

9. *What a leader "says" is not always what followers "hear."* People sometimes manufacture narratives. People take what leaders say, reinterpret it, and take it in a direction or to a degree leaders did not intend. Both friends and critics do this, so leaders need to communicate and communicate often. These circumstances are common to leadership challenges and part of casting a new vision in a new direction, in part because some people do not like change. Brevity is beautiful, they say, when it comes to speaking, but repetition is beautiful too because it's how people hear accurately and learn.

10. *Great leaders recognize leadership is not so much about personality or power as about purpose and passion.* Leadership is an art not a science, more akin to music and poetry than to routine endeavor.[377] So, great leaders keep their eyes fixed on vision, not kudos.

Great leaders keep their eyes fixed on vision, not kudos.

Leadership is a privilege. And it is a stewardship before God. Great leaders know this, remembering, "It is the LORD who goes before you. He will be with you; he will not leave you or forsake you. Do not fear or be dismayed" (Deut. 31:8).

Leaders Don't Wait, They Lead

Leadership is needed today. Leadership is for today. Sooner or later, God gives everyone leadership opportunities, and it is then for us to respond. Would that we would respond like Jabez in the Old Testament. "Jabez called upon the God of Israel, saying, 'Oh that you would bless me and enlarge my border, and that your hand might be with me, and that you would keep me from harm so that it might not bring me pain!' And God granted what he asked" (1 Chron. 4: 10).

Jabez did not shy from opportunity. He asked for more, not out of arrogance or greed but a desire to serve God. To pray like Jabez, to request "an expansion of territory (is to pray for) victory and prosperity in all our endeavors and that our life be marked by increase. The presence of God's hand. This was Jabez's way of asking for the guidance of God and His strength to be evident in his daily existence."[378]

Leonard Sweet talked about *Carpe Mañana*, "Seize Tomorrow." He noted that "if there was ever a time for on-the-edge, over-the-top, out-of-the-box leadership, it is now."[379]

John R. W. Stott chastised the Christian community. "Don't be content with the mediocre! Don't settle for anything less than your full God-given potential! Be ambitious and adventurous for God! God has made you a unique person by your genetic endowment, upbringing, and education. He has himself created you and gifted you, and he does not want his work to be wasted. He means you to be fulfilled not frustrated. His purpose is that everything you have and are, should be stretched in his service and in the service of others. This means that God has a leadership role of some degree and kind for each of us."[380]

For Christians, leadership is not an option; it's an opportunity. "We all make a difference. The question is, what kind of difference do we want to make?"[381]

> **For Christians, leadership is not an option; it's an opportunity.**

Church and culture need right-thinking, right-behaving leaders, and God will use you as an unlikely leader for his purposes. Are you ready to make a difference?

What Will Your Epitaph Be?

If you want to make a difference, regardless of your age now, start thinking about things long term. Where do you see yourself in ten years? What does your goal line look like? Or how will you finish well?

"Start by defining what finishing well means and creating a plan to achieve your goals. Then, build a robust support system, prioritize your health and well-being, and continuously learn and grow."[382]

"The better you finish your current season, the better you begin your next season. . . . We honor the organization and the people we've served by finishing strong."[383]

Maybe, think about what your epitaph will be.

Leaders leave legacies, sometimes captured in a long-remembered pithy synopsis of their life. Teddy Roosevelt, "Speak softly and carry a big stick." General Douglas MacArthur, "I shall return." Margaret Thatcher, "You may have to fight a battle more than once to win it." Muhammad Ali, "I am the greatest," and in boxing in his day, he was.

Or consider this actual epitaph on the gravesite of John F. Kennedy, "Let every nation know . . . that we shall pay any price, bear any burden . . . to assure the survival and the success of liberty."

For a long time, I have been interested in epitaphs. The word "epitaph" comes from Greek, *epi* meaning "upon," and *taph* meaning "tomb." So, an epitaph is something written upon a tomb.

I know it makes me a little strange, but I enjoy going to old cemeteries from time to time and reading the epitaphs. A gravestone in Thurmont, Maryland says: "Here lies an atheist. All dressed up and no place to go." Or how about this one from the tombstone of a husband and wife buried in Barlinine Cemetery, Glasgow, England:

Here beneath this stone, we lie
Back-to-back my wife and I
And when the angel's trump shall trill
If she gets up, then I'll lie still.

Either they had a great sense of humor or a poor relationship.

In the Bible we can find some wonderful epitaphs. Moses and Joshua, for example, were each given strong tributes by the biblical authors. David was called a man after God's own heart (1 Sam. 13:14; Acts 13:22). Even before his death, John the Baptist was eulogized by Christ as the greatest prophet born of women (Matt. 11:11).

Bad epitaphs are recorded in Scripture too. Ancient Israel's King Ahab and Queen Jezebel are among the worst of the Old Testament royalty: "There was none who sold himself to do what was evil in the sight of the Lord like Ahab, whom Jezebel his wife incited. He acted very abominably in going after idols" (1 Kings 21:25–26). In time, God said of Ahab, "In the place where dogs licked up the blood of Naboth shall dogs lick your own blood," and of his wife Jezebel, God said, "The dogs shall eat Jezebel within the walls of Jezreel" (1 Kings 21:19, 23). How's that for a summation of your life?

And when you read the life and death of Samson, you think his epitaph must read, "What might have been!"

One of my favorite epitaphs is on the West Point grave of Lt. Col. Herbert Bainbridge Hayden. It reads: "In appreciation of a loyal friend, a square man, an efficient officer, in every way a thoroughbred." Now that's a life well lived.

In 2 Kings, we read of good King Hezekiah's epitaph. "He trusted in the Lord, the God of Israel, so that there was none like him among all the kings of Judah after him, nor among those who were before him. For he held fast to the Lord. He did not depart from following him but kept the commandments that the Lord commanded Moses. And the Lord was with him; wherever he went out, he prospered" (2 Kings 18:5–7).

Hezekiah lived a life worth living, and he died a man honored for his service for the Lord. I'm convinced that the greatest epitaph a person could hope to have is simply, "Here lies the body of a godly man/woman."

I've sometimes wondered what my epitaph will be. What would my associates or my family write? What will God write?

What will your leadership epitaph be? As an unlikely leader, if you are faithful to the Lord, like King Hezekiah, God will work through you to accomplish his purposes. If you "work heartily, as for the Lord and not for men, knowing that from the Lord you will receive the inheritance as your reward. You are serving the Lord Christ" (Col. 3:23–24), then the Lord will also use your legacy to accomplish his will.

> **What will your leadership epitaph be?**

Your epitaph as one of God's unlikely leaders is not generally something you will write or can control, but how you live your life will create that epitaph word by word. Let it be our aim in leadership to someday say with the apostle Paul, "I have fought the good fight, I have finished the race, I have kept the faith" (2 Tim. 4:7).

Great Gifts, Great Needs, Great Opportunities

Tom Brokaw described an entire generation as leaders. In his bestselling book, *The Greatest Generation*, Brokaw saluted this generation of Americans who came of age during the Great Depression and fought in World War II or contributed on the home front.[384] His core message was that this generation displayed extraordinary values like duty, honor, courage, self-sacrifice, and humility, and that these qualities defined the American spirit at a critical moment in history.

- They were ordinary people who rose to extraordinary challenges. Many of them didn't consider themselves heroes, but they responded with resilience and a strong sense of responsibility when their country needed them.
- They didn't seek fame or fortune but quietly built the foundations of postwar America—through hard work, family, and community involvement.
- Their values contrasted sharply with what Brokaw saw as more self-centered or cynical aspects of later generations, including a growing focus on individualism and materialism in modern America.

The Greatest Generation led by example, commitment, and participation and they answered the call, time and again. These men and women took the measure of their challenges and in many cases gave "the last full measure of devotion" to defend what they believed and the homeland and people they loved. They helped preserve freedom for you and me today. Brokaw wondered if others in future generations would possess the moral fortitude to take the Greatest Generation's place of leadership.

You can be an unlikely leader, a legion of one.

We cannot predict much less control what given generational cohorts may do. But we know what we can do. The late Mother Teresa said, "If you can't feed a hundred people, then feed just one."[385] You can be an unlikely leader, a legion of one.

Jim Collins, renowned for his book, *Good to Great*,[386] offered this insightful, motivating observation in one of his later books, *Great by Choice*: "We are not imprisoned by our circumstances. We are not imprisoned by the luck we get or the inherent unfairness of life. We are not imprisoned by crushing setbacks, self-inflicted mistakes or past success. We are not imprisoned by the times in which we live, by the number of hours in the day or even the number of hours we're granted in our very short lives. In the end, we can control only a tiny sliver of what happens to us. But even so, we are free to choose, free to become great by choice."[387]

Collins is not intentionally expressing a Christian worldview, but the way he describes the independence and empowerment God vested in created human beings is an admirable reminder. God created us in his image, "a little lower than the heavenly beings and crowned him with glory and honor" (Ps. 8:5), vesting us with purpose, moral capacity, and an ability to reason. He bestowed upon us immense and eternal value and he gave us dominion over the entirety of creation. As *imago Dei* we are, therefore, not controlled or determined by economics or society or culture or language or political ideology or psychology or sex or ethnicity or even religion. God granted us the ability to discern and, in his providence, to change our future.

> **God granted us the ability to discern and, in his providence, to change our future.**

You can choose to lead. You can be an unlikely leader. You can be an effective, perhaps great leader, in part because God has already extended to us an abundance of great blessings.

There are *two great questions* that God gave us the free will to answer. I believe these two questions are the greatest questions we will face in life. What do you think of Christ? How should we then live?

Each of us is born in sin (Rom. 3:10). We are sinners in need of forgiveness and salvation (Rom. 3:23; 6:23). But God blesses us with good news presented in John 3:16, "For God so loved the world, that he gave his only Son, that whoever believes in him should not perish but have eternal life." This question is for each created human being. What do you think of Christ? Is he just a historical figure, or is he the Son of God and our Lord and Savior?

Redemption is a gift, but we must choose to believe. "Because, if you confess with your mouth that Jesus is Lord and believe in your heart that God raised him from the dead, you will be saved. For with the heart one believes and is justified, and with the mouth one confesses and is saved" (Rom. 10:9–10). If we believe, the Lord saves us: "Everyone who believes that Jesus is the Christ has been born of God" (1 John 5:1).

Once we have become a believer, a Christ follower or Christian, then we can respond to the question, "how should we then live?" This comes from Ezekiel 33:10 in the King James Version of the Bible that the late Francis A. Schaeffer popularized in the title of his book, *How Should We Then Live? The Rise and Decline of Western Thought and Culture*.[388] The point is clear. Once we have become a believer embracing biblical values, we must decide how we are going to live our life.

For our considerations here, how will our relationship with the Lord and his Word influence our leadership? The apostle Peter asked the question in different words, "What sort of people ought you to be in lives of holiness and godliness?" (2 Peter 3:11).

Like our choice of salvation, God grants us the blessing of freedom of choice in how we live our lives. Nowhere in Scripture is Christianity presented as an enemy of freedom but rather as the source and bulwark of what today we call religious liberty on the national level and what the founder of Rhode Island, Roger Williams, called soul liberty on the personal level.

We are given the *greatest opportunities* in life; despite unpredictable markets, despite the politics of envy and greed that characterize our age, still, we enjoy unparalleled economic abundance and technological advances, and the longest life expectancy in history. We have no excuses; nothing holding us back.

We are presented with the *greatest need* on earth. Over 8 billion people walk the earth, a more than 300 percent increase since I was born. Though Christianity is the world's largest religion, spread across about 31 percent of the population, many portions of the globe remain untouched by evangelism. And even with twenty-first-century communications and transportation technology available to us, still, about 40 percent of the world's population—roughly 2–3 billion people—are estimated to have never heard the gospel of Jesus Christ or to have had little to no exposure to the gospel in a meaningfully presented way.[389] So, this is humanity's greatest need: people the world over who are captured by religious isms, people who do not know Jesus—the way, the truth, and the life—people who are lost and without hope. This then is our opportunity to carry the message of hope, to be ambassadors of Christ, sharing the message of reconciliation (2 Cor. 5:11–21).

You can be one of God's unlikely leaders in this moment, like these not-well-known-but-courageous individuals in Scripture who became leaders when their opportunity arrived. Shiphrah and Puah were Hebrew midwives who defied Pharaoh when he ordered them to kill Hebrew baby boys. They feared God more than Pharaoh, risked their lives, and preserved Israel's future (Ex. 1:15–21).

Think of Naaman's Israelite slave girl, who told Naaman, her Syrian master, about the prophet Elisha who could heal him.

She trusted God's power and extended compassion to an enemy (2 Kings 5:23). Or consider Ebed-Melech, an Ethiopian eunuch in King Zedekiah's palace who bravely rescued the prophet Jeremiah from a muddy pit where he was left to die. Ebed-Melech acted with integrity and courage, trusting God over political pressure (Jer. 38:7–13).

These individuals were not elites, nor were they famous, wealthy, "accomplished," or admired, yet they exercised their faith, using their abilities and access to become influential leaders and advance the kingdom of God.

In one of my favorite quotes, Michelangelo once said, "The *greatest danger* for most of us is not the fact that our aim is too high and we miss it, but that it is too low, and we reach it." This quote appeals to me for a lot of reasons, one of them being that Michelangelo's aim reached as high as the ceiling of the Sistine Chapel.

I do not know if Michelangelo ever read the biblical accounts of the midwives, the unnamed slave girl, or the eunuch, but given his philosophy of aiming high, I think he would have affirmed them. They aimed high and achieved their goals because they trusted God. They are excellent examples of how God often chooses the unlikely to accomplish the exceptional, not because of status, but because of surrender. And God often calls ordinary people to do extraordinary things, not because they are great, but because he is.

> **God often calls ordinary people to do extraordinary things, not because they are great, but because he is.**

The midwives, slave girl, and eunuch were ordinary people through whom God did extraordinary things. They were humble people, like the man who became known as the "father of modern missions," the eighteenth-century missionary to India, "William Carey, who said 'expect great things from God and attempt great things for God.'"[390]

For the Christian, leadership and greatness are not off-limits because it's not about them. It's "for the Lord and not for men" (Col. 3:23). It's about excellence.

"We used to think greatness came from outside—power, position, prestige, wealth. We now know greatness comes from within—spirit, character, loyalty, honesty, soul."[391] It's not mystical or magical. It's not secular. It's simply God's *imago Dei* within us, a desire to aspire toward accomplishing good things for the Lord and his people.

What are your aspirations? Desiring to lead for the right reasons is an admirable aspiration. Scripture tells us this: "The saying is trustworthy: If anyone aspires to the office of overseer, he desires a noble task" (1 Tim. 3:1). Being a leader is an honorable pursuit.

> **Desiring to lead for the right reasons is an admirable aspiration.**

Any of us who are privileged to lead are all "unlikely leaders." But to do great things for God, we must be God's unlikely leaders.

God's favor is essential to our vision, plans, perseverance, accomplishments, effectiveness, and success. Nehemiah knew this, concluding his work with these seven words, "Remember me, O my God, for good" (Neh. 13:31).

LEADERSHIP LESSONS

1. You can lead for such a time as this.
2. We need leaders who stand for something, leaders who try, who do, who take risks, who inspire others to aspire.
3. Leaders don't just go *anywhere*; they go *somewhere*.
4. Great leaders keep their eyes fixed on vision, not kudos.
5. For Christians, leadership is not an option; it's an opportunity.
6. What will your leadership epitaph be?
7. You can be an unlikely leader, a legion of one.
8. God granted us the ability to discern and, in his providence, to change our future.
9. God often calls ordinary people to do extraordinary things, not because they are great, but because he is.
10. Desiring to lead for the right reasons is an admirable aspiration.

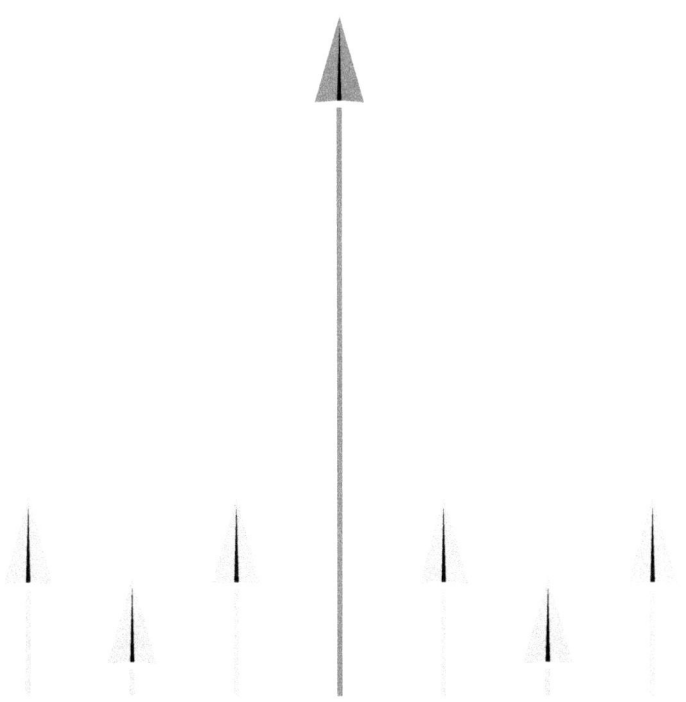

LEADERSHIP LESSONS

PROLOGUE
1. Leaders are more often made than born.
2. Good leaders leave a legacy of faithfulness.
3. Effective leaders rise to the spiritual challenge of their day.
4. Readers make leaders.
5. Proper public prayer is an act of leadership in a pluralistic culture.
6. The leadership experience is similar in all kinds of organizations.
7. Leaders can be both professionally tenacious and gracious.
8. Leaders learn to work in productive partnerships.
9. Leaders need mentors too.
10. Leaders should strive to finish well.

1 CHOICES
1. Leadership is a gift of God.
2. If you don't lead someone else will.
3. Leadership is.
4. Leaders don't have all the answers.
5. Holding a leadership position isn't the same as leading.
6. Leadership is a high-wire act without a net.
7. The church is neither leading nor developing leaders.
8. All people possess untapped leadership potential.
9. God looks for people who *will be* leaders.
10. You can be one of God's unlikely leaders.

2 CREDIBILITY

1. Sooner or later, everyone is presented with the "need to lead."
2. Leadership is the act of inspiring others toward a goal.
3. Leadership is one way to *stand out* and *step up* as God's ambassadors.
4. Believe leadership myths; fail to reach leadership potential.
5. Leaders are as different in personality and gifts as leaves in a forest of trees.
6. Every follower of Christ is given at least one spiritual gift.
7. Nowhere in the Bible does God say women should not or cannot lead.
8. Human beings are free moral agents who can use leadership for good or for evil.
9. Leadership always gets back to character.
10. Jesus never condemned authority or use of power but led with love.

3 CONFUSION

1. Leadership isn't capitalized in the Bible.
2. Leading a family is still leadership.
3. Uneducated and common doesn't disqualify people from leadership.
4. God's unlikely leaders took risks and made mistakes.
5. Men and women of God must be godly men and women.
6. Character and competence count more than countenance or connections.
7. Don't get hung up on a presumed lack of talent but vigorously use the talents God provides.
8. Access the power of prayer.
9. Stand for something.
10. Lead when others are not yet following.

4 CHARACTER

1. "Life-ship" is central to leadership.
2. A leader's private choices inevitably affect his or her public actions.
3. Leaders cannot rise above the level of their own character.
4. Be guided by a conscience instructed by God's standard of holiness.
5. Confidence is born of experience with one's God-given abilities.
6. Those who toot their own horns don't have much to toot about.
7. Leadership is not machoism.
8. Leaders with character, confidence, and courage accomplish most for God.
9. Great challenges are great opportunities wearing a mask.
10. Character defines leadership; courage distinguishes it.

5 CAUSE

1. Moses truly became a leader when he learned to delegate.
2. Purpose implies *mission*; vision implies *movement*.
3. Leaders reach beyond technique, themselves, today, and tomorrow.
4. Leaders don't just go *anywhere*; they go *somewhere*.
5. There's no place for mediocrity in leadership.
6. Excellence is a perpetual goal.
7. Leading is no cakewalk.
8. After a while, the chief obstacle to innovation can be the chief innovator.
9. Leaders should be optimistic realists.
10. A Sovereign God and luck are mutually exclusive concepts.

6 COMMUNICATION

1. Godly, effective leadership is in short supply.
2. Passion is contagious.
3. Effective leaders don't demand but enthuse.
4. Leaders inspire others to aspire.
5. Leaders help followers think the impossible is possible.
6. Use symbolism more often than statistics.
7. Leaders who teach make things happen.
8. The central importance of telling an organization's story cannot be overstated.
9. Communicate vision clearly, concisely, practically, passionately, repeatedly.
10. Lead with your words.

7 COMMITMENT

1. Leaders lead by example.
2. Leaders look for a better way.
3. Leaders hold principles tightly, ideas loosely.
4. Attitude enables ability.
5. Competence is polished talent.
6. A leader's work ethic becomes the staff's gold standard.
7. Great leaders set out to "do good" not just to "feel good."
8. Rapid change puts a premium on transformational leadership.
9. One of the most important decisions leaders make is who sits in the seats nearest to them.
10. Leaders turn their followers into leaders.

8 COMMUNITY

1. Be a person after God's own heart.
2. Faith empowers leadership.
3. Never fail to return to the Lord.

4. Flawed person, faithful follower of God, fearless leader.
5. Strong leaders need—want—help.
6. Strong leaders should be developed at *all* levels of the organization.
7. Identify the right people with the right stuff.
8. Make the "hard decision" about struggling personnel.
9. Develop unlikely leaders by giving them opportunity.
10. Leaders not only think "big" but long-term.

9 CRISES
1. Criticized? Welcome to leadership.
2. Leaders must know the facts before they act.
3. Leaders lead best when they listen.
4. *How* leaders respond is as important as *what* they say.
5. What leaders say in cyberspace never goes away.
6. Leaders who were wrong should say so.
7. Criticism hurts most when it comes from our own.
8. Spiritual opposition always follows spiritual opportunity.
9. No leader is invulnerable to crises.
10. Crisis is not only a threat but an opportunity for leaders who lead.

10 CONDUCT UNBECOMING
1. Bad choices and bad character trump great ability and advantages.
2. Leaders are role models.
3. Failing is not fatal to leadership; falling frequently spells the end.
4. Man looks on the outward appearance, but the Lord looks at the heart.
5. Leaders who succeed learn how to fail forward.
6. Correction is open to anyone.

7. Submitting the heart is personally liberating and professionally energizing.
8. Leaders who fall make willful, sinful choices.
9. No one is invulnerable to sexual temptation or immorality.
10. Leadership is a privilege.

11 CONTINUITY
1. No leader leads forever.
2. Legacies are an imprint of the leader's vision.
3. Creating living legacies is what a leader's life should be about.
4. Ignoring sacred cows can create a culture of complacency.
5. Nothing good is served by hiding skeletons in a closet.
6. Changing the culture is the quickest way to get the organization moving toward the leader's vision.
7. Think about what the organization will look like without you.
8. Leadership transition is a matter of stewardship.
9. Ceremony creates credibility for the new leader.
10. Better for a former leader to lead and leave than to lead and grieve.

12 CONCLUSION
1. You can lead for such a time as this.
2. We need leaders who stand for something, leaders who try, who do, who take risks, who inspire others to aspire.
3. Leaders don't just go *anywhere*; they go *somewhere*.
4. Great leaders keep their eyes fixed on vision, not kudos.
5. For Christians, leadership is not an option; it's an opportunity.
6. What will your leadership epitaph be?
7. You can be an unlikely leader, a legion of one.
8. God granted us the ability to discern and, in his providence, to change our future.

9. God often calls ordinary people to do extraordinary things, not because they are great, but because he is.
10. Desiring to lead for the right reasons is an admirable aspiration.

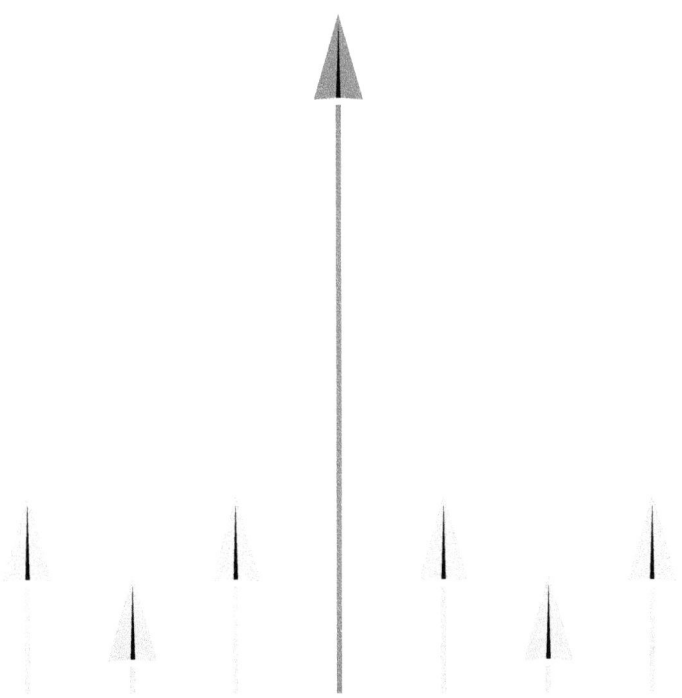

ACKNOWLEDGMENTS

In addition to the people mentioned in the prologue, many others taught me about leadership and influenced the contents of this book.

Over a few years, several people provided comments and insight that helped improve this book, among them: Debbie Brink, Doug Fagerstrom, Steve and Cathey Prudhomme, John VerBerkmoes, Dennis Wiens, John Frick.

My son Andrew, a young writer and editor, made comments that helped polish some text. And he later provided helpful advice about presentation and marketing.

Sarah, my wife, was and is a never-failing source of kindness, love, and support. Among her spiritual gifts are encouragement and hospitality. I cannot think of any of my project ideas to which she has not responded, "Go for it." More than that, she was right there, the counsel and strength for every move to a new place and new position, every leadership endeavor. Her gifts are not my gifts and without her generous contributions, in support of my work or on her own, my service would not have been possible.

Finally, I salute the trustees, personnel, students, and friends of the Christian colleges, universities, mission agency, and other organizations with whom I've worked. You taught me much.

Of course, the final product is mine, so I bear the ultimate responsibility.

The only way I can thank the people who've influenced my life, work, and thinking is to attempt to live by the Christian values dear to them and to try to instill those values in others. Forgive me for where I've failed. May God bless and keep you all as you lead others.

SELECTED BIBLIOGRAPHY

Abraham, Fares. *Next Gen Leaders: Learning Today How to Change Tomorrow.* Washington, DC: Levant Media, 2017.

Abrashoff, D. Michael. *It's Your Ship.* NY: Warner Books, 2002.

Allen, Scott D. *Why Social Justice Is Not Biblical Justice: An Urgent Appeal to Fellow Christians in a Time of Crisis.* Grand Rapids: Credo House Publishers, 2020.

Ambrose, Stephen E. *Eisenhower: Soldier and President.* NY: Touchstone, 1990.

Amidon, Rick E., and Rex M. Rogers. *Today You Do Greatness: A Parable on Success and Significance.* Unlikely Leaders, 2011.

Armerding, Hudson T. *The Heart of Godly Leadership.* Wheaton, IL: Crossway Books, 1992.

Army Leadership: Be, Know, Do. Field Manual 22–100. Washington, DC: Headquarters, Department of the Army. August 1999.

Atteberry, Mark. *The Caleb Quest: What You Can Learn from the Boldest Dreamer in the Bible.* Nashville: Thomas Nelson, 2006.

Autry, J. *Love and Profit: The Art of Caring Leadership.* NY: Morrow, 1991.

Baird, Bruce B. *Legendary Leadership: How Ordinary People Become Uncommon Leaders.* Chicago: Muse Literary, 2022.

Banks, Robert, and Kimberly Powell, eds. *Faith in Leadership: How Leaders Live Out Their Faith in Their Work and Why It Matters.* San Francisco: Jossey-Bass, 2001.

Barber, Robert Lee. *Leading by Design: The Leadership Secret No One Tells You.* Chattanooga, TN: Paratus Consulting LLC, 2025.

Barna, George. *Leaders on Leadership.* Ventura, CA: Regal Books, 1997.

Barna, George. *The Power of Vision.* Ventura, CA: Regal Books, 1992.

Bassous, Michael G. *Leadership . . . in Crisis: A Global Perspective on Building Resilience, Stamina, Agility, and Confrontation.* Eugene, OR: Wipf and Stock Publishers, 2022.

Beals, Timothy J., ed. *The Essential Engstrom: Proven Principles of Leadership— Ted W. Engstrom.* Colorado Springs, CO: Authentic Publishing, 2007.

Behm, Dan. *Chief Culture Officer: Attract Top Talent, Grow Like Crazy, and*

Have an Insane Amount of Fun Doing It. Grand Rapids: Credo House Publishers, 2018.

Bennis, Warren. *On Becoming a Leader.* Reading, MA: Addison-Wesley, 1989.

Bennis, Warren. *Why Leaders Can't Lead.* San Francisco: Jossey-Bass, 1989, orig. 1976.

Bennis, Warren, and Joan Goldsmith. *Learning to Lead: A Workbook on Becoming a Leader.* Cambridge, MA: Perseus Books, 1997.

Bennis, Warren, and Bert Nanus. *Leaders: Strategies for Taking Charge.* NY: HarperBusiness, 1997.

Biehl, Bob. *31 Days to Confident Leadership.* Nashville, TN: Broadman and Holman Publishers, 1998.

Blanchard, Kenneth. *The Heart of a Leader: Insights on the Art of Influence.* Tulsa: Honor Books, 1999.

Blanchard, Kenneth, and Phil Hodges. *Lead Like Jesus Revisited: Lessons from the Greatest Leadership Role Model of All Time.* Nashville, TN: Thomas Nelson, 2016.

Blanchard, Kenneth, Bill Hybels, and Phil Hodges. *Leadership by the Book.* Nashville: Abingdon, 1996.

Block, P. J. *Stewardship.* San Francisco: Berrett-Koehler, 1993.

Bogue, E. G. *Leadership by Design.* San Francisco: Jossey-Bass, 1994.

Bolman, L. G., and Terrence E. Deal. *Leadership with Soul: An Uncommon Journey of Spirit.* San Francisco: Jossey-Bass, 2001.

Bolman, L. G., and Terrence E. Deal. *Reframing Organizations: Artistry, Choice, and Leadership.* San Francisco: Jossey-Bass, 1997.

Bowen, W., and H. Shapiro, eds. *Universities and Their Leadership.* Princeton, NJ: Princeton University Press, 1998.

Bower, Marvin. *The Will to Lead: Running a Business with a Network of Leaders.* Boston: Harvard Business School Press, 1997.

Brokaw, Tom. *The Greatest Generation.* NY: Random House, 1998.

Brooks, Arthur C. *Love Your Enemies: How Decent People Can Save America from the Culture of Contempt.* NY: Broadside Books, 2019.

Brown, Brene. *Dare to Lead: Brave Work. Tough Conversations. Whole Hearts.* NY: Random House, 2018.

Bryant, Adam. *The Leap to Leader: How Ambitious Managers Make the Jump to Leadership.* Boston: Harvard Business Review Press, 2023.

Burns, James MacGregor. *Leadership.* NY: HarperCollins, 1978.

Burns, James MacGregor. *Transforming Leadership: A New Pursuit of Happiness.* NY: Atlantic Monthly Press, 2003.

Callahan, K. *Effective Church Leadership.* San Francisco: Jossey-Bass, 1990.

Carver, John. *Boards That Make a Difference: A New Design for Leadership in Nonprofit and Public Organizations.* San Francisco: Jossey-Bass, 2006.

Chambers, Oswald. *Spiritual Leadership.* Chicago: Moody Press, 1967.

Chestnut, Beatrice. *The 9 Types of Leadership: Mastering the Art of People in the 21st Century.* NY: Post Hill Press, 2017.

Clark, David R. *Steward Leadership: Jesus' Leadership Model.* Cincinnati, OH: Glad House Publishing, 2023.

Clinton, Robert. *The Making of a Leader.* Colorado Springs, CO: NavPress, 1988.

Collins, Jim. *Good to Great: Why Some Companies Make the Leap . . . and Others Don't.* NY: Harper Collins, 2001.

Collins, Jim, and Morten T. Hansen. *Great by Choice: Uncertainty, Chaos, Luck—Why Some Thrive Despite Them All.* NY: Harber Business, 2011.

Conger, Jay, and Beth Benjamin. *Building Leaders: How Successful Companies Develop the Next Generation.* San Francisco: Jossey-Bass, 1999.

Covey, Stephen. *Principle Centered Leadership.* NY: Simon & Schuster, 1991.

Csorba, Les T. *Trust: The One Thing That Makes or Breaks a Leader.* Nashville: Thomas Nelson, 2004.

Dale, Robert. *Leading Edge: Leadership Strategies from the New Testament.* Nashville: Abingdon, 1996.

Dallas, Joe. *Christians in a Cancel Culture: Speaking with Truth and Grace in a Hostile World.* Eugene, OR: Harvest House Publishers, 2021.

DeFrank, Thomas M. *Write It When I'm Gone: Remarkable Off-the-Record Conversations with Gerald R. Ford.* NY: G. P. Putnam's Sons, 2007.

De Pree, Max. *Leadership Is an Art.* NY: Dell, 1989.

De Pree, Max. *Leadership Jazz.* NY: Doubleday, 1992.

De Pree, Max. *Leading Without Power: Finding Hope in Serving Community.* San Francisco: Jossey-Bass, 1997, 2003.

DeVries, James H., and Rick Sessions. *Christ-Centered Leadership at Work: Called to Serve on Mondays.* Grand Rapids: Credo House Publishers, 2021.

D'Souza, Dinesh. *Ronald Regan: How an Ordinary Man Became an Extraordinary Leader.* NY: Free Press, 1997.

Dungy, Tony, and Nathan Whitaker. *Quiet Strength: The Principles, Practices, and Priorities of a Winning Life.* Carol Stream, IL: Tyndale House Publishers, 2007.

Edinger, Scott K., and Laurie Sain. *The Hidden Leader: Discover and Develop Greatness Within Your Company.* NY: AMACOM, 2015.

Eisner, Michael. *Work in Progress.* NY: Random House, 1998.

Finzel, Hans. *The Top Ten Mistakes Leaders Make.* Wheaton, IL: Victor Books, 1994.

Ford, Leighton. *Transforming Leadership: Jesus' Way of Creating Vision, Shaping Values, and Empowering Change.* Downers Grove, IL: InterVarsity Press, 1991.

Frei, Frances, and Anne Morriss. *Unleashed: The Unapologetic Leader's Guide to Empowering Everyone Around You.* Boston: Harvard Business Review Press, 2020.

Fullan, Michael. *Leading in a Culture of Change.* San Francisco: Jossey-Bass, 2001.

Gardner, Howard. *Leading Minds: Anatomy of Leadership.* NY: Books, 1995.

Gardner, John W. *Excellence*: Can We Be Equal and Excellent Too? NY: W. W. Norton & Company, 1987.

Gardner, John W. *On Leadership.* NY: Free Press, 1990.

Gergen, David. *Eyewitness to Power: The Essence of Leadership, Nixon to Clinton.* NY: Simon & Schuster, 2000.

Gerstner, Louis V., Jr. *Who Says Elephants Can't Dance? Inside IBM's Historic Turnaround.* NY: HarperBusiness, 2002.

Getz, Gene A. *Nehemiah: Becoming a Disciplined Leader.* Nashville: Broadman and Holman, 1995.

Giuliani, Rudolph W. *Leadership.* NY: Miramax Books, 2002.

Godin, Seth. *Tribes: We Need You to Lead Us.* NY: Portfolio, 2008.

Goleman, Daniel. *What Makes a Leader: Why Emotional Intelligence Matters.* Florence, MA: More Than Sound, LLC, 2017.

Goleman, Daniel, Richard E. Boyatzis, and Annie McKee. *Primal Leadership, Unleashing the Power of Emotional Intelligence.* Brighton, MA: Harvard Business Review Press, 2013.

Goodall, Wayde. *Why Great Men Fall: 15 Winning Strategies to Rise Above It All.* Green Forest, AR: New Leaf Publishing Group, 2005.

Goodwin, Doris Kearns, *The Bully Pulpit: Theodore Roosevelt, William Howard Taft, and the Golden Age of Journalism.* NY: Simon & Schuster, 2013.

Goodwin, Doris Kearns. *Leadership: In Turbulent Times.* NY: Simon & Schuster, 2018.

Goodwin, Doris Kearns. *Team of Rivals: The Political Genius of Abraham Lincoln.* NY: Simon & Schuster, 2005.

Greenleaf, Robert K. *The Servant as Leader.* Indianapolis: The Robert K. Greenleaf Center, 1970, 1991.

Greenleaf, Robert K. *Servant Leadership: A Journey into the Nature of Legitimate Power and Greatness.* NY: Paulist Press, 1977.

Grove, Andy. *Only the Paranoid Survive.* NY: Doubleday, 1996.

Guinness, Os, ed., *Character Counts: Leadership Qualities in Washington, Wilberforce, Lincoln, and Solzhenitsyn.* Grand Rapids: Baker Books, 1999.

Habecker, Eugene B. *The Other Side of Leadership: Coming to Terms with the Responsibilities That Accompany God-Given Authority.* Wheaton, IL: Scripture Press Publications (Victor Books), 1987.

Habecker, Eugene B. *The Softer Side of Leadership: Essential Soft Skills That Transform Leaders and the People They Lead.* Sisters, Oregon: Deep River Books, 2018.

Harari, Oren. *The Leadership Secrets of Colin Powell.* NY: McGraw-Hill, 2002.

Hayward, Steven F. *Churchill on Leadership: Executive Success in the Face of Adversity.* Rocklin, CA: Forum, 1997.

Heath, Chip, and Dan Heath. *Switch: How to Change Things When Change Is Hard.* New York: Crown Business, 2010.

Heifetz, R. A. *Leadership Without Easy Answers.* Cambridge, MA: Belknap/Harvard, 1994.

Herman, Robert D., and Associates. *The Jossey-Bass Handbook of Nonprofit Leadership and Management.* San Francisco: Jossey-Bass, 1994.

Hunter, J. C. *The Servant: A Simple Story About the True Essence of Leadership.* Rocklin, CA: Prima, 1998.

Hybels, Bill. *Courageous Leadership.* Grand Rapids: Zondervan, 2002.

Ibarra, Herminia. *Act Like a Leader, Think Like a Leader.* Boston: Harvard Business Review Press, 2015.

Ingram, Chip. *Good to Great in God's Eyes: Ten Practices Great Christians Have in Common.* Grand Rapids: Baker Books, 2007.

Inrig, Gary. *A Call to Excellence.* Wheaton: Victor Books, 1985.

Jennings, Ken, and John Stahl-Wert. *The Serving Leader: 5 Powerful Actions to Transform You, Your Team, and Your Community.* San Francisco: Berrett-Koehler Publishers, Inc., 2003, 2016.

Johnson, Tim. *Crisis Leadership: How to Lead in Times of Crisis, Threat, and Uncertainty.* London: Bloomsbury Business, 2018.

Jones, Laurie Beth. *Teach Your Team to Fish: Using Ancient Wisdom for Inspired Teamwork.* NY: Crown Wisdom, 2002.

Kaplan, Robert Steven. *What You Really Need to Lead.* Boston: Harvard Business Review Press, 2015.

Kessler, Ronald. *A Matter of Character: Inside the White House of George W. Bush.* NY: Sentinel, 2004.

Klann, Gene. *Crisis Leadership: Using Military Lessons, Organizational Experiences, and the Power of Influence to Lessen the Impact of Chaos on the People You Lead.* Greensboro, NC: Center for Creative Leadership, 2003.

Korda, Michael. *Ulysses S. Grant: The Unlikely Hero.* NY: HarperCollins, 2004.

Kotter, John P. *Leading Change.* Boston: Harvard Business School Press, 1996, 2012.

Kotter, John P. *John P. Kotter on What Leaders Really Do.* Boston: Harvard Business School Press, 1999.

Kouzes, James M., and Barry Z. Posner, ed. *Christian Reflections on the Leadership Challenge.* San Francisco: Jossey-Bass, 2004.

Kouzes, James M., and Barry Z. Posner. *Credibility: How Leaders Gain and Lose It, Why People Demand It.* San Francisco: Jossey-Bass, 1993.

Kouzes, James M., and Barry Z. Posner. *Encouraging the Heart: A Leader's Guide to Rewarding and Recognizing Others.* San Francisco: Jossey-Bass, 1999.

Kouzes, James M., and Barry Z. Posner. *The Leader's Legacy.* San Francisco: Jossey-Bass, 2006.

Kouzes, James M., and Barry Z. Posner. *The Leadership Challenge: How to Get Extraordinary Things Done in Organizations.* San Francisco: Jossey-Bass, 1987.

Kouzes, James M., and Barry Z. Posner. *The Leadership Challenge Planner: An Action Guide to Achieving Your Personal Best.* San Francisco: Jossey-Bass/Pfeiffer, 1999.

Kouzes, James M., and Barry Z. Posner. *The Truth About Leadership: The No-fads, Heart-of-the-Matter Facts You Need to Know.* San Francisco: Jossey-Bass, 2010.

Lansing, Alfred: *Endurance: Shackleton's Incredible Voyage.* NY: Basic Books, 2008.

Lawless III, Edward E., and Christopher G. Worley. *Built to Change: How to Achieve Sustained Organizational Effectiveness.* San Francisco: Jossey-Bass, 2006.

Lawrenz, Mel. *Spiritual Influence: The Hidden Power Behind Leadership.* Grand Rapids: Zondervan, 2012.

Lee, Terrance. *Quiet Voice Fearless Leader: 10 Principles for Introverts to Awaken the Leader Inside.* Frenchtown Publishing, 2021.

Malphurs, Aubrey. *Developing a Vision for Ministry.* Grand Rapids: Baker Books, 1992.

Malphurs, Aubrey. *Values-Driven Leadership: Discovering and Developing Your Core Values for Ministry.* Grand Rapids: Baker Books, 1996.

Marcus, Leonard J., Eric J. McNulty, Joseph M. Henderson, and Barry C. Dorn. *You're It: Crisis, Change, and How to Lead When It Matters,* NY: PublicAffairs, 2019.

Marshall, Tom. *Understanding Leadership.* UK: Sovereign World, 1991.

Maxwell, John C. *Developing the Leader Within You.* Nashville, TN: Thomas Nelson, 1993.

Maxwell, John C. *Developing the Leaders Around You.* Nashville, TN: Thomas Nelson, 1995.

Maxwell, John C. *Failing Forward.* Nashville: Thomas Nelson, 2000.

Maxwell, John C. *The 5 Levels of Leadership.* NY: Center Street, 2011.

Maxwell, John C. *High Road Leadership: Bringing People Together in a World That Divides.* Duluth, GA: Maxwell Leadership, 2024.

Maxwell, John C. *How Successful People Lead.* NY: Center Street, 2013.

Maxwell, John C. *Leadership 101: What Every Leader Needs to Know.* Nashville: Thomas Nelson, 2002.

Maxwell, John C. *Running with the Giants: What Old Testament Heroes Want You to Know About Life and Leadership.* NY: Warner, 2002.

Maxwell, John C. *The 17 Indisputable Laws of Teamwork.* Nashville: Thomas Nelson, 2001.

Maxwell, John C. *Sometimes You Win, Sometimes You Learn.* NY: Center Street, 2013.

Maxwell, John C. *The 21 Indispensable Qualities of a Leader.* Nashville: Thomas Nelson, 1999.

Maxwell, John C. *The 21 Irrefutable Laws of Leadership.* Nashville: Thomas Nelson, 1998.

Mayberry, Matt. *The Transformational Leader: How the World's Best Leaders Build Teams, Inspire Action, and Achieve Lasting Success.* 1st ed. NY: Wiley, 2024.

McIntosh, Gary L., and Samuel D. Rima Jr. *Overcoming the Dark Side of Leadership.* Grand Rapids: Baker Books, 1997.

McKenna, David. *The Leader's Legacy: Preparing for Greater Things.* Newberg, OR: Barclay Press, 2006.

McMillan, Robert C. *The Next Gen Leader: Cutting Edge Strategies to Make You the Leader You Were Born to Be.* Pompton Plains, NJ: Career Press, 2014.

Meacham, Jon. *Franklin and Winston: An Intimate Portrait of an Epic Friendship.* NY: Random House, 20003.

Mellon, Liz. *Inside the Leader's Mind: Five Ways to Think Like a Leader.* Harlow, England: Financial Times Prentice-Hall, 2011.

Meylan, Daniel. *The Compound Effect: The Transformational Power of Business Competency & Spiritual Maturity.* Colorado Springs, CO: Dawson Media, 2011.

Michael, Larry G. *Spurgeon on Leadership.* Grand Rapids: Kregel, 2003.

Moore, Steve. *The Top 10 Leadership Conversations in the Bible.* Atlanta: Nexleader Foundation, 2017.

Morgan, Robert. *Lions of the West: Heroes and Villains of the Westward Expansion.* Chapel Hill, NC: Algonquin Books, 2011.

Nanus, Bert, and Stephen M. Dobbs. *Leaders Who Make a Difference: Essential Strategies for Meeting the Nonprofit Challenge.* San Francisco: Jossey-Bass, 1999.

Nouwen, Henri. *In the Name of Jesus.* NY: Crossroads, 1991.

Novak, David. *How Leaders Learn: Master the Habits of the World's Most Successful People.* Boston: Harvard Business Review Press, 2024.

Oster, Merrill J. *Vision-Driven Leadership.* San Bernardino: Here's Life Publishers, 1991.

O'Toole, James. *Leading Change: Overcoming the Ideology of Comfort and the Tyranny of Custom.* San Francisco: Jossey-Bass, 1995.

O'Toole, James. *Leading Change: The Argument for Values-Based Leadership.* NY: Ballantine Books, 1995.

Parrott, Roger. *The Longview: Lasting Strategies for Rising Leaders.* Colorado Springs, CO: David C. Cook, 2009.

Pascarella, Perry. *Christ-Centered Leadership: Thriving in Business by Putting God in Charge.* Rocklin, CA: Prima Publishing, 1999.
Phillips, Donald T. *Lincoln on Leadership.* NY: Warner Books, 1992.
Phillips, R. D. *The Heart of an Executive: Lessons on Leadership from the Life of King David.* NY: Doubleday, 1999.
Pollard, William. *The Soul of the Firm.* NY: Harper Business, 1996.
Putnam, Howard D., and Gene Busnar. *The Winds of Turbulence: A CEO's Reflections on Surviving and Thriving on the Cutting Edge of Corporate Crisis,* 1991.
Rainer, Thom S. *Who Moved My Pulpit? Leading Change in the Church.* Nashville: B&H Publishing Group, 2016.
Rinehart, S. T. *Upside Down: The Paradox of Servant Leadership.* Colorado Springs, CO: NavPress, 1998.
Robinson, William. *Incarnate Leadership.* Grand Rapids: Zondervan, 2009.
Rodin, R. Scott. *The Steward Leader: Transforming People, Organizations and Communities.* Downers Grove, IL: InterVarsity Press, 2010.
Romney, Mitt. *Turnaround: Crisis, Leadership, and the Olympic Games.* Washington, DC: Regnery Publishing, Inc., 2004.
Rosenbach, W. E., and R. L. Taylor, eds. *Contemporary Issues in Leadership.* Boulder, CO: Westview Press, 1993.
Ross, Alan M., and Cecil Murphey. *Unconditional Excellence: Answering God's Call to Be Your Professional Best.* Avon, MA: Adams Media Corp., 2002.
Sample, Steve B. *The Contrarian's Guide to Leadership.* San Francisco: Jossey-Bass, 2002.
Sandberg, Sheryl. *Lean In: Women, Work, and the Will to Lead.* New York: Knopf, 2013.
Sandborn, Mark. *You Don't Need a Title to Be a Leader: How Anyone, Anywhere Can Make a Positive Difference.* NY: Doubleday, 2006.
Sanders, J. Oswald. *Spiritual Leadership.* Chicago: Moody Press, 1994.
Schaeffer, Francis A. *How Should We Then Live? The Rise and Decline of Western Thought and Culture.* Ada, MI: Fleming H. Revell, 1976.
Schein, Edgar H. *Organizational Culture and Leadership.* San Francisco: Jossey-Bass, 2010.
Schweizer, Peter. *Reagan's War: The Epic Story of His Forty-Year Struggle and Final Triumph over Communism.* NY: Doubleday, 2002.
Shackleton, Ernest. *South: The Endurance Expedition.* NY: Penguin Putnam, 1919, 2004.

Sinek, Simon. *Leaders Eat Last: Why Some Teams Pull Together and Others Don't.* London: Penguin Random House, 2017.

Sinek, Simon. *Start with Why: How Great Leaders Inspire Everyone to Take Action.* New York: Portfolio, 2009.

Southerland, Dan. *Transitioning: Leading Your Church Through Change.* Grand Rapids: Zondervan, 1999.

Spaulding, Tommy. *The Heart-Led Leader: How Living and Leading from the Heart Will Change Your Organization and Your Life.* NY: Crown Business, 2015.

Spears, L. C., ed. *Reflections on Leadership: How Robert K. Greenleaf's Theory of Servant-Leadership Influenced Today's Top Management Thinkers.* NY: Wiley, 1995.

Spears, L. C., ed. *Insights on Leadership: Service, Stewardship, Spirit, and Servant-Leadership.* NY: Paulist, 1998.

Sweet, Leonard. *Carpe Mañana: Is Your Church Ready to Seize Tomorrow?* (Grand Rapids: Zondervan, 2001.

Thomas, Viv. *Future Leaders.* UK: Paternoster Press, 1999.

Thornton, Paul B. *Be the Leader: Make the Difference.* Torrance, CA: Griffin Publishing Group, 2002.

Tichy, Noel M.. *The Leadership Engine.* NY: HarperCollins, 1997.

Tichy, Noel M., and Warren G. Bennis. *Judgment: How Winning Leaders Make Great Calls.* NY: Portfolio, 2007.

Tichy, Noel M., and Nancy Cardwell. *The Cycle of Leadership: How Great Leaders Teach Their Companies to Win.* NY: Harper Business, 2002.

Walsh, Kenneth T. *Air Force One: The History of the Presidents and Their Planes.* NY: Hyperion, 2003.

Wiersbe, Warren W. *The Integrity Crisis.* Nashville: Thomas Nelson, 1988.

Wiersbe, Warren W. *Life Sentences: Discover the Key Themes of 63 Bible Characters.* Grand Rapids: Zondervan, 2007.

Wilkes, C. Gene. *Jesus on Leadership: Discovering the Secrets of Servant Leadership from the Life of Christ.* Wheaton, IL: Tyndale House Publishers, 1998.

Willink, Jocko, and Leif Babin. *Extreme Ownership: How U.S. Navy Seals Lead and Win.* NY: St. Martin's Press, 2017.

Wills, Garry. *Uncertain Trumpets: The Call of Leaders.* NY: Simon & Schuster, 1994.

Wooden, John, and Steve Jamison. *Wooden on Leadership.* NY: McGraw-Hill, 2005.
Woodward, Bob. *Bush at War.* NY: Simon & Schuster, 2002.
Woolfe, Lorin. *The Bible on Leadership: From Moses to Matthew—Management Lessons for Contemporary Leaders.* NY: American Management Association, 2002.
Wright, Walter C. *Relational Leadership.* UK: Paternoster Press, 2000.
Zigarelli, Michael A. *Ordinary People, Extraordinary Leaders.* Gainesville, FL: Synergy Publications, 2002.
Ziglar, Zig. *Top Performance.* NY: Berkley Books, 1987.

ENDNOTES

1. Don Warrick, Cornerstone University Second Annual Leadership Symposium, April 8–9, 2003.
2. Warren Bennis, Why Leaders Can't Lead (San Francisco: Jossey-Bass, 1989), p. 142.
3. Noel Tichy and Nancy Cardwell, The Cycle of Leadership: How Great Leaders Teach Their Companies to Win, (NY: HarperBusiness, 2002), p. xxiv.
4. Burt Nanus and Stephen M. Dobbs, Leaders Who Make a Difference: Essential Strategies for Meeting the Nonprofit Challenge (San Francisco: Jossey-Bass, 1999), p. 5.
5. George Barna, Leaders on Leadership (Ventura, CA: Regal Books, 1997), p. 18.
6. Barry Z. Posner, Cornerstone University Inaugural Leadership Symposium, April 15, 2002.
7. Posner, Cornerstone University Inaugural Leadership Symposium.
8. Tichy and Cardwell, The Cycle of Leadership, p. xxii.
9. Noel Tichy, The Leadership Engine (NY: HarperCollins, 1997), p. 8.
10. Louis V. Gerstner Jr., Who Says Elephants Can't Dance? Inside IBM's Historic Turnaround (NY: HarperBusiness, 2002), pp. 29, 68, 78, 199.
11. Gerstner, Who Says Elephants Can't Dance?, pp. 50–51.
12. Laurie Beth Jones, Teach Your Team to Fish: Using Ancient Wisdom for Inspired Teamwork (NY: Crown Wisdom, 2002), p. 133.
13. Richard L. Morrill, "Integral Strategy as Process of Leadership," Selected Presentations, 2003 President's Institute, The Council of Independent Colleges (January 4–7, 2003), p. 12.
14. Morrill, "Integral Strategy as Process of Leadership," p. 11.
15. David Harpool, Survivor College (Chula Vista, CA: Aventine Press, 2003), p. 88.
16. Frank H. T. Rhodes, "The Art of the Presidency," A.C.E. (Spring, 1998), p. 14.
17. Kenneth T. Walsh, Air Force One: The History of the Presidents and Their Planes. NY: Hyperion, 2003, pp. 102, 124–129, 140.
18. https://winstonchurchill.org/resources/speeches/1940-the-finest-hour/blood-toil-tears-sweat/

19 Warren W. Wiersbe, The Integrity Crisis (Nashville: Thomas Nelson, 1988), p. 72.
20 Barna, Leaders on Leadership, p. 29.
21 Kenneth Briggs, "Looking for Leaders, Preferably with Most of Them Under 30," In Trust (Summer, 2002), p. 8.
22 Kenneth O. Gangel, "What Leaders Do," in George Barna, Leaders on Leadership, p. 31.
23 Larry G. Michael, Spurgeon on Leadership (Grand Rapids: Kregel, 2003), p. 74.
24 Stephen E. Ambrose, Eisenhower: Soldier and President (NY: Touchstone, 1990), p. 81.
25 Tichy, The Leadership Engine, p. 6.
26 John C. Maxwell, Leadership 101: What Every Leader Needs to Know (Nashville: Thomas Nelson, 2002), pp. 11–12, 16.
27 Posner, Cornerstone University Inaugural Leadership Symposium.
28 Posner, Cornerstone University Inaugural Leadership Symposium.
29 Maxwell, Leadership 101, p. 43.
30 C. Gene Wilkes, Jesus on Leadership: Discovering the Secrets of Servant Leadership from the Life of Christ (Wheaton: Tyndale House Publishers, 1998), p. 145.
31 James O'Toole, Leading Change: The Argument for Values-Based Leadership (NY: Ballantine Books, 1995), p. x.
32 James O'Toole, Leading Change, p. 5.
33 https://winstonchurchill.org/resources/speeches/1940-the-finest-hour/blood-toil-tears-sweat/.
34 During the past fifty years, scholars have conducted more than 1,400 studies and developed some 65 classification systems about leadership. Cited in Peter G. Northouse, Leadership Theory and Practice, 3rd ed. (Thousand Oaks: Sage, 2004), p. 2. See also http://www.etymonline.com/index.php?term=lead.
35 Barry Z. Posner, Cornerstone University Inaugural Leadership Symposium, April 15, 2002.
36 Noel Tichy, The Leadership Engine (NY: HarperCollins, 1997), p. 45.
37 Robert K. Greenleaf, The Servant as Leader (Indianapolis: Robert K. Greenleaf Center, 1970, 1991), p. 8.
38 Tichy, The Leadership Engine, p. 44.
39 John Maxwell, Developing the Leader Within You (Nashville: Thomas Nelson, 1993), p. 1.

40 Zig Ziglar, Top Performance (NY: Berkley Books, 1987), p. 31.
41 Stephen E. Ambrose, Eisenhower: Soldier and President (NY: Touchstone, 1990), p. 82.
42 John P. Kotter, "What Leaders Really Do," Harvard Business Review on Leadership (Boston: Harvard Business School Publishing, 1998), p. 41.
43 John P. Kotter, John P. Kotter on What Leaders Really Do (Boston: Harvard Business School Press, 1999), p. 10.
44 Posner, Cornerstone University Inaugural Leadership Symposium.
45 Steve B. Sample, The Contrarian's Guide to Leadership (San Francisco: Jossey-Bass, 2002), p. 107.
46 James MacGregor Burns, Transforming Leadership: A New Pursuit of Happiness (NY: Atlantic Monthly Press, 2003), p. 2.
47 Page, "Needed: A Theology of Christian Leadership for Christian Colleges and Universities," Faculty Dialogue (Fall, 1994), p. 116.
48 Don Page, "Needed: A Theology of Christian Leadership," p. 119.
49 This paragraph owes much to Dr. Guy Saffold, Trinity Western University, Vancouver, British Columbia, Canada, from an email offering comments on a biblical theology of leadership, (May 9, 2002).
50 J. Oswald Chambers, Spiritual Leadership (Chicago: Moody Press, 1967, 1980), pp. 12–13. See also Rick Amidon and Rex M. Rogers, Today, You Do Greatness (Grand Rapids: Unlikely Leaders, 2011).
51 Greenleaf, The Servant as Leader, p. 27.
52 Posner, Cornerstone University Inaugural Leadership Symposium.
53 Warren Bennis, On Becoming a Leader: A Soundview Classic (Concordville, PA: Soundview Executive Book Summaries, 1990), p. 7.
54 Warren Bennis, Why Leaders Can't Lead (San Francisco: Jossey-Bass, 1989), p. 18.
55 Gary D. Badcock, The Way of Life: A Theology of Christian Vocation (Grand Rapids: Eerdmans, 1998), pp. 4–9; 82–83. See also Garry Friesen, Decision Making and the Will of God: A Biblical Alternative to the Traditional View (Portland, OR: Multnomah Press, 1980) or Henlee H. Barnette, Christian Calling and Vocation (Grand Rapids: Baker Books, 1965).
56 George Barna, Leaders on Leadership (Ventura, CA: Regal Books, 1997), p. 24.
57 Barna, Leaders on Leadership, p. 25.
58 See Martin Luther, "An Open Letter to the Christian Nobility of the German Nation Concerning the Reform of the Christian Estate," (1520) in

William C. Placher, ed., Callings: Twenty Centuries of Christian Wisdom on Vocation (Grand Rapids: Eerdmans, 2005), pp. 211–213; http://books.google.com/books?id=nyJSVgcX4SIC&pg=PA211&lpg=PA211&dq=martin+luther+the+spiritual+estate&source=web&ots=ZnUlYA_8p6&sig=hFA6q9xYhDZkJUaXaIv-GKvqkxY&hl=en&sa=X&oi=book_result&resnum=4&ct=result.

59 Badcock, The Way of Life, p. 126.
60 Os Guinness, The Call: Finding and Fulfilling the Central Purpose of Your Life (Nashville: Word Publishing, 1998), p. 31.
61 Guinness, The Call, p. 31.
62 Sheryl Sandberg, Lean In: Women, Work, and the Will to Lead (New York: Knopf, 2013).
63 Greenleaf, The Servant as Leader. See also http://en.wikipedia.org/wiki/Servant_leadership.
64 David R. Clark, Steward Leadership: Jesus' Leadership Model (Cincinnati: Glad House Publishing, 2023).
65 Clark, Steward Leadership, p. 35.
66 Page, "Needed: A Theology of Christian Leadership," p. 124.
67 Kenneth Blanchard, The Heart of a Leader: Insights on the Art of Influence (Tulsa: Honor Books, 1999), pp. 128–129.
68 Another type of Christian leadership model called "shepherd leadership" may be more useful than servant leadership. This approach is taken from Isaiah 40:11 where leaders are enjoined to feed, care, and lead the sheep, preferably in that order. Throughout Scripture, shepherds, among the most unlikely examples of leadership in biblical times one could cite, are "used to describe leaders and those responsible for the care and oversight of others, and the term shepherd was used as a noble term to describe kings, governors, priests, and prophets" (Ezek. 34:1–10; 1 Peter 5:4). Don Warrick, Cornerstone University Second Annual Leadership Symposium, April 8–9, 2003; also Don Warrick's unpublished paper, "Introduction to Shepherding," undated.
69 John C. Maxwell, Developing the Leader Within You (Nashville: Thomas Nelson, 1993), p. 100.
70 NIV translates Acts 1:20, "May another take his place of leadership."
71 This fictional letter has been bouncing around the Internet for years and may be found on numerous sites, including https://tonycooke.org/stories-and-illustrations/jerusalem-management/. See also Tim Hansel, Eating Problems

for Breakfast (Nashville: Word Publishing, 1988), pp. 194–95, or Gene A. Getz, The Apostles (Nashville: Broadman and Holman, 1998), pp. 3–4.
72 Michael A. Zigarelli, Ordinary People, Extraordinary Leaders (Gainesville, FL: Synergy Publications, 2002), p. 75.
73 Larry G. Michael, Spurgeon on Leadership (Grand Rapids: Kregel, 2003), p. 43.
74 Herbert Lockyer, All the Men of the Bible (Grand Rapids: Zondervan, 1958), p. 202.
75 Warren W. Wiersbe, Life Sentences (Grand Rapids: Zondervan, 2007), p. 74.
76 Lorin Woolfe, The Bible on Leadership: From Moses to Matthew—Management Lessons for Contemporary Leaders (NY: American Management Association, 2002), p. 23.
77 James M. Kouzes and Barry Z. Posner, ed., Christian Reflections on the Leadership Challenge (San Francisco: Jossey-Bass, 2004), p. 120. See also James M. Kouzes and Barry Z. Posner, Credibility: How Leaders Gain and Lose It, Why People Demand It (San Francisco: Jossey-Bass, 1993).
78 Les T. Csorda, Trust: The One Thing That Makes or Breaks a Leader (Nashville: Thomas Nelson, 2004), p. xv. Notation "(or her)" added.
79 David Gergen, Eyewitness to Power: The Essence of Leadership, Nixon to Clinton (NY: Simon & Schuster, 2000), p. 347.
80 R. D. Phillips, The Heart of an Executive: Lessons on Leadership from the Life of King David (NY: Doubleday, 1999), p. 234.
81 Warren Bennis, On Becoming a Leader: A Soundview Classic (Concordville, PA: Soundview Executive Book Summaries, 1990), p. 4.
82 Quoted in Ravi Zacharias, Beyond Opinion: Living the Faith That We Defend (Nashville: Thomas Nelson, 2007), p. 304.
83 J. Oswald Chambers, Spiritual Leadership (Chicago: Moody Press, 1967, 1980), pp. 225–40.
84 https://en.wikipedia.org/wiki/List_of_federal_political_sex_scandals_in_the_United_States.
85 https://en.wikipedia.org/wiki/Me_Too_movement.
86 See http://en.wikipedia.org/wiki/Monica_Lewinsky, accessed April 9, 2008.
87 Ronald Kessler, A Matter of Character: Inside the White House of George W. Bush (NY: Sentinel, 2004), p. 289.
88 Quoted in Csorba, Trust, p. 55.
89 Gergen, Eyewitness to Power, p. 346.
90 Kenneth T. Walsh, Air Force One: The History of the Presidents and Their Planes. NY: Hyperion, 2003, pp. 80–86.

91 Rick Warren, The Purpose Driven Life (Grand Rapids: Zondervan, 2002).
92 David McKenna, The Leader's Legacy: Preparing for Greater Things (Newberg, OR: Barclay Press, 2006), p. 55.
93 Gergen, Eyewitness to Power, pp. 143, 179.
94 Quoted in Noel Tichy, The Leadership Engine (NY: HarperCollins, 1997), p. 81.
95 Charles Swindoll, Elijah (Nashville: W Publishing Group, 2000), p. 103.
96 Stephen E. Ambrose, D-Day (NY: Simon & Schuster, 1994), p. 61.
97 Tony Dungy and Nathan Whitaker, Quiet Strength: The Principles, Practices, and Priorities of a Winning Life (Carol Stream, IL: Tyndale House Publishers, 2007).
98 Marc Eliot, Jimmy Stewart: A Biography (NY: Three Rivers Press, 2006).
99 John C. Maxwell, The 21 Irrefutable Laws of Leadership (Nashville: Thomas Nelson, 1998), p. 42.
100 Gleaves Whitney, "Gleaves Whitney on Leadership: What Is Leadership and How Can We Tell Who an Effective Leader Is?" https://scholarworks.gvsu.edu/cgi/viewcontent.cgi?article=1019&context=ask_gleaves.
101 https://www.fordlibrarymuseum.gov/digital-research-room/library-collections/topic-guides/nixon-pardon#:~:text=%E2%80%9CI%20was%20one%20of%20those,are%20proud%20of%20his%20achievement.%E2%80%9D.
102 Bennis, On Becoming a Leader, p. 8.
103 Phillips, The Heart of an Executive, p. 61.
104 Leighton Ford, Transforming Leadership: Jesus' Way of Creating Vision, Shaping Values, and Empowering Change (Downers Grove, IL: InterVarsity Press, 1991), p. 53. See also http://www.leightonfordministries.org/.
105 Walter Kiechell III, "Wanted: Corporate Leaders, Must Have Vision and Ability to Build Corporate Culture. Mere Managers Need Not Apply," Fortune (May 30, 1983), p. 38.
106 Many Christian writers talking about leadership cite Proverbs 29:18: "Where there is no vision, the people perish" (KJV), contending this verse speaks directly to the need for vision in leadership. Some theologians, however, debate the appropriateness of this interpretation. Interestingly, the King James Version rendering of this verse is best suited to leadership discussions, yet virtually all individuals using it for leadership discussions have long since moved to later versions of the Bible.
107 Robert K. Greenleaf, The Servant as Leader (Indianapolis: The Robert K. Greenleaf Center, 1970, 1991), p. 18.

108 Ronald Kessler, A Matter of Character: Inside the White House of George W. Bush (NY: Sentinel, 2004), p. 277.
109 An organization's purpose is often written in what have come to be called "Mission Statements," while organizational visions are sometimes written in "Vision Statements" (which too often sound like Mission Statements). Such statements have long been incorporated in strategic plans, printed in marketing brochures, or posted on websites. These statements can be useful, and some organizational leaders wield them effectively. But it's probably more common for Purpose/Mission and Vision Statements, often developed by strategic planning committees, to lose their compelling power. When this happens, they become little more than background noise in the organization's bureaucracy. Purposes or visions are far more engaging when leaders inject them with passion and use them to lead.
110 Doris Kearns Goodwin, Team of Rivals: The Political Genius of Abraham Lincoln (NY: Simon & Schuster, 2005), p. 205.
111 James M. Kouzes and Barry Z. Posner, Encouraging the Heart: A Leader's Guide to Rewarding and Recognizing Others (San Francisco: Jossey-Bass, 1999), p. xvii.
112 James MacGregor Burns, Leadership (NY: HarperCollins, 1978), p. 455.
113 Leonard Sweet, Summoned to Lead (Grand Rapids: Zondervan, 2004), pp. 105–6.
114 Max De Pree, Leadership Is an Art (NY: Dell, 1989), p. xix.
115 David Gergen, Eyewitness to Power: The Essence of Leadership, Nixon to Clinton (NY: Simon & Schuster, 2000), p. 347.
116 See Martin Luther King's "I Have a Dream" at https://youtu.be/smEqnnklfYs?feature=shared.
117 See http://en.wikiversity.org/wiki/Victor_Hugo_quote.
118 DePree, Leadership Is an Art, p. 73.
119 Rick E. Amidon and Rex M. Rogers, Today You Do Greatness: A Parable on Success and Significance (Grand Rapids: Unlikely Leaders, 2011).
120 James M. Kouzes and Barry Z. Posner, The Leadership Challenge: How to Get Extraordinary Things Done in Organizations (San Francisco: Jossey-Bass, 1987), pp. 31, 132.
121 See https://time.com/archive/6732597/margaret-thatcher-2/.
122 See https://www.reddit.com/r/GetMotivated/comments/9cac80/text_the_quality_of_a_mans_life_is_in_direct/#:~:text=%5BText%5D%20%E2%80%9CThe%20quality%20of,therap321.

123 Chip Ingram, Good to Great in God's Eyes: Ten Practices Great Christians Have in Common (Grand Rapids: Baker Books, 2007), p. 8.
124 Don Warrick, Cornerstone University Second Annual Leadership Symposium, April 8–9, 2003.
125 Gary Inrig, A Call to Excellence (Wheaton: Victor Books, 1985), pp. 10, 16–17.
126 Gergen, Eyewitness to Power, p. 140.
127 Posner, Cornerstone University Inaugural Leadership Symposium, April 15, 2002.
128 Burns, Leadership, p. 461.
129 See https://www.u2interference.com/threads/bono-model-leader-and-change-agent.191100/.
130 Edward E. Lawless III, and Christopher G. Worley, Built to Change: How to Achieve Sustained Organizational Effectiveness (San Francisco: Jossey-Bass, 2006).
131 Michael Eisner, Work in Progress (NY: Random House, 1998).
132 John C. Maxwell, Developing the Leader Within You (Nashville: Thomas Nelson, 1993), p. 52.
133 Newt Gingrich, Real Change: From the World That Fails to the World That Works (Washington, DC: Regnery Publishing, 2008), p. 73.
134 W. Chan Kim and Renee Mauborgne, "Tipping Point Leadership," HBR OnPoint (Harvard Business School Publishing, 2003), p. 10.
135 John P. Kotter, John P. Kotter on What Leaders Really Do (Boston: Harvard Business School Press, 1999), p. 92.
136 Jim Collins, Good to Great: Why Some Companies Make the Leap . . . and Others Don't (NY: HarperCollins, 2001).
137 Maxwell, Developing the Leader Within You, p. 51.
138 John C. Maxwell, The 21 Irrefutable Laws of Leadership (Nashville: Thomas Nelson, 1998).
139 Thomas L. Friedman, The World Is Flat: A Brief History of the Twenty-First Century (NY: Farrar, Straus and Giroux, 2005), and cited in Mark R. Stromberg, "Learning and Leading," Imprints 6, no. 2 (Spring 2008): p. 1.
140 Rudolph W. Giuliani, Leadership (NY: Miramax Books, 2002), p. 359.
141 Steven F. Hayward, Churchill on Leadership: Executive Success in the Face of Adversity (Rocklin, CA: Forum, 1997), pp. 26, 28–29.
142 Greenleaf, The Servant as Leader, p. 8.

143 Herbert Lockyer, All the Men of the Bible (Grand Rapids: Zondervan, 1958), pp. 205–7.
144 Warren W. Wiersbe, Life Sentences (Grand Rapids: Zondervan, 2007), p. 97.
145 Wiersbe, Life Sentences, p. 99.
146 Barry Z. Posner, Cornerstone University Inaugural Leadership Symposium, April 15, 2002.
147 Louis V. Gerstner Jr., Who Says Elephants Can't Dance? Inside IBM's Historic Turnaround (NY: HarperBusiness, 2002), p. 236.
148 James MacGregor Burns, Leadership (NY: HarperCollins, 1978), p. 439.
149 R. D. Phillips, The Heart of an Executive: Lessons on Leadership from the Life of King David (NY: Doubleday, 1999), pp. 32–33, 37, 41.
150 Quoted in Steve B. Sample, The Contrarian's Guide to Leadership (San Francisco: Jossey-Bass, 2002), p. 150.
151 Posner, Cornerstone University Inaugural Leadership Symposium.
152 Dinesh D'Souza, Ronald Reagan: How an Ordinary Man Became an Extraordinary Leader (NY: Free Press, 1997), pp. 28–29.
153 Phillips, The Heart of an Executive, p. 96.
154 Robert L. Debruyn, Causing Others to Want Your Leadership (Manhattan, KS: Master Teacher, 1976), pp. 122–24.
155 Lorin Woolfe, The Bible on Leadership: From Moses to Matthew—Management Lessons for Contemporary Leaders (NY: American Management Association, 2002), p. 44.
156 James O'Toole, Leading Change: The Argument for Values-Based Leadership (NY: Ballantine Books, 1995), p. x.
157 Rudolph W. Giuliani, Leadership (NY: Miramax Books, 2002).
158 Gerstner, Who Says Elephants Can't Dance?, p. 77.
159 Laurie Beth Jones, Teach Your Team to Fish: Using Ancient Wisdom for Inspired Teamwork (NY: Crown Wisdom, 2002), p. 101.
160 Jon Meacham, Franklin and Winston: An Intimate Portrait of an Epic Friendship (NY: Random House, 2003), pp. 9–10.
161 Meachem, Franklin and Winston, pp. 10, 15.
162 Larry G. Michael, Spurgeon on Leadership (Grand Rapids: Kregel, 2003), p. 40.
163 Noel Tichy, The Leadership Engine (NY: HarperCollins, 1997), pp. 173–75.
164 James M. Kouzes and Barry Z. Posner, Encouraging the Heart: A Leader's Guide to Rewarding and Recognizing Others (San Francisco: Jossey-Bass, 1999), pp. 105, 147.

165 Jay A. Conger, Rabindra N. Kanungo, and associates, Charismatic Leadership: The Elusive Factor in Organizational Effectiveness (San Francisco: Jossey-Bass, 1988), p. 316.
166 D'Souza, Ronald Reagan, pp. 31, 249.
167 http://en.wikipedia.org/wiki/Anthony_McAuliffe.
168 Kenneth T. Walsh, Air Force One: The History of the Presidents and Their Planes (NY: Hyperion, 2003), pp. 49–50, 62.
169 D'Souza, Ronald Reagan, pp. 31, 53, 82.
170 Noel Tichy and Nancy Cardwell, The Cycles of Leadership: How Great Leaders Teach Their Companies to Win (NY: HarperBusiness, 2002), pp. 75–76, 97.
171 Tichy and Cardwell, The Cycle of Leadership, pp. 10–11.
172 The observations in this paragraph come from Sample, The Contrarian's Guide to Leadership, p. 144.
173 Sample, The Contrarian's Guide to Leadership, pp. 144, 148.
174 This paragraph comes from Howard Gardner, Leading Minds: Anatomy of Leadership (NY: Basic Books, 1995), pp. 111–29.
175 Richard L. Morrill, "Integral Strategy as a Process of Leadership," Selected Presentations, 2003 President's Institute, The Council of Independent Colleges (January 4–7, 2003), pp. 16–17.
176 Five versions of the "Gettysburg Address" remain, ranging from 246 to 272 words, http://en.wikipedia.org/wiki/Gettysburg_Address. See also http://en.wikipedia.org/wiki/Edward_Everett.
177 Kenneth Blanchard, The Heart of a Leader: Insights on the Art of Influence (Tulsa: Honor Books, 1999), pp. 144–147.
178 Blanchard, The Heart of a Leader, pp. 70–71.
179 https://simple.wikipedia.org/wiki/The_Eleventh_Commandment_(Ronald_Reagan).
180 Posner, Cornerstone University Inaugural Leadership Symposium.
181 Gardner, Leading Minds, p. 12.
182 Mary Kay Murphy, The Advancement President and the Academy: Profiles in Institutional Leadership (Phoenix: A.C.E., 1997), pp. 13–14.
183 Paul B. Thornton, Be the Leader: Make the Difference (Torrance, CA: Griffin Publishing Group, 2002), p. 32.
184 These paragraphs on Churchill are from Steven F. Hayward, Churchill on Leadership: Executive Success in the Face of Adversity (Rocklin, CA: Forum, 1997), pp. 97–102.

185 Herbert Lockyer, All the Men of the Bible (Grand Rapids: Zondervan, 1958), p. 88.
186 Steven F. Hayward, Churchill on Leadership: Executive Success in the Face of Adversity (Rocklin, CA: Forum, 1997), pp. 6–8.
187 http://thinkexist.com/quotation/there_are_many_ways_of_going_forward-but_only_one/10791.html.
188 Barry Z. Posner, Cornerstone University Inaugural Leadership Symposium, April 15, 2002.
189 W. Chan Kim and Renee Mauborgne, "Tipping Point Leadership," Harvard Business Review On Point, no. 3353 (April 2003).
190 Richard L. Morrill, "Integral Strategy as a Process of Leadership," Selected Presentations, 2003 President's Institute, The Council of Independent Colleges (January 4–7, 2003), p. 10.
191 http://www.brainyquote.com/quotes/quotes/t/theodorero403358.html.
192 Burt Nanus and Stephen M. Dobbs, Leaders Who Make a Difference: Essential Strategies for Meeting Nonprofit Challenges (San Francisco: Jossey-Bass, 1999), p. 97.
193 Dinesh D'Souza, Ronald Regan: How an Ordinary Man Became an Extraordinary Leader (NY: Free Press, 1997), p. 30.
194 Noel Tichy, The Leadership Engine (NY: HarperCollins, 1997), p. 99.
195 https://www.terenceascott.com/dare-to-believe.
196 Cathey Prudhomme, Cornerstone University Leadership Development Seminar, Grace Adventures, November 2002.
197 John W. Gardner, Excellence: Can We Be Equal and Excellent Too? (NY: W. W. Norton & Company), 1987.
198 Leslie Lenkowsky, "Service, Leadership, and Generation Nine-One-One," The Public Interest, No. 149, (July 24, 2002).
199 Kenneth T. Walsh, Air Force One: The History of the Presidents and Their Planes (NY: Hyperion, 2003), pp. 102, 124–29, 140, 178.
200 James MacGregor Burns, Leadership (NY: HarperCollins, 1978). See also http://en.wikipedia.org/wiki/Transformational_leadership.
201 Burns, Leadership, p. 4.
202 James MacGregor Burns, Transforming Leadership: A New Pursuit of Happiness (NY: Atlantic Monthly Press, 2003), p. 24.
203 Burns, Transforming Leadership, pp. 24–25.
204 Burns, Leadership, p. 4.
205 Burns, Leadership, p. 455.

206 James MacGregor Burns quoted in James M. Kouzes and Barry Z. Posner, The Leadership Challenge: How to Get Extraordinary Things Done in Organizations (San Francisco: Jossey-Bass, 1987), p. 133.
207 Leighton Ford, Transforming Leadership: Jesus' Way of Creating Vision, Shaping Values, and Empowering Change (Downers Grove, IL: InterVarsity Press, 1991), pp. 15–16.
208 Bill Hybels, Courageous Leadership (Grand Rapids: Zondervan, 2002), p. 38.
209 Stephen E. Ambrose, Eisenhower: Soldier and President. (NY: Touchstone), 1990, pp. 139–40.
210 https://www.leadingwithhonor.com/colin-powell-leadership-point/#:~:text=The%20principle%20is%20%E2%80%9CCommand%20is,%2C%20prepare%20to%20be%20lonely.%E2%80%9D.
211 Steve B. Sample, The Contrarian's Guide to Leadership (San Francisco: Jossey-Bass, 2002), p. 74.
212 Sample, The Contrarian's Guide to Leadership, pp. 71–72, 81.
213 Bob Woodward, Bush at War (NY: Simon & Schuster, 2002), pp. 136, 256.
214 Hayward, Churchill on Leadership, p. 89.
215 Harari, The Leadership Secrets of Colin Powell.
216 John C. Maxwell, Developing the Leaders Around You (Nashville, TN: Thomas Nelson, 1995).
217 James M. Kouzes and Barry Z. Posner, Encouraging the Heart: A Leader's Guide to Rewarding and Recognizing Others (San Francisco: Jossey-Bass, 1999).
218 Robert K. Greenleaf, The Servant as Leader (Indianapolis: The Robert K. Greenleaf Center, 1970, 1991), p. 9.
219 Herbert Lockyer, All the Men of the Bible (Grand Rapids: Zondervan, 1958), p. 89.
220 R. D. Phillips, The Heart of an Executive: Lessons on Leadership from the Life of King David (NY: Doubleday, 1999), pp. 62, 69.
221 Phillips, The Heart of an Executive, p. 158.
222 Warren W. Wiersbe, Life Sentences (Grand Rapids: Zondervan, 2007), p. 140.
223 Kenneth Blanchard, The Heart of a Leader: Insights on the Art of Influence (Tulsa: Honor Books, 1999), pp. 14–15.
224 Phillips, The Heart of an Executive, p. 50.
225 Reprinted in Oren Harari, The Leadership Secrets of Colin Powell (NY: McGraw-Hill, 2002).

226 Bob Allen, https://baptistnews.com/article/southern-baptist-leader-steps-down-over-moral-indiscretion/#.XH03PS3MwWo; Bob Smietana, https://www.christianitytoday.com/news/2018/april/bill-hybels-resigns-willow-creek-misconduct-allegations.html; Stoyan Zaimov, https://www.christianpost.com/news/celebrity-pastors-falling-hard-evangelicals-must-be-more-suspicious-theologian.html; Patrick M. O'Connell and Morgan Greene, https://www.chicagotribune.com/news/ct-met-harvest-bible-chapel-james-macdonald-turmoil-20190211-story.html.

227 Doris Kearns Goodwin, Team of Rivals: The Political Genius of Abraham Lincoln (NY: Simon & Schuster), 2005.

228 Daniel Goleman, Richard Boyatzis, and Annie McKee, Primal Leadership (Boston: Harvard Business School Press, 2002), p. xiii.

229 John C. Maxwell, The 17 Indisputable Laws of Teamwork (Nashville: Thomas Nelson, 2001), p. 223.

230 Laurie Beth Jones, Teach Your Team to Fish: Using Ancient Wisdom for Inspired Teamwork (NY: Crown Wisdom, 2002), p. xv.

231 Garry Wills, Uncertain Trumpets: The Call of Leaders (NY: Simon & Schuster, 1994), p. 34.

232 Bob Woodward, Bush at War (NY: Simon & Schuster, 2002), p. 255.

233 Larry L. Thompson, sermon entitled "Leaders Make a Difference," preached at First Baptist Church, Ft. Lauderdale, FL, January 12, 2003.

234 Steve B. Sample, The Contrarian's Guide to Leadership (San Francisco: Jossey-Bass, 2002), p. 122.

235 Sheryl Sandberg, Lean In: Women, Work, and the Will to Lead (New York: Knopf, 2013).

236 Doris Kearns Goodwin, The Bully Pulpit: Theodore Roosevelt, William Howard Taft, and the Golden Age of Journalism (NY: Simon & Schuster, 2013).

237 David A. Heenan and Warren Bennis, Co-Leaders: The Power of Great Partnerships (NY: John Wiley and Sons, 1999), p. 17.

238 Sample, The Contrarian's Guide to Leadership, p. 125.

239 Noel Tichy, The Leadership Engine (NY: HarperCollins, 1997), p. 11.

240 J. Collins, Good to Great: Why Some Companies Make the Leap . . . and Others Don't (NY: HarperCollins, 2001).

241 Rudolph W. Giuliani, Leadership (NY: Miramax Books, 2002), p. x.

242 Paul B. Thornton, Be the Leader: Make the Difference (Torrance, CA: Griffin Publishing Group, 2002), p. 36.

243 Quoted in Maxwell, Leadership 101: What Every Leader Needs to Know (Nashville: Thomas Nelson, 2002), p. 47.
244 James M. Kouzes and Barry Z. Posner, The Leadership Challenge Planner: An Action Guide to Achieving Your Personal Best (San Francisco: Jossey-Bass/Pfeiffer, 1999), p. 17.
245 James M. Kouzes and Barry Z. Posner, Encouraging the Heart: A Leader's Guide to Rewarding and Recognizing Others (San Francisco: Jossey-Bass, 1999), p. 9.
246 Maxwell, Leadership 101, p. 35.
247 Lorin Woolfe, The Bible on Leadership: From Moses to Matthew—Management Lessons for Contemporary Leaders (NY: American Management Association, 2002), pp. 64, 69.
248 Don Warrick, Cornerstone University Second Annual Leadership Symposium, April 9, 2003.
249 Robert K. Greenleaf, The Servant as Leader (Indianapolis: Robert K. Greenleaf Center, 1970, 1991), p. 13.
250 Kouszes and Posner, The Leadership Challenge: How To Get Extraordinary Things Done in Organizations, (San Francisco: Jossey-Bass, 1987), p. xxv.
251 See http://leadership.ohioscpa.com/Main.aspx?MenuItem=59.
252 Barry Z. Posner, Cornerstone University Inaugural Leadership Symposium, April 15, 2002
253 John P. Kotter, John P. Kotter on What Leaders Really Do (Boston: Harvard Business School Press, 1999), p. 51.
254 Maxwell, Leadership 101, p. 39; John C. Maxwell, Developing the Leader Within You (Nashville: Thomas Nelson, 1993), p. 136.
255 Don Warrick, Cornerstone University Leadership Retreat, September 9, 2000.
256 Zig Ziglar, Top Performance (NY: Berkley Books, 1987), p. 88.
257 Alan M. Ross and Cecil Murphey, Unconditional Excellence: Answering God's Call to Be Your Professional Best (Avon, MA: Adams Media Corp., 2002), pp. 5, 21.
258 John P. Kotter, "What Leaders Really Do," Harvard Business Review on Leadership (Boston: Harvard Business School Publishing, 1998), p. 48.
259 Kotter, John P. Kotter on What Leaders Really Do, p. 63.
260 Thornton, Be the Leader, p. 82.
261 Harari, The Leadership Secrets of Colin Powell, p. 369.
262 Jones, Teach Your Team to Fish, p. 57.

263 Tichy, The Leadership Engine, p. 3.
264 Kotter, "What Leaders Really Do," p. 53.
265 Louis Gerstner Jr., Who Says Elephants Can't Dance? Inside IBM's Historic Turnaround (NY: HarperBusiness, 2002), p. 235.
266 Andrew J. DuBrin, The Complete Idiot's Guide to Leadership (NY: Alpha Books MacMillan, 1998), p. 125.
267 Warren Bennis, Why Leaders Can't Lead (San Francisco: Jossey-Bass, 1989), p. 15.
268 Harari, The Leadership Secrets of Colin Powell.
269 Bennis, Why Leaders Can't Lead, pp. 17, 23.
270 Steven F. Hayward, Churchill on Leadership: Executive Success in the Face of Adversity (Rocklin, CA: Forum, 1997), p. 8.
271 Jim Collins, Good to Great, Why Some Companies Make the Leap . . . and Others Don't, (NY: HarperCollins, 2001).
272 Paul B. Thornton, Be the Leader: Make the Difference (Torrance, CA: Griffin Publishing Group, 2002), pp. 44, 80.
273 Philips, The Heart of an Executive, p. 163.
274 James O'Toole, Leading Change: The Argument for Values-Based Leadership (NY: Ballantine Books, 1995), p. 5.
275 Louis Gerstner Jr., Who Says Elephants Can't Dance? Inside IBM's Historic Turnaround, (NY: HarperBusiness, 2002), pp. 181–82.
276 Gerstner, Who Says Elephants Can't Dance?, p. 188.
277 Gerstner, Who Says Elephants Can't Dance?, pp. 29, 78, 108.
278 Gerstner, Who Says Elephants Can't Dance?, pp. 187–88.
279 Max DePree, Leadership Is an Art (NY: Dell, 1989), p. 11.
280 D. Michael Abrashoff, It's Your Ship (NY: Warner Books, 2002), pp. 36, 52.
281 Gene Goulooze shared his wisdom in a leadership development session at Cornerstone University. After he stepped out of corporate life, Gene continued to lead for the Lord, founding a nonprofit Christian ministry called New Creations, for evangelism and discipleship in prisons. Gene serves as the ministry's executive director, marshaling a workforce of over one hundred volunteers. God has allowed Gene to lead scores of prisoners to Christ.
282 Dinesh D'Souza, Ronald Reagan: How an Ordinary Man Became an Extraordinary Leader (NY: Free Press, 1997), p. 30.
283 Warren W. Wiersbe, The Integrity Crisis (Nashville: Thomas Nelson, 1988), p. 72.

284 Herbert Lockyer, All the Men of the Bible (Grand Rapids: Zondervan, 1958), pp. 255–56.
285 Wiersbe, The Integrity Crisis, p. 79.
286 Wiersbe, The Integrity Crisis, p. 80.
287 Steven F. Hayward, Churchill on Leadership: Executive Success in the Face of Adversity (Rocklin, CA: Forum, 1997), p. 89.
288 Jim C. Collins, Good to Great: Why Some Companies Make the Leap . . . and Others Don't (NY: HarperCollins, 2001).
289 Barry Z. Posner, Cornerstone University Inaugural Leadership Symposium, April 15, 2002.
290 Steve B. Sample, The Contrarian's Guide to Leadership (San Francisco: Jossey-Bass, 2002), pp. 26–31.
291 Hayward, Churchill on Leadership, p. 6.
292 Sample, p. 163.
293 https://leighpowers.com/2017/11/17/criticism-hurts/.
294 https://chosenrebel.me/2022/04/26/when-christian-leaders-are-criticized/.
295 R. D. Phillips, The Heart of an Executive: Lessons on Leadership from the Life of King David (NY: Doubleday, 1999), p. 51.
296 Glenn Llopis, https://www.forbes.com/sites/glennllopis/2015/08/11/4-constructive-ways-leaders-can-handle-criticism/?sh=3867a6b55615.
297 George Barna, Leaders on Leadership (Ventura, CA: Regal Books, 1997), p. 27.
298 Charles Swindoll, Elijah (Nashville: W Publishing Group, 2000), p. 15.
299 Laurie Beth Jones, Teach Your Team to Fish: Using Ancient Wisdom for Inspired Teamwork, (NY: Crown Wisdom), 2002, pp. 85-86.
300 From the foreword by Warren Bennis in Steve B. Sample, The Contrarian's Guide to Leadership (San Francisco: Jossey-Bass, 2002), p. xiii.
301 Kenneth Blanchard, Heart of a Leader: Insights on the Art of Influence (Tulsa: Honor Books, 1999), pp. 48–49.
302 Posner, Cornerstone University Inaugural Leadership Symposium.
303 Gene Klann, Crisis Leadership: Using Military Lessons, Organizational Experiences, and the Power of Influence to Lessen the Impact of Chaos on the People You Lead. Greensboro, NC: Center for Creative Leadership, 2003, p. 34.
304 Jones, p. 60.
305 Zara Abrams, "Leadership in Times of Crisis," https://www.apa.org/monitor/2020/07/leadership-crisis.

306 Michael G. Bassous, Leadership . . . in Crisis: A Global Perspective on Building Resilience, Stamina, Agility, and Confrontation (Eugene, OR: Wipf and Stock Publishers, 2022), pp. 120–21.
307 Lorin Woolfe, The Bible on Leadership: From Moses to Matthew—Management Lessons for Contemporary Leaders (NY: American Management Association, 2002), p. 48.
308 Patrick D. Miller, "Toward a Theology of Leadership: Some Clues from the Prophets," in Israelite Religion and Biblical Theology: Collected Essays (Sheffield: Sheffield Academic Press, 2000), p. 666.
309 https://business.udemy.com/resources/udemy-in-depth-2018-workplace-distraction-report/?utm_source=google&utm_medium=organic-search.
310 Bassous, p. 7.
311 Warren W. Wiersbe, Life Sentences (Grand Rapids: Zondervan, 2007), p. 114.
312 James MacGregor Burns, Transforming Leadership: A New Pursuit of Happiness (NY: Atlantic Monthly Press, 2003), p. 28.
313 https://www.express.co.uk/sport/golf/1126804/tiger-woods-first-wife-120-women-elin-nordegren-tiger-woods-marriage-affair-pga-championsh?utm_source=chatgpt.com.
314 https://www.today.com/popculture/why-did-martha-stewart-go-to-prison-rcna176755.
315 https://en.wikipedia.org/wiki/Catholic_Church_sexual_abuse_cases.
316 R. D. Phillips, The Heart of an Executive: Lessons on Leadership from the Life of King David (NY: Doubleday, 1999), pp. 36–37, 41.
317 Phillips, The Heart of an Executive, pp. 62–64.
318 Phillips, The Heart of an Executive, pp. 32–33, 49.
319 Phillips, The Heart of an Executive, p. 158.
320 https://hbr.org/2013/11/the-reinvention-imperative.
321 https://sloanreview.mit.edu/article/why-good-leaders-fail/.
322 Wiersbe, Life Sentences, pp. 99–100.
323 https://www.indeed.com/career-advice/career-development/failure-of-leadership.
324 https://www.gcu.edu/blog/business-management/why-failure-important-leadership.
325 Barry Z. Posner, Cornerstone University Inaugural Leadership Symposium, April 15, 2002.
326 https://brilliantio.com/what-causes-leadership-failure/.
327 https://online.hbs.edu/blog/post/failing-well.

328 https://www.gcu.edu/blog/business-management/why-failure-important-leadership

329 Michael Eisner, Work in Progress (NY: Random House, 1998), p. 237.

330 Steven F. Hayward, Churchill on Leadership: Executive Success in the Face of Adversity (Rocklin, CA: Forum, 1997), p. 29.

331 Lorin Woolfe, The Bible on Leadership: From Moses to Matthew—Management Lessons for Contemporary Leaders (NY: American Management Association, 2002), p. 16.

332 https://www.englishclub.com/ref/esl/Sayings/T/Truth_will_out_942.php#:~:text=Origin%3A%20This%20saying%20was%20already,the%20end%20truth%20will%20out.%22.

333 https://www.businessinsider.com/people-who-lost-power-clout-respect-in-the-2010s?op=1#in-september-2019-antonio-brown-one-of-the-best-wide-receivers-in-the-nfl-said-he-would-no-longer-play-after-his-trainer-accused-him-of-rape-43.

334 https://raybwilliams.medium.com/the-downfall-of-leaders-how-unethical-and-amoral-behavior-leads-to-failure-2762fb533cce.

335 I owe this understanding of the sequential steps involved in a typical path to sexual immorality to Rev. Wes Dupin, formerly of Daybreak Church, Grand Rapids, Michigan.

336 https://www.psychologytoday.com/us/blog/why-bad-looks-good/202109/the-impact-of-watching-pornography-at-work.

337 https://www.barna.com/research/pastors-pornography-use/; https://www.covenanteyes.com/blog/porn-and-leadership/.

338 https://www.washingtonpost.com/archive/lifestyle/1994/05/30/clintons-loose-cannon/4606f204-3d1b-431f-8c32-b28c23471ad3/?utm_source=chatgpt.com.

339 https://www.chicagotribune.com/2015/12/30/a-guide-to-the-allegations-of-bill-clintons-womanizing/.

340 Simon, Sinek, Leaders Eat Last: Why Some Teams Pull Together and Others Don't (London: Penguin Random House, 2017), p. x.

341 Charles Swindoll, Elijah (Nashville: W Publishing Group, 2000), p. 111.

342 Noel Tichy and Nancy Cardwell, The Cycle of Leadership: How Great Leaders Teach Their Companies to Win (NY: HarperBusiness, 2002), p. xxiv.

343 Jim Bakker, I Was Wrong (Nashville: Thomas Nelson, 1996).

344 William Martin, A Prophet with Honor: The Billy Graham Story (NY: Quill, 1991), p. 107.

345 https://billygrahamlibrary.org/blog-celebrating-75-years-of-the-modesto-manifesto/?utm_source=chatgpt.com.
346 Steve Moore, The Top 10 Leadership Conversations in the Bible (Atlanta: Nexleader Foundation), 2017, pp. 6, 45.
347 David A. Heenan and Warren Bennis, Co-Leaders: The Power of Great Partnerships (NY: John Wiley and Sons, Inc., 1999), pp. 7–8.
348 Lorin Woolfe, The Bible on Leadership: From Moses to Matthew—Management Lessons for Contemporary Leaders (NY: American Management Association, 2002), pp. 32, 35, 42.
349 John C. Maxwell, Leadership 101: What Every Leader Needs to Know (Nashville: Thomas Nelson, 2002), pp. 95–96.
350 Woolfe, The Bible on Leadership, p. 216.
351 Maxwell, Leadership 101, pp. 98–99.
352 https://charitableadvisors.com/sacred-cows-they-may-not-be-worth-it/.
353 https://fortune.com/2008/03/05/the-trouble-with-steve-jobs/.
354 https://stephanmeyer.com/killing-sacred-cows-why-its-time-to-question-your-companys-untouchables/.
355 https://fortune.com/2008/03/05/the-trouble-with-steve-jobs/.
356 https://thenonprofittimes.com/npt_articles/american-red-cross-sued-claiming-haitian-relief-funds-misused/.
357 https://en.wikipedia.org/wiki/Sexual_abuse_cases_in_Southern_Baptist_churches; https://www.baptistpress.com/resource-library/news/dojs-closes-investigation-of-sbc/.
358 https://research.lifeway.com/2025/04/30/southern-baptists-membership-decline-continues-amid-other-areas-of-growth/?utm_source=chatgpt.com.
359 https://www.nbcnews.com/news/us-news/lawyer-demands-boy-scouts-open-perversion-files-n997786.
360 https://www.usatoday.com/story/news/nation/2025/02/08/boy-scouts-of-america-celebrate-115th-birthday/78298452007/.
361 https://www.betterworks.com/magazine/changing-organizational-culture-comprehensive-guide/.
362 Edgar H. Schein, Organizational Culture and Leadership (San Francisco: Jossey-Bass, 2010), p. 5.
363 https://en.wikipedia.org/wiki/The_king_is_dead,_long_live_the_king!
364 Wallace Erickson, "Transition in Leadership," in George Barna, Leaders on Leadership (Ventura, CA: Regal Books, 1997), p. 298.

365 Quoted in Maxwell, Leadership 101, p. 95.
366 Noel Tichy and Nancy Cardwell, The Cycle of Leadership: How Great Leaders Teach Their Companies to Win (NY: HarperBusiness, 2002), p. 152.
367 Erickson, "Transition in Leadership," p. 298.
368 Reprinted in Oren Harari, The Leadership Secrets of Colin Powell (NY: McGraw-Hill, 2002).
369 Maxwell, Leadership 101, p. 95.
370 Fares Abraham, Next Gen Leaders: Learning Today How to Change Tomorrow (Washington, DC: Levant Media, 2017), p. 106.
371 Edith Deen, All the Women of the Bible (NY: Harper and Row, 1955), pp. 146–52.
372 https://jwa.org/blog/risingvoices/queen-esther-quiet-leader.
373 Daniel Goleman, Richard E. Boyatzis, and Annie McKee, Primal Leadership, Unleashing the Power of Emotional Intelligence (Brighton, MA: Harvard Business Review Press, 2013), p. 101.
374 Leonard J. Marcus, Eric J. McNulty, Joseph M. Henderson, and Barry C. Dorn, You're It: Crisis, Change, and How to Lead When It Matters (NY: PublicAffairs, 2019), p. 59.
375 Perry Pascarella, Christ-Centered Leadership: Thriving in Business by Putting God in Charge (Rocklin, CA: Prima Publishing, 1999), p. 27.
376 Paraphrased from Lewis Carroll, Alice's Adventures in Wonderland (London: Macmillan and Company, 1865), chapter 6.
377 Steve B. Sample, The Contrarian's Guide to Leadership (San Francisco: Jossey-Bass, 2002), p. 18.
378 https://www.gotquestions.org/prayer-of-Jabez.html.
379 Leonard Sweet, Carpe Mañana: Is Your Church Ready to Seize Tomorrow? (Grand Rapids: Zondervan, 2001), p. 19.
380 John R. W. Stott, Involvement: Social and Sexual Relationships in the Modern World (Old Tappan, NJ: Fleming H. Revell, 1985), p. 264.
381 Barry Z. Posner, Cornerstone University Inaugural Leadership Symposium, April 15, 2002.
382 https://www.gregwoodard.com/blog/how-to-finish-well-as-a-leader-the-four-steps-you-need-to-take.
383 https://www.globalleadership.org/article/the-case-for-finishing-well.
384 Tom Brokaw, The Greatest Generation (NY: Random House, 1998).
385 https://www.brainyquote.com/quotes/mother_teresa_105649.

386 Jim Collins, Good to Great: Why Some Companies Make the Leap . . . and Others Don't (NY: Harper Collins, 2001).

387 Jim Collins and Morten T. Hansen, Great by Choice: Uncertainty, Chaos, Luck—Why Some Thrive Despite Them All (NY: Harber Business, 2011), p. 183.

388 https://en.wikipedia.org/wiki/Francis_Schaeffer. Francis A. Schaeffer, How Should We Then Live? The Rise and Decline of Western Thought and Culture (Ada, MI: Fleming H. Revell, 1976).

389 https://www.globalcp.org/statistics?utm_source=chatgpt.com.

390 Leighton Ford, Transforming Leadership: Jesus' Way of Creating Vision, Shaping Values, and Empowering Change (Downers Grove, IL: InterVarsity Press, 1991), p. 97.

391 Leonard Sweet, Summoned to Lead (Grand Rapids: Zondervan, 2004), p. 79.

www.ingramcontent.com/pod-product-compliance
Lightning Source LLC
Chambersburg PA
CBHW062042080426
42734CB00012B/2536